The
JIM
MURRAY
Collection

ALSO BY JIM MURRAY
The Best of Jim Murray
The Sporting World of Jim Murray

Series Editor, Carlton Stowers

The
JIM
MURRAY
Collection

Introduction by
VIN SCULLY

TAYLOR PUBLISHING COMPANY
Dallas, Texas

Published by Taylor Publishing Company
1550 West Mockingbird Lane
Dallas, Texas 75235

Library of Congress Cataloging-in-Publication Data

Murray, Jim.
    The Jim Murray collection.

    (Contemporary American sportswriters)
    Includes index.
    1. Sports.   2. Newspapers—Sections, columns, etc.—
Sports.   I. Title.   II. Series.
GV707.M775   1988   070.4'49796   87-33613
ISBN 0-87833-607-9

Printed in the United States of America

0   9   8   7   6   5   4   3   2   1

For every guy who ever struck out with
the bases loaded, took a 10-count, fumbled
on the goal line, double-faulted, missed
a layup at the buzzer, pulled a 3-foot
putt and bet into a pat hand of aces full
. . . and every guy who ever closed a
bar alone at 2 o'clock in the morning.

Introduction

The memory of the event has never left me.

It happened over thirty-five years ago and although that doesn't place it in time like the invention of the wheel, you've got to admit that it was not exactly yesterday afternoon. It was just moments after the Brooklyn Dodgers had lost a bitter one-run game to the New York Giants at Ebbets Field. As fate would have it, Jackie Robinson was involved in a very close play at second base for the final out, and he was steaming. Even though most if not all of his teammates felt that he had been *rightfully* called out, Jackie was hollering at the top of his lungs about the unfair call, punctuating every steamy sentence by hurling furniture, equipment, and anything else he found handy into his locker.

Now to really get the picture you had to understand the home team clubhouse in Brooklyn. The pecking order and star status on the team placed the big-name players' lockers near the front door somewhat the way a wise restaurateur sets up his celebrity tables for all to see. Gil Hodges, Pee Wee Reese, Roy Campanella, Preacher Roe, Duke Snider, and Jackie were prominently displayed. After that, according to rank, a player was assigned a locker that befit his status on the team. In the farthest corner of the room, near the showers and the ice box that held the beer and soft drinks, was the locker of a somewhat obscure black pitcher named Dan Bankhead. The fans didn't know much about ol' Dan but his teammates did. Bankhead was not one to waste words and when he did have something to say, he had the immediate attention of all concerned.

On this day as Robinson ranted and raved and hurled his bootless cries to the heavens, his was the only sound heard in the room. In the far corner Bankhead sprawled off the stool in front of his cubicle, naked but for a towel across his loins, hands folded at his stomach and reading glasses perched precariously at the end of his nose. Right in the middle of Robinson's harangue Bankhead said softly, "Robinson . . ." Jackie stopped in mid-sentence, adverbs and adjectives hanging in the air like wisps of smoke. "Robinson," said Bankhead, now that he had complete silence in the room, "Robinson . . . you are not only *wrong* . . . you is *loud wrong.*"

Jackie stood and stared at ol' Dan for a moment, and then his handsome ebony features broke into a wide grin. The storm had passed, the point taken, and the wisdom well received. Immediately murmurs turned to laughter, everyday noise welled up in the room, and what passed for normalcy returned to the Dodger clubhouse.

I have often thought of that moment, especially since I make my living with the spoken word, doing a high-wire act across a chasm bottomed with the boulders of national criticism, knowing all the while that a slip of the tongue, a mistake in judgment, an inappropriate expression, and I am off the wire without a net. Even though he has the luxury of checking his copy before it's published, Jim Murray climbs up on that wire with me several hundred times a year and has a chance to be loud in his nationally syndicated column. Yet I have never known him to be "loud wrong."

He has made his readers laugh and cry, all the while peppering them with enough one-liners to (in the old days) land you a week at the Palace. He can level cities with tongue-in-cheek descriptions, humanize by hyperbole, and puncture the pompous with his literary lance. I cried when he wrote of the passing of his lovely wife, Gerry, and I marveled at his sensitivity when he wrote about losing the use of an eye as if he had just lost an old friend. And then there was the old friend that we both lost, a gentle man named Vic Hunter who loved to play golf and died while busily engaged with his favorite hobby. Who else but Jim Murray could have begun that column, "My friend Vic Hunter picked up a number 2 at Riviera . . ."?

All of us in the media are similar yet different at the same time. We all deal in words, but in different ways. The play-by-play man does his best to stay with and describe events that are happening now. The writer makes his notes throughout whatever contest he is watching and writes after the fact. But the columnist, ah, there's the rub. Every day the same challenge, the same blank piece of paper tauntingly unfurled and hanging out of the typewriter like a mocking tongue, daring him to be different, fresh, funny, and incisive. And every day for better than twenty-five years, Jim Murray has not only accepted that challenge but triumphed.

Years ago the noted British playwright Noel Coward was rushing through a Canadian airport pursued by anxious writers eager for an interview. While running to keep up with Coward, a *Toronto Star* reporter hollered breathlessly, "Mr. Coward, Mr. Coward . . . Do you have a word for the *Star?*" "Certainly," said the British wit, "Twinkle."

Twinkle, in a word, is exactly what Jim Murray does, and he does it day in and day out. Year after year. He is, without a doubt, a star of the first magnitude in the firmament that is sportwriting, and well worth the looking. This is no Halley's Comet that bursts across the sky and is gone in an instant. We're talking permanence right in the middle of the constellation. So pull up a chair and have a look. You'll be glad you did.

Vin Scully
Pacific Palisades, California

Contents

Preface / xv

Personally Speaking / 1

AS WHITE AS THE KU KLUX KLAN / 2

IT'S BUSINESS AS USUAL / 5

"MARRING" THE RACES / 8

THANKFUL, BUT . . . / 10

DON'T BLAME LITTLE LEAGUE / 12

MISSING: An Ocean of Joy / 15

OF HUMAN BONDAGE / 18

BLASTING A GOLF TRAIL / 21

WEIRD SITE FOR A FIGHT / 24

THE TERROR OF INDY / 27

SCORE IT NONSENSE / 31

A MATTER OF BLIND FAITH / 34

THE HALL OF WHAT? / 37

LAWS OF MURRAY / 40

THE SAME OLD SONG / 43

THE JOY OF SEEING / 46

TRANSLATING THE QUOTES / 50

IF YOU'RE EXPECTING ONE-LINERS / 53

RECRUITING SALES TALK / 56

CONTENTS

ONE MAN'S OPINION / 60

INSTANT CELEBRITY / 62

A CAR TO REMEMBER / 65

ALL-TIME GREATEST NAME / 68

IT WASN'T TOO BAD / 71

BO, YOU HAVE COMPANY / 74

WE JUST HAVE IT TOO GOOD / 77

IT'S SEEN AND NOT HEARD / 80

IT DOESN'T SUIT THEM / 83

SOME NIGHTS I STAY UP THROUGH
    THE NEWS / 86

LET'S BE HONEST ABOUT THE MASTERS / 89

BREEDING COUNTS BUT DOESN'T ADD UP / 92

THE SPORT THAT TIME LEAVES ALONE / 95

JUST ONCE, I'D LIKE TO SEE . . . / 98

WHO LET LAWYERS IN THE BALLPARK? / 100

NO BOSOX TEA PARTY / 103

RED-BLOODED RUNNERS / 105

TRIBUTE TO ABE / 108

GOLF IS TO FOOTBALL AS PALM SPRINGS IS
    TO PITTSBURGH / 110

NO GRUNDGES IN THE KUMQUAT BOWL / 113

A TRANSIENT BUSINESS / 116

FROM RUSSIA WITH LOVE OR . . . I'LL NEVER
    SMILE AGAIN / 120

CONTENTS

Portraits / 125

MAN WITHOUT A FUNNYBONE / 126

IDOL WHOSE TIME IS PAST / 129

CATCHIN' UP WITH SATCH / 132

A WOMAN OF THE CENTURY / 135

HE EARNED HIS WAY / 138

HE DARED STAND ALONE / 141

DR. J CAME TO PLAY / 144

BASEBALL'S SHOWBOAT / 147

THE PIRATE HAS HEART / 150

BABY-FACE BOMBER / 153

THAT'S SHOE BIZ / 156

COMANECI OLYMPICS / 158

WHO IS THIS GUY? / 162

A REJECTED LANDMARK / 165

THE COWBOY'S LAMENT / 169

ALZADO IS RAZOR SHARP / 172

FAME BUT NO HALL / 175

A SALUTE TO GILLIAM / 178

THE PEOPLE'S CHAMP / 181

TROUBLE HITS TAPE / 184

LIEUTENANT FAIR-AND-SQUARE / 187

A COLLEGE GRADUATE / 191

A TOUGH LITTLE LADY / 195

FIRST TEST-TUBE LINEBACKER / 198

MAKING OF A MAN / 202

THE ONE AND ONLY / 205

PERFECT TIMING / 208

WORLD CLASS LEPRECHAUN / 211

THE ONE THAT COUNTS / 214

ANOTHER ROCKY STORY / 217

MASTER OF THE CITY GAME / 220

AN AMERICAN LEGEND / 224

TRACK AND FIELD'S HOTTEST DOUBLE
  FEATURE / 227

YOU'D NEVER THINK SHE IS ONE OF THEM / 230

COACH OF THE LIVING DEAD / 233

PATCHING AN IMAGE / 235

HE NEEDN'T TAKE NUMBER; IT'S HIS / 238

AN ACTOR ON CANVAS / 241

THE ETERNAL COWBOY / 244

Fond Farewells / 247

LIFE FINALLY CAUGHT MARCIANO WITH A
  SUCKER PUNCH / 248

LAST OF THE VICTORIANS / 251

HE NEVER GREW UP / 254

CONTENTS

DEATH OF AN HEIRLOOM / 256

A PORTRAIT IN COURAGE / 259

THE CALL OF A SIREN / 262

HE MADE A NAME OF RED SMITH / 264

Index / 267

Preface

Each year about this time, as regular as the crocuses, the return of spring is heralded by a significant new entry in my mail. The full-throated, patch-elbowed, blue-jean college work-shirker is abroad in the land, the guy who has been dozing through lectures all winter and now must find someone to do his final paper for him or he'll flunk the course.

The letters are all alike. They read either, "Dear Sir: Will you please explain the role of sports journalism in a changing world today in your own words and please return to the writer at Shiftless U by May 15," or, they enclose a questionnaire which they explain has been sent to you as one of a select group of citizens chosen to help them "partially fulfill my assignment and complete my thesis."

It sure beats cribbing, or stealing exam papers, or paying some "greasy grind" (which is what we used to call anyone who got better marks than you did) which we had to do in my day.

To save stamps, I will offer here a sample questionnaire I have filled out for a young man in the Midwest who got me (and a few dozen other suckers) to do his homework for him for nothing.

Dear Mr. Murray:
1. Did you attend college? (Yes.) If so, what institution? (Trinity College.)
2. In your opinion, what university or educational institution in the United States has the finest school of journalism? (The New York Daily News.) Why? (Institutions with ivy on their walls have no courses for: a) stealing pictures of the corpse in a murder off the dresser of a weeping mother; b) being able to convince yourself a talentless ruffian is "colorful," a boor is "humorous," an opportunist is a "sportsman," and that, in sports, you use "great" for "mediocre," "sensational" for "poor" and "immortal" for "competent." Universities suffer from

the quaint notion people want information, not entertainment, which shows they haven't even been studying their own student bodies.)

3. What are your working hours? (Depends, I try to get the World Series by the fourth inning or two hours after the game starts, whichever comes first. Basketball, the last 10 seconds is enough. Football, you only have to get in the game about as often as the Cypriot placekicker. In auto racing, you just call the coroner periodically and he does your work for you. In college, you just spend 10 minutes a year licking stamps on questionnaires.)

4. What day(s) off, if any, do you have? (Every.)

5. When you cover an event, what material do you take? (Paper, pencil, eyes, ears—and a good book to read in case it gets dull.)

6. To what magazines, periodicals, etc., do you subscribe? (*Playboy, Modern Screen, True Confessions, The Shadow Magazine, Street & Smith's Wild West* and *Colliers.*)

7. What other materials do you feel are valuable to you (reference books, etc.)? (*Modern Theories of Cricket, The Great Commissioners of Baseball,* Clifford Irving's biography of Duane Thomas, and *The Religious Experiences of Leo Durocher.* I've only got a 12-inch bookshelf.)

8. What is your favorite spectator sport? (Before *Oh, Calcutta!* it was golf.) What is your favorite particpant sport? (Polo.)

9. What is your favorite assignment? (Locker room interviews in ladies' tennis.)

10. (CONFIDENTIAL) In what range does your annual salary fall? (It falls just short of confidential.)

11. Regarding your future, do you have any ambitions? (I'd like to break 90.)

12. What tips would you give a person who wants to make a career of sports writing? (Disregard all of the above and start doing your own homework. You can't cover the Super Bowl by questionnaire. If you could, I would.)

Personally Speaking

AS WHITE AS THE KU KLUX KLAN

APRIL 6, 1969

GREENSBORO—OK, rest easy, Jefferson Davis! Put down the gun, John Wilkes Booth. Let's hear a chorus of Dee-eye-ex-eye-eee! Run up the Stars and Bars. You won't have to blindfold that Confederate general's statue after all. Downtown Tobacco Road is still safe from the 20th century.

The Masters golf tournament is as white as the Ku Klux Klan. Everybody in it can ride in the front of the bus.

There's nothing the Supreme Court can do about it. Integration fell about 18 strokes or 20 Masters points short. Integration missed the cut.

The one break Charlie Sifford couldn't read and compensate for was the one which made him, like, an eighth-generation American, if only a third-generation free man. "Only in America," as the fellow says. Twenty golf champions had a clear shot at redressing a longtime wrong but they drove it in the deep rough. They double-bogeyed a chance to do something for golf, for themselves, for their country.

Charlie Sifford should have been Chinese, I guess, instead of Carolinian. An accident of birth keeps his clubs in the trunk of the car this week.

The circumstances are well known, but I will recount them briefly here, to the accompaniment of the *Battle Hymn of the Republic* and a recitation of the Gettysburg Address.

Charlie Sifford is a golfer, an American, a gentleman. He is not, however, a Caucasian. Until 1961, this seriously interfered with his life, liberty, and pursuit of happiness, to say nothing of his occupation—because golf was a "Members Only" club till

2

then. They didn't publish the 14th Amendment in *Golf Digest*. It wasn't covered under the "free drop" rule.

Charlie was almost 40 years old before he got to play with the big boys. You can make book Arnold Palmer couldn't have overcome a handicap like that. You would have thought the other guys would give him two-a-side at first, just to be fair.

Charlie didn't need them. Even though some tournaments still had the bedsheet on—retreating behind the "invitational only" subterfuge, Charlie had become dangerous competition. He won two important tournaments, the Hartford and Los Angeles. If you think that's easy, you don't know golf. If you think that's even possible (with Charlie's late start), you're an optimist.

Now, the Masters is an unusual tournament. It was Bobby Jones' dream—and a man is entitled to do in his dreams what he wishes. What Bobby wished was to make it a sort of glorious annual reunion for certified legends of the game—never mind that some of them became fossilized.

The country took to the tournament. So did the world. Golf journalists from two continents wrote tone poems about the course. It became a "bonus" event. Winning it was like getting a seat on the Stock Exchange.

Bobby had to change it—or it would've become known as the "Fossils" instead of the "Masters." He kept six positions for non-legends, touring pros who never made any of the rich-kid amateur teams, guys who might leave their spoons in their coffee while they drank.

The Masters didn't *bar* black people. Frankly, it wasn't thought necessary. In fact, it did let them carry the bags.

Now, one way you can get in the Masters is by winning the championship of Formosa or making a good showing at Kuala Lumpur. Plus, you can be *invited* by a vote of former champions.

Former champions have often voted out of sentiment. Cronies who had fallen on evil days—to say nothing of in sand traps and lateral water hazards—got in on this kind of pass.

As a two-time tour winner, a guy who had been a victim of 20 years of injustice, and a surrogate for his people who have been victims of 200 years of same, it occurred to me, a sense of shame might have directed that vote to Charlie Sifford this year. Charlie is not *any* black man, and this would not be tokenism, he is a tour winner under circumstances as adverse as for any athlete who ever lived. Like a Bulgarian immigrant getting in a spelling bee.

Art Wall Jr.—and let's hear it for him!—voted for Charlie Sifford. As far as I know, that gave Charlie a total of one. The other guys voted for Bob Murphy.

Now, I'm all for the Irish. But we've been in the country clubs for a long time now. Not as long as West Virginians, to be sure, but long enough.

What's more, Bob Murphy was already safely in the Masters! He was second on a point list that would admit all the way through six! It was like sending money to Rockefeller or rice to China.

The Masters invites select foreigners, as noted. The official position of the Masters is that they "allow ourselves a bit more latitude with foreign players because, in most cases, they do not have the opportunity to prove themselves against USA players."

How's that again, fellows?! Who was more "foreign" than Charlie Sifford till he was over 40? He could play if he was raised on a camel or a fjord or a castle in Spain. In a tobacco patch in Carolina, no.

But, pshaw! He had an unnatural advantage: He was raised in America.

Charlie had one last chance down here at Greensboro. At the age of 46, all he had to do was beat out this field of 141 young studs. Charlie threw a 74 at the course in the opening round. On this easy track it might as well be 94.

Charlie signed his scorecard, then turned and said to this reporter bitterly: "Now they can keep their tournament down there lily-white."

Wait a minute, Charlie! You forgot the caddies.

IT'S BUSINESS AS USUAL

JULY 21, 1972

Every year about this time, I have the same dream. I go down to the Shriners' Crippled Children's Hospital and it's closed. There's this big sign outside, "For Lease Or Rent, Will Remodel To Suit Tenant."

The grass is clear up to the windows, some of which are broken. There are cracks in the mortar and, as you go inside, there's dust on the telephones and there's cobwebs on the wheelchairs.

The operating room obviously hasn't been used in years and the surgical tools are rusted. When you yell in the corridors, all you get is an echo. The beds with the prison-bar rails are empty and rusted and only a little stuffed doll, not a live one, sits in a corner of a crib.

"Is anybody here?" I shout, looking around for the guys in those funny little fezzes with the rhinestones on them, or for a nurse carrying a little package of bones that could have been a child once.

Then a woman appears and shines a light on me and says, "Are you interested in renting this place?" And I say, "No—but what happened to the children?" "We don't know," she says, "but, one day, they just stopped coming. We couldn't believe it, so we went out looking—and you know what we found out? For a period of 12 months, there hadn't been a single crippled child born into the world! A miracle had happened! They got the assembly line fixed up there or the quality control and, for years now, every kid comes into the world with his legs pointing down and with toes on them. And they can all throw baseballs with their arms and dance with their feet or go roller-skating. And their spines are all straight, and their bones are all strong and don't snap in a high wind the way those kids with osteo-

5

genesis' bones did. Heaven must have had a callback on all the defective models before they let them out."

Then I wake up. And drive down to the Shriners' Crippled Children's Hospital and—damn!—there they still are.

The hospital's in use, all right. There isn't a cobweb in the place. The operating rooms are still operating on full shifts. The phones are ringing. It was on one of those operating tables little Steve died this year. Just kind of gave up. Everyone else had given up on him in his seven years. They abandoned him to medicine, but by the time the Shriners got to him, there wasn't much left to work with. You see, kids in casts have to be convinced it's worthwhile to breathe deep. Otherwise, they get pneumonia and die. Pretty blonde nurses like Bonnie get them to do it with balloons. "They got machines for it," she says. "But kids prefer balloons to machines."

There's little Monica—or was that Amy? She pointed to her little artificial legs fastened to the stumps she was born with. "These legs can't break," she said proudly, tapping them. No, but hearts can.

There was little Gracie, red-headed, gay, but with that tell-tale pallor that tells of a too-fragile grip on life. Gracie is about two feet tall but she's seven years old. She has that brittle-bone disease. She has steel rods for bones, otherwise she would be just a head and a box of pieces. The hospital fights for time because the bones sometimes get marrow in them, or whatever the strength-giving substance is, when the child gets to be a teenager. Also, if.

I went through the hospital with the North-South All-Star football squads, boys who will be playing in the annual charity football game at the Coliseum Thursday night which pays for Gracie's rods and her stall for time. Everywhere these healthy football players looked were God's fumbles.

Bart didn't have a helmet on when massive tackle Scott Avery came up to him. Bart had what appeared to be a scaffolding of steel screwed into his brain. His pillow is a set of steel bars which keep his head steady so they can fuse a spine into him. They call it a "halo" traction, but it looks like something out of Torque-mada's dungeon. Months of captivity in this iron mask stagger the imagination. If I had to wear that iron pillow for one day, I would confess every crime in the world. I would tell them my wife did it if I were caught as a spy and put in this torture chamber. But Bart has to wear the bars for a year. He calls them "Bart's Antlers." You don't know anything about pluck till you've seen how these kids go through the hall of horrors that is life for them.

There's no danger of the Crippled Children's Hospital going up for sale or lease for lack of clientele. As someone said, all you have to have is no legs and no money to get in—and the Lord knows there are plenty of these all over the world.

But there is always danger of a house of mercy like this being padlocked and cobwebbed for lack of money. That would make my dream a nightmare. So, please buy a ticket. Be glad you have fingers to do it, and that you don't have to see life through a steel bird cage. One of these years they may be able to turn this place into a parking lot. But not until they plug that awful leak in that great assembly line where broken babies come from.

"MARRING"
THE RACES

AUGUST 1, 1973

If an auto race writer were covering the story of the Titanic, how would he handle it?

Simple. His story would start: "The maiden voyage of the S.S. Titanic was 'marred' today when the luxury liner hit an iceberg and sank with all hands." Or, it might be "The S.S. Titanic broke all lap and qualifying records for the North Atlantic run Monday before a severely damaged front end forced it out of the race."

You are tempted to conjure up a few "mars" of history. "A weekend visit of school teacher Nathan Hale to British lines was 'marred' Sunday by a hanging—his." I guess the docking of the Hindenburg was "marred."

"The performance of *Our American Cousin* at Ford's Theater in Washington, D.C., last evening was 'marred' by an unscheduled curtain call by the actor John Wilkes Booth." Or "Saturday afternoon in Altoona was 'marred' this week when a dam broke in Johnstown and drowned 2,205 persons."

All this is occasioned by a story Sunday out of a place called Zandvoort, The Netherlands, which I bring you in all its pristine, straight-faced reporting: "Scotsman, Jackie Stewart reached a milestone in Formula I racing today with his 26th career victory in the Dutch Grand Prix, an event marred by the death of British driver Roger Williamson."

The story went on to say that Stewart took the lead in point standings. I swear I think the "Good News, Bad News" jokes were inspired by auto race writers.

The tragedy underscores something generally overlooked in this country, in auto race commentary: not all the holocausts take place at the closed circuit of Indianapolis. The pastoral roads of Europe have their quotas of death-by-automobile, too. In the past decade or two, Formula I has run neck-and-neck

8

with American oval racing (to say nothing of heart trouble) in "mars." The Marquis de Portago, Count Wolfgang von Trips, Jimmy Clark, Jochen Rindt have all perished in European race cars, to name only the more famous. Death speaks five languages, too.

When a tragedy occurs you can do one of two things, if you're a race track official. You can snarl, "What about the deaths in football?" Or, "What about the drownings on the Fourth of July?!"

The other tack is less soul-satisfying. It requires track management to say, "Yes, we made some serious mistakes. We are sanctioning cremation. Now, what we must do is make this a sport again, not a blaze."

Indianapolis, for instance, is removing box seats from Charcoal Alley, raising the concrete rim around the track, removing the pill-box-like abutment which turned Swede Savage's car into a furnace on impact, and is keeping a low profile on name-calling. People in burning buildings shouldn't throw coals.

The drivers in the Dutch Grand Prix had warned the promoters the course was unsafe and, for two years, had refused to die in it. The fire engines took eight minutes to get to the pyre Sunday. You wonder what country the fire house was in. You couldn't save Chicago if you gave fire an eight-minute head start.

When journalists tell them their race courses are unsafe, promoters can be pardoned for sniffing, "What do you guys know about it?" (Even though you don't have to be an automotive engineer to count the dead.) But when 30 or more of the world's best drivers tell them their course is unsafe, and then go out and prove it, it's time for a change.

The excuse for auto racing is, it will cut down on the highway carnage, not improve on it. The futility of this argument is shown by the fact that, after 60 years of auto racing, fire trucks can't get to a fire before it's an ash.

As usual, they got the wrong vehicles going 200 m.p.h. What I would like to see is a good fire "marred" by the timely arrival of fire trucks.

THANKFUL, BUT . . .

NOVEMBER 22, 1973

Let's see—Thanksgiving Day, right? OK.

I'm thankful the Old South finally got blacks in university backfields and lines—but I'd be more thankful if the rooting sections would put away those Confederate flags. To a black, that must have all the warmth and charm of a swastika.

I'm thankful George Foreman won the heavyweight championship—but I'd be more thankful if he fought somebody who could fight back.

I'm thankful for all the 1,000-yard runners, the O. J. Simpsons, Mercury Morrises, Floyd Littles and Larry Browns, in football—but I'd be more thankful if there were a few Slinging Sammy Baughs, Sid Luckmans, Otto Grahams and Bob Waterfields to go along with them and do something besides hand the ball to somebody all afternoon.

I'm thankful for the higher scoring in hockey—but I'd be more thankful if I could see one of them some night. Seeing a goal scored in hockey is like picking your mother out of a crowd shot at the Super Bowl.

I'm thankful for all the foreign-born placekickers they send over here—but we'd rather have janitors.

I'm thankful for Monday Night Football—but not three hours of bedsheets saying "Hi Dandy!"

I'm thankful they relaxed the requirements to let underprivileged kids into college—but I wish some of them would become doctors instead of Green Bay Packers.

I'm thankful the Rams are playing in the Coliseum—but if they want a new stadium, they should build it, not us. I don't know about you, but I've got all the mortgages I want.

I'm thankful all those seven-foot basketballers can make millions jumping contracts—but I wish the people I sign contracts with would afford me the same liberty. Or the same judges.

I'm thankful for the Heisman Trophy—but I wish they'd give it to someone who graduates.

I'm thankful for the New York Mets' pennants—but I wish they'd play their games in a demilitarized zone.

I'm thankful for the Masters—but I wish Lee Elder could win it.

I'm thankful for Jack Nicklaus—but I wish Arnold Palmer could win one more U.S. Open.

I'm thankful for Ralph Nader—but not very.

I'm thankful for Secretariat—but I wish he had to keep working for a living like the rest of us. Early retirement might be OK—but at age *three?!*

I'm thankful for open tennis—but I wish they'd have it.

I'm thankful for $500,000 golf tournaments—but I wish someone like Dr. Schweitzer could win one.

I'm thankful Henry Aaron is going to be the one to break Babe Ruth's record—period.

I'm thankful I can give thanks today—it beats working.

DON'T BLAME LITTLE LEAGUE

NOVEMBER 30, 1973

Little League baseball is a much-maligned institution at the mercy of any psychiatrist in search of a headline. For him, it comes out as a combination of Hitler Youth and child labor and they usually recommend a constitutional amendment to ban it in favor of something they call "unstructured play."

What upsets them, usually, is that the culture of Bora Bora or some other place where they put bones in their noses—places psychologists for some reason set a great store by—have no exact equivalent of Little League. Ergo, they wonder why New York City does.

I take issue with these people. I have no romantic notions about the lifestyles of primitive people because I come from a long line of them and, believe me, I'd rather go to the opera. For one thing, the people smell nicer.

I had a mini-quarrel with a psychologist on the subject once. It didn't last long because the longest word I knew was "Yastrzemski." And, besides, he smoked a pipe. So, everyone knew right away he was smarter than I was. And he had never played baseball. Neither had Freud.

I sent him a front page from the *New York Daily News* a few days later showing where some kids, in a burst of unstructured play, had tied another kid to a hydrant and set fire to him.

I rested my case there, but I'm sure he found a way to blame it on Little League. I bring this up because Dr. Creighton Hale, president of Little League, is in town. He's only been president a month, and already he must feel as if he's spreading typhoid, or as if Little League were hazardous to your health. You half expect to see pickets demanding "Free Little League" or "Release Our Kids." He must feel like the Pied Piper piping rats *into* town.

Dr. Hale is a Ph.D. and a physiologist who pioneered the

Little League flap helmet, now required equipment even in the big leagues, and a chest protector and catcher's mask which are standard equipment for the big leagues. Still, you would think Little League was polluting the environment or advising the overthrow of the government by force and violence.

Now, it's NOW (National Organization of Women) that wants to knock Little League out of the box. It's pushing for the admission of girls. Little League is fearful of the medical bills and lawsuits if they succeed. "Speed is the most important element in force—and boys run faster and hit harder than girls on the basepaths," warns Dr. Hale.

Nonetheless, NOW produced a psychiatrist in New Jersey who argued that, unless Little League integrates girls in its boys' program, why, then, he would call for the elimination of Cub Scouts, Boy Scouts, Camp Fire Girls, Brownies, and (I'm sure) Daughters of the American Revolution.

These suits have to be fought with Little League money, although the plaintiff organization gets civil rights lawyers and civil rights funds at no cost to them. I know a lot of people I'd sue under those conditions.

The misconception that Little League is a highly profitable organization must always be met. "It's not only nonprofit, it's a deficit operation," Dr. Hale says. The $10 per team in 8,000 leagues raises about $320,000 a year, or less than half the annual nut.

Little League is the only organization other than the Boy Scouts chartered by Congress and, while it's as American as apple pie, four of the last five "World Series" have been won by Taiwan, the baseball-mad island off China which has been so good Little League has been forced to send teams of investigators to check the ages of the contestants. The Chinese, though deeply hurt, have behaved with typical forbearance in the face of this American barbarity.

There are 2 million youngsters worldwide (Mexico won twice and Puerto Rico twice) in Little League. While no athletic program is 100 percent safe, Little League has more fatalities from lightning than from baseball.

But, it's the nonphysical trauma that the shrinks cavil about. Says Dr. Hale: "We know kids are not harmed by these pressures. A kid is crying two minutes after a game, but 10 minutes after a game he's in the pool playing with the guy who struck him out. It's the managers and the coaches who are sitting in the dugout brooding."

No one has ever been scarred for life because he missed the third strike or dropped a pop fly in Little League, but Dr. Hale better get used to the boo stories. I remember once a friend told me about the kid in our Little League who cried and sulked and climbed into a tree and stayed there all night because they wouldn't let him pitch. Gravely worried, we brought this problem to his uncle.

"That's right," he admitted. "But did they also tell you he cries and sulks and climbs into a tree all night if they won't let him play with knives or put his little sister in a trunk or the cat in the disposal?"

MISSING:
An Ocean of Joy

This Christmas morning, for the first time in 18 years, I walk out my front door and an old friend is no longer there. My ocean.

I have abandoned my great shining sea for the ease and access of the city. I have left the ramparts for the soft center. I have left my love for my comforts. I have left the sunset land and wild acres for the sedate, the secure.

I have traded white caps for white houses. I shall never be exactly the same person again.

Did you ever watch a sun sink into a molten sea? Have you ever had a chance to watch the changeling moods of a mighty ocean—*the* mightiest of oceans?

An ocean is like a person—now stormy, raging, passionate, dangerous, reckless, now spent and placid and resting from its labors of anger.

They say the moon once dwelled where the Pacific landfalls appeared, ripped from its bed by some cataclysmic rage of nature in antiquity. The floor of the ocean is the same substance as the core of the earth, the only body of water with a carpeting of basalt.

A view of the ocean is a great healer in bad times. Its very immutability is a reminder that what has gone wrong in your little life is not a flyspeck on the grand and mysterious design of things. It can be an ocean of tears. But in the best of times, it can be an ocean of joy.

It cools the land. It brings the rain. It is probably the real mother of man. Or the father of life. It is bountiful, forgiving. Or cruel and merciless. It is never boring. Beneath its placid surface lurk the most fascinating creatures on the planet.

It is full of caprice. It can take the life of a bather caught in a rip in four feet of water—or it can spare a man who bobs on

15

its surface on a plank for two months 2,000 miles from the nearest land.

To the person who bought my house, I leave more than the land, the bricks, the mountain backdrop to the north and east. I leave a vista where, as far as the eye or the glass can see, there is nothing between you and Japan but a few seal-covered islands.

I leave a headland surrounded by the deepest water of the Southern California littoral. Robert Louis Stevenson country. Herman Melville land. Four-masters anchored here. Smugglers in stocking caps prowled Paradise Cove. The proper name of the promontory is Pt. Dume (originally pronounced "Du-may" after a French smuggler or pirate), but I always preferred "Pt. Doom."

On nights when fog creeps across the fingers of land, and the deep-water buoy off the rocks sounds its mournful dirge, you'll know why. It becomes a British moor, sound is muffled, lights are snuffed, in the gray invasion from the sea.

You will want to watch the whales this time of the year. God's most majestic and awesome creatures—they would make an elephant look like a poodle or the toy of the breed—make their stately way south in their annual migration to replenish their endangered species in the waters of Mexico's Magdalena Bay. They frolic down. They roll languidly back, their passion spent. Sometimes they press into the rocks off the point to scrape barnacles off their massive sides, looking like giant submarines. There is a living Disney movie rolling past your front door. A whale is the most humbling sight a man can see.

It is not paradise. Those devil winds from the north and east, as hot as a dragon's breath, will howl, down the mountain passes about seven times a year and you will huddle inside and curse them. They were worse before I put those eucalyptus trees behind the house. Would you believe those soaring branches were in pots when I put them in? A "Santana" can be as unnerving as being in a Great Plains blizzard. But, as a friend pointed out, "you don't have to shovel wind the next day."

The trouble was, all this was 45 miles from the clangor of the marketplace. It was an explosive love affair. The cost was in time. It is easily spent when you are 35 years old. You have lots of it. But a weekend beach traffic jam ages a man who has to get to a ballpark, or a ballplayer, through it.

Still, I will envy you when I hear rain falling on pavement, and I know you are watching *my* storm come in—long gray veils of rain sweeping in from the tossing sea, leaving the temples of the mountains with the hoar of mist, what the poet calls the "compassionate sweet laughter of the rain, the gray-eyed daughters of the mist above the flawed and driven tide."

Then, and not only then, but mostly then, will I miss my lovely, lost land, my sunset, my ocean, my 18 Christmases by the side of my beloved sea.

OF HUMAN BONDAGE

MAY 8, 1974

To the guy who stole my golf clubs, the guy who bought them off him, or the police who are looking for them:

You won't need the registration number (47939). Just take them out and play them—or follow someone who is trying to.

Take the No. 1 wood first. This is a club which, no matter how you come to the ball, or with what swing, opens up precisely at impact. And sends the ball bananaing crazily out of bounds or into the deep rough on the right.

There is no correction you can make. I've tried them all. The only time it will avail you to aim down the left side is if there's water there. In that case, the club will automatically adjust itself into a smoother hook and go smack into the middle of the hazard with a large splash. The club has a natural instinct for trouble. It's a born outlaw. If it were human, it'd be robbing banks.

The putter only looks steel. Actually, it's a 4½-foot garter snake which comes to life over 3-foot putts. It has a built-in tremor. I think it eats mice at night.

There is no way in the world the 7-iron will get a ball in the air. The club's sole retracts three inches into the shaft as it comes into the ball. It has never hit a ball anywhere but on the skull. It has scalped more objects than the Plains Indians.

The sand wedge has a great little sense of humor. In the first place, it checks to see if you've put greasy kid stuff in your hair. In that case, it always turns so you are facing into the wind in a bunker. It is programmed never to hit in the vicinity of the ball on the first swing. Rather, it sends a shower of sand into your hair where it will stick for six months. Now, on its *next* shot, it *does* hit the ball. Over a tree and into the parking lot. For an encore, it might throw cayenne pepper in your eyes or give you a hotfoot. If it extricates a ball from a trap in one shot, it's not my club.

It's academic anyway—because the guy who stole, fenced, or got my clubs out of hock has long since wrapped them around a tree or sunk them in a lake or driven a truck over them or used them as fire pokers.

Still, you grow attached. Like Leslie Howard in *Of Human Bondage,* you're unable to help yourself. They may turn out to be strumpets and faithless and deceive you every time and treat you like a cowering cripple, but you can't help it. They're the only clubs in the world for you, fickle, cruel, shallow though they might be. You're like Don Jose in Carmen. You go around begging them to hurt you some more, and, when they're gone, you miss them.

Now, you start the hunt for a set that will beat you, torment you, mock you, turn on you. You want a set just like the set that didn't marry dear old dad.

I don't know whether you know it or not, but a golfer on the scent of new clubs makes Don Juan look like a dependable, 9-to-5 type, the marrying kind. A golfer looking for new clubs is like Joe Namath on a pickup. He'll dance with every girl at the prom.

I first tried the latest rage, the Simmons International Golf Tech Honeycombs. These have the cellular structure of a bee-hive, a metal honeycomb that a bear would try to lick if he found it hanging on a tree. Pat Simmons, president of the company, pressed a set on me over at Calabasas.

I hit a 7-iron and the ball rose in the air 50 feet, hit the green and *backed up*—as if Sammy Snead had hit it! The 3-wood flew out there 200 yards. It didn't even *look* over towards the right rough. "You can land an iron shot on the side of the Empire State Building and stop it," boasted Pat.

I didn't know how to break it to him. The clubs were not for me. I mean, what will I do with clubs that don't have an automatic "top" built in? How can I explain to my pals a ball that doesn't scream across the green like a train going off a trestle? I'll have to get a whole new set of friends if I start coming out of sandtraps in one.

Simmons was shocked. It was like turning down a date with Elizabeth Taylor.

I went through four or five other sets. What I was looking for was a Bette Davis, if you know what I mean. Sticks that would never get me below a 20 handicap.

Alas, that thief who stole my clubs stole my heart. Toney Penna makes clubs that should hang in Tiffany's windows. You screw a jeweler's glass in your eye to play them. Toney makes clubs the way Stradivarius made fiddles.

"Toney," I told him, "I can't be seen on a golf course with some things that could shoot 69 all by themselves. I need a bagful of mean spirited cayuses. One-legged pirates. Cheating dames, if you know what I mean."

"Wait a minute," said Toney. "Let's see your swing." I showed him. The famous, fluid eight-piece takeaway, the $3^{1}/_{2}$-piece return to the ball, the fall-away downswing, the jump shot, the dunk lunge, the dribble—the whole arsenal of the born 23-handicapper.

Toney whistled. "Listen," he said, "don't change a thing! I'll guarantee you your clubs will start to drink, stay out all night, chase around—*anything* to get away from you. Don't worry. By the end of six months, these clubs won't be hitting the ball anywhere but into trouble on you. They'll start cutting balls on you out of spite, putting sand in you hair, quivering to get out of your hand, screaming silently in the bag, and pretending to get stuck in the webbing—anything to keep you from getting your hands on them."

I felt better already. Only the other day, my 3-wood lost six new balls on me. And I think I heard it laughing. We're going to get along just fine. I felt just like Leslie Howard when Bette Davis threw a drink in his face and went off with a sailor.

BLASTING A GOLF TRAIL

AUGUST 25, 1974

Some guys want to climb the Matterhorn. Others dream of singing opera. Still others wish they could quarterback the Rams. But my life's ambition has always been to hold the course record somewhere. You know, like Sam Snead holds the course record, 59, at Greenbrier, and Mike Souchak had a 60 at Breckenridge Park in San Antonio. And so on.

I always wanted to have people point me out as I tee it up somewhere and have them whisper, "That's Jim Murray. You know, he holds the course record at L.A. North. Shot a 56. In the rain."

I *know*, of course, I could never hold the course record at Riviera. The best I've ever done there is 103. Still, it's nice to dream.

My friend, John Marin, didn't know any of this when he called me the other weekend. "How'd you like to be the *first* ever to play a new course up on Mulholland Drive?" he asked.

My first inclination was to say "No." I'm between swings, at the moment, changing over from a Gay Brewer loop to a Doug Ford duck hook. Then, a light went on.

"Wait a minute," I said. "You mean *nobody's* played it—*ever?*"

"That's right," he said. "Never had a cleat mark on it. Won't open for a couple of months. Mountain Gate, 6,900 yards of sylvan beauty. Might have to chase the deer off if they're in our line."

My mind reeled. If I played it, I would have the course record!

"I'll get a foursome," John pledged.

"No, no, don't do that!" I implored him. "There'll just be the two of us. *Please!* Uh, how're you playing?"

"Haven't had a club in my hand in six months," John said cheerfully. "I got this little loop in my backswing."

"Get your clubs!" I screamed. "I'll meet you at the first tee!"

Now, do you have any idea what a thrill it is to stand on a tee and *know* you're going to set a competitive course record? To know that *every* shot is history?

Egad! I know what the captain of the *Titanic* felt like when he sailed out of Liverpool, what Napoleon must have thought crossing into Russia.

I wondered if Snead took a mulligan when he shot his 59. Never mind. I did.

Johnny Marin beat me on the first hole. The little double-crosser threw a six at me. I got very cross with him. "Well," I said. "If you're going to go around bogeying all day, we might as well wind this up right now. You told me you were off your game."

"Look at it this way," John said. "You had the first eight ever recorded at Mountain Gate."

A minute later. I had the first lost ball. Then, I had the first-ball-to-bounce-off-a-tree and the first-man-ever-hit-in-the-face-by-his-own-golf-ball.

A hole or two later I became the first golfer ever at Mountain Gate to take seven shots to the edge of a green and say out loud, "Let's see, I lie three to here." The first, but not the last.

I set a whole bunch of firsts. First ever to hit a ball onto the San Diego Freeway, first ever to go off in the knee-high brush, first ever to dribble a new ball out of my pocket while pretending to bend down and then say, "Here it is! Hey, I got an open shot!"

I was the first guy ever to mark a ball and then move the marker three feet when my opponent turned his back. I became the first ever to get a 56-foot "gimme" and the first to pocket my ball 14 feet from the hole and say, when my partner arrived on the green, "It was in the leather."

John became the first guy ever to whiff there but he got kind of huffy when I noted the honor. "It wasn't a whiff," he insisted. "The ball fell backwards off the tee one inch. It's the first *backward* shot, is what it is."

"No, it isn't," I reminded him. "That tree I hit on No. 2, the ball bounced *backward* 80 yards. Yours is the *shortest* backward shot but not the first."

I was the first guy to leave a ball in a sand trap, the first guy ever to hit a provisional and then sneak ahead and pretend to have found my first shot. "Here it is! It's 'in' after all" I shouted, thus becoming the first liar.

I hold the 9-hole record, the 18-hole record. I hold the record score for holes 2, 3, 4, 5, 8, 10, 13, 14, 15, 16, 17. Marin, the louse, halved or won the rest. I'm the first guy to kick an opponent's ball *into* the rough while teeing up my own ball there. I'm the first one ever to say, "I think it breaks left about 10 inches" of a putt of his which I knew perfectly well was straight in or, if anything, broke right.

I threw a 45 at him the front nine with a dazzling display of footwork (the feet are the most important part of the game as any golfer can tell you and as I have proven over and over again by kicking balls out of sand traps or into preferred lies).

I threw a little 48 at the back nine. That'll give the boys something to shoot at. A 93 gross. It'll be months before anyone breaks that. They'll have to put my picture in the clubhouse as soon as they build one. Bobby Jones may have a record at the "Auld Course," Nicklaus may have the record at Scioto or some place, but I have the record at the New Course.

Don't think it was a walk in the park. Johnny threw a 111 score at me. I couldn't let up.

Come to think of it, I'm the club champion! All these years I've been envying those guys who get their names in silver on the club trophy and a little write-up in the club magazine and now, here I am, club champion, gross and net, and holder of the course record. I think I'll bring out an instructional book. *The Course Record And How to Win It,* or, *The Importance of Timing in Winning the Club Championship.*

And, some day, when they hold the U.S. Open there, I can go around and people will point at me and say, "Did you know old Jim used to hold the course record around here? Shot the lights out of it back in '74, they tell me."

Move over, Sammy, Jack, Arnold, Bobby and Ben. Make way for the Master of Mountain Gate! One of the all-time immorals of the game! The Golden Bore!

I wonder if this gets me in the Masters?

WEIRD SITE
FOR A FIGHT

SEPTEMBER 15, 1974

EN ROUTE TO DARKEST AFRICA—All right, my good man, hand me my jodhpurs and pith helmet and polish my monocle. Get the elephant ready. Fire up the African Queen. Phone Berlitz and see what they have in the way of Swahili. Get Tarzan and Jane on the drum and see what they're doing Tuesday. See what you can find out about the tsetse fly. Call me Bwana. Let's hope Grace Kelly and Ava Gardner get to fight over me in the steaming jungle night.

They're holding the world heavyweight championship fight in the Congo, I guess because the top of Mt. Everest was busy. I don't know why they can't hold it in Yankee Stadium like everybody else. The only African word I know is "Cheetah." I always thought "Kinshasa" was one of the Gabor sisters. "Zaire" sounds like an NFL placekicker.

It took the Mann Act to run the Jack Johnson–Jess Willard fight to Havana. It took the governor of California, taken down with an attack of high-minded morality, to run the Johnson-Jeffries fight to Reno.

They have fought on barges, in Mississippi swamps. They ran the Muhammad Ali–Sonny Liston bout clear up to Lewiston, Maine, before they found somebody who wouldn't padlock it. But nobody ever thought of the equator before.

Dempsey and Gibbons fought in Shelby, Montana, because the state solons wanted to put Shelby on the map. When Dempsey's manager got through with it, they had put it off the map. Dempsey was the first fighter in history to knock out seven banks in one fight.

But, ordinarily, promoters from Tex Rickard to Mike Jacobs preferred to keep the thing on a subway ... until lately when the "Have Fight, Will Travel" syndrome cropped up. George Foreman won his title in Jamaica, defended it in Tokyo and

24

Venezuela. Ali picks Madison Square Garden only after he has exhausted all the other romantic places on the globe—like Frankfurt, Zurich, Houston, Lewiston and Las Vegas.

Here, perhaps, is a chance to top Dempsey, to break a country. Except that Swiss banks are putting up the line of credit and American pay-TV is almost sure to sell out—at $25 a seat tops.

For those with a stake in the Congo, it is viewed as a chance to prove it is not the 17th-century happy hunting ground of the gorilla, the tsetse fly, and asp, pygmy blowgun and purple people-eaters of the *Trader Horn* and *Africa Speaks* movies; not the Ernest Hemingway country where the hyenas prowl the expedition tents by night and the vultures circle by day and the jungle drums in the soundtrack mean that 8-foot warriors with rings through their noses and stone spears are coming.

It is a dark and bloody ground like Boone's Kentucky. Before the blood was off the walls, the UN, Kasavubu, Tshombe, Lumumba and Mobutu had warred over the land when they threw the Belgians out. Dag Hammerskjold died there.

It is worth fighting over. Tin and gold, copper and diamonds are found there. Madame Curie got her radium there. Pythons, tree cobras, puff adders, tigerfish, electric eels, gorillas, elephants, hippopotamus, rhinoceros, leopards and the dreaded tsetse are also found there. Dr. Livingstone, I presume, was found there.

It is a 200-tribe complex which lay comfortably in the Stone Age until the white man began the search for the headwaters of the Nile. The elephants' graveyard, theme of many Edgar Rice Burroughs ape-man movies, lies there.

It is an audacious idea, a heavyweight title bout in the shadow of the Ruwenzori. For ink-stained wretches, more used to the dark interior of Madison Square Garden whose only knowledge of Africa comes from reading *The Short Happy Life of Francis Macomber,* the experience may be unsettling enough so that many will never return and be found unshaven and delirious wandering the brush looking for the Eighth Avenue subway or Robinson Crusoe.

The fight will be held at the witching hour of 3:30 A.M., a time zone for millions of spontaneous fights over the years but never one contracted beforehand. Usually you have to steal someone's girl or drink to get in a fight at that hour. These guys are only going to steal $5 million apiece. This will be the first fight at that hour where the principals wore gloves.

Well, if you're sure Clyde Beatty and Cecil Rhodes and Martin and Osa Johnson got their start this way, hand me my quinine and I'll unlock the secrets of the Dark Continent—like, do they use the 5-point must system of scoring there? Do you stop a fight because of malaria? What language is the count in? Arthur Brisbane once said of a title fight, "A gorilla could lick both of them." Unless they post guards at the gate at Kinshasa, we may find out.

THE TERROR OF INDY

MAY 23, 1975

INDIANAPOLIS—Some people never sample the wine of life. Some people stay down in the valley. Some people opt for the rocking chair, the crossword puzzle, the briefcase and 9-to-5 job.

Not your correspondent. The blood of adventurers courses through these veins. The scent of excitement runs through my life. Let others pine for the safe, the comfortable. Give me the ramparts, the unclimbed, the mysterious beauty of the unknown.

I have never faced Sandy Koufax' fastball, Muhammad Ali's left jab, Larry Csonka's rhinoceros charge. I have never hunted the lion, rode the shark or walked a jet wing.

But I have braved the terror in the corners of Indy. I have joined the Knights of the Roaring Road. I have gone hell-bent down the terrible straights of the Brickyard. I have joined the immortals of racing, the Rickenbackers. Barney Oldfields. They may make a movie about my life—starring Jim Garner or Paul Newman. I drove the dreaded Indianapolis Motor Speedway, the graveyard of many brave young men.

"Goggles" Murray, the scourge of the Speedway. Foyt turns pale at the sound of my engines revving up to speed. Rutherford would rather see a train bearing down on him than catch old Goggles in his rear-view mirror.

I went through the turns at a fearsome speed of 12.5 mph. I was a blur on the straightaways at 22.5. I came near to frying the clutch in my pit stop.

The car I climbed in was the one Mario Andretti set the world speed record in a couple of years ago, a closed-circuit mark of 214.158 mph I quickly ascertained that the temperature of the track wouldn't handle that kind of speed, that I had to save the car and not run too lean a mixture. All the great drivers save their cars.

As I was strapped in the car by Andretti and Parnelli Jones, I heard a hush fall over the Speedway. Stopwatches clicked along the pit wall. People came out of every garage in Gasoline Alley. Old Zero was on the track.

I checked out the pedals carefully like all the great ones do. "Where's the cigarette lighter?" I asked. Like Foyt, I'm a perfectionist. "You're going to smoke?!" demanded Parnelli. "In a 'Viceroy' car?" I asked. "I thought it was required. Well, if I can't smoke, how about a bottle of champagne?"

I was soon out of the pits and onto the track. I waved one finger exultantly in the air. I checked my instruments. The car was handling nicely at a steady 15 mph.

Suddenly, in my rear-view mirror I saw a track sweeper truck bearing down on me. I realized unless I did something he would dive under me in the groove and take the lead. I upped the boost to 22 mph and held him safely in my sights.

I went past Hell's Corner where Pat O'Connor was killed in '58, past the crash sites of a dozen drivers, brave men, all.

I lapped the track sweeper, coming dangerously close to the wall—80 feet. Into the short chute, I charged. I had to make several split-second decisions—whether to eat the peanut-butter sandwiches I had brought aboard, whether to abort the run. I could tell one of the cylinders was running raggedly and the wing wasn't holding the car on the track.

As I pitted, I climbed out of the car the way Foyt does when things aren't going right, slammed my helmet to the ground, unbuttoned my flameproof suit and said, "Dammit! I told you to check that boost. The car was fishtailing like a salmon as I got up to speed—22 mph."

"Congratulations!" said Parnelli. "You have just completed the first Speedway run in history that could be timed by a sun dial and a calendar." "What are you talking about!" I yelled. "I almost bought it in Turn One! Andretti would have gone right into the crowd if a car did that to him! I saved you a $100,000 automobile." Parnelli was disgusted. "At the speed you were going, you could have run over a bee and not bruised it."

"Listen, Jones!" I told Parnelli. "Don't you realize there's an energy crisis?! Just ask yourself—did I conserve on fuel and tires? Did I punish the chassis? Did anybody slip in my oil? Was the yellow light on any part of my trip?"

"Yellow light?!" screamed Parnelli. "I thought we were going to have to go out and look for you! You would have finished fourth in the Kentucky Derby!"

Of course, there's more to race driving than just standing on it in the turns. "There's a million things to check in that cockpit. Tires, heat gauge, oil pressure, wind direction, the groove," I told him. "You could have read a book!" protested Parnelli. I wasn't about to give up. "Did you ever have to blow off a track sweeper in Turn Three?" I asked him.

When you make it at the Speedway, the United States Auto Club acknowledges you have arrived by printing up a small bio of you in its USAC sanction book. Mine will now read:

"Murray, James ('Goggles')

"Age: 55, height 6', weight, refuses to give.

"Marital standing: Dubious. Wife, Geraldine. Four children.

"1967—Won the pole on the Santa Monica Freeway off-ramp at Harbor in a blown Cougar with front-end suspension.

"1968—Rear-ended a 1947 Ford driven by an uninsured pensioner with a hard-luck story.

"1969—Black-flagged by wife after noisy party for throwing oil and trying to put car key in cigarette lighter.

"1970—Got lost while running 15th, phoned Auto Club for directions.

"1971—Set record for getting up hill from Rose Bowl after New Year's Day game breaking old mark of six hours and five minutes by 10 seconds.

"1972—Found a parking spot in Beverly Hills the first time around the block.

"1973—Saw and reported a car in Westwood *not* driven by a woman.

"1974—Got to a destination on directions given by sister-in-law.

"1975—Ran out of gas on Hollywood Freeway during rush hour.

"May 22—Ran the slowest lap on the Indianapolis Speedway by any car not steered by tiller or any four-wheeled vehicle not pulled or pedaled."

I am super-qualified.

I braved *their* track. I'd like to see them on mine—the dreadful stretch from the Harbor to the Santa Monica at five o'clock at night with your glasses sweaty, your shocks worn—and two California highway patrolmen in your rear-view mirror behind on their quotas.

SCORE IT NONSENSE

SEPTEMBER 21, 1975

Tennis is a game in which love counts nothing, deuces are wild and the scoring system was invented by Lewis Carroll.

It has never made much headway with the poor people, and I think I know why. It's not a game, it's a multiplication table. The guys who invented it clearly wanted to keep out anybody who couldn't do square roots. You don't play it, you compute it. Data systems with nets.

Why would you guess the first point would be scored 15? The second, 30? And the third, 40? If you spot a trend there, go directly to the Theory of Relativity.

Six games win a set. But only if you stay two games ahead of your opponent. Why? You can win a baseball game by one run, a fight by one punch, a football game by one point. In soccer, that's about all you usually do score.

Tennis weaves around in the upper reaches of calculus. My guess is it was made up by the kind of guys who roll dice in their own hats and tell you that you lost. My theory is the kings kept rigging the game till the peasants got a headache.

The scoring system is so arcane, just short of logarithms, that joining tennis is like joining the House of Lords. It's really not a sport, it's a club, a ritual, like the Masons.

The game is as old as the pharaohs but it never really got out of the castles or the railroad barons' casinos in Newport. For thousands of years, everyone who played it wore or was white, and had a whole bunch of hyphens or Roman numerals in his name or was a baron or an earl. There wasn't a guy in it didn't have two or more syllables in his first name. You couldn't understand him unless you went to Groton.

I don't know why there should be a score like 40–40 in the

first place, but how it adds up to deuce, I leave for Alice in Wonderland to figure out.

Why is a Davis Cup round called a tie? Obviously, so the lorgnette set can spot a tradesman in their midst, and get the coachman to usher him out.

Are all those obscure definitions really necessary? I mean, it may look to you like some guy just hitting the damn ball but to them it's a drop volley or ground stroke (which, by the way, is just hitting a bouncing ball).

Why should you get two serves? You don't get two at-bats one right after the other in an inning. If you hit a foul pop-up, you're out. If you miss the putt in golf, that's it. The service ace is probably the single most boring thing in sports next to the foul tip anyway, but tennis encourages it by giving you a mulligan on your serve, so you can go for it on the first serve. I wonder what king thought *that* one up?

Who do you suppose started the let ball? The let that ticks the net is silly enough. If a guy can't keep his serve from skidding off the top of the net—well, too bad. He should play it as it lies. But the let—played when a point is in dispute or the umpire didn't get a good look at it or the queen was on her way to the royal box—is really laughable. Imagine a close play at home plate in the World Series where the umpire frowns, bites his lip, appeals to others, and then says, "OK, everybody back to where they were. We're going to play a let on that." Tennis does this all the time. Probably Charlemagne had trouble keeping the serves high enough.

A few years ago, a man named Jimmy Van Alen came along with a system for simplifying the game. They gave him short shrift. Thing is, they don't *want* to make it decipherable to truck drivers. God knows manners are in enough trouble in this day and age without tampering with something sacred like tennis.

But they did adopt—with a pained look—something called the tie-breaker. This is tennis' version of showdown poker. You play it at stately, ritualistic gavotte pace till the score is 6–6, and then you give each side a lot of free punches at each other.

The point is, if they can do this on the goal line, so to speak, why not on the kickoff? If it's OK in the bottom of the ninth, why not in the top of the first?

I plan to go out to the Pacific Southwest finals at Pauley

Pavilion today with my own simplified scoring system. Each guy gets one point a winner, no more and no less. I expect to have every monocle on my side of the court fogged up in anger. But I'll keep the game in my mathematical range, not Einstein's.

A MATTER OF
BLIND FAITH

MARCH 16, 1978

For years, I have had a secret ambition in life. It's simple. Some guys want to climb the Matterhorn. Others want to shoot 69. Some want to corner the market. Me? All I want to do is see a hockey goal.

I guess I've been watching the sport off and on for 30 years. And I've never seen a goal. If they don't light that red light, I'm in trouble. My compliments to the guy who lights it. He must be part hawk. When I see a 4–3 hockey game, I take it on blind faith there were seven goals scored. I didn't see any of them.

I mean, look! I have seen home runs in baseball, bombs in pro football. I can dig a service ace in tennis. I can catch a layup in basketball, a short KO punch in boxing. But, when 11 players get around the net in hockey with two linesmen thrown in for good measure, that puck might as well be white.

You know what I think? I don't think goals are *scored* at all. They bounce off pipes, ricochet off skates, slide in by themselves. They usually award a goal and two assists when this happens. Some guys get assists who haven't touched the puck in hours. If I were a hockey player, I'd just kind of skulk around the net, skating back and forth till a crowd collected, and, the minute I saw the light start to go around, I'd throw my hands and stick up in the air and act like I did it.

I was there the night Phil Esposito set the record for most goals—or most points—or both—in a season. Know how he did it? He *slid* into the net. The puck was somewhere on him. It was kind of like a catcher making a tag with his gloved hand in baseball. But it was kind of disappointing. Like Babe Ruth *bunting* a home run, if you know what I mean.

I think the 11-inch touchdown is the most uninteresting play in football, next to the shovel pass. But, in hockey, that's all you get. I keep going to games hoping to see the midcourt slap shots go in the crease. They never do. They hit the goalie, the glass, the pipes or the wall. Laid end to end, all the hockey goals in one season wouldn't reach to the blue line.

I mean, what does a goal look like? What color is it? What does it sound like? Is it bigger than a breadbox? Does it even exist? Or was hockey really invented by Lewis Carroll?

I figured if anyone knew what a hockey goal looked like it would be Gary Simmons. Gary Simmons is the backup goalie on the Los Angeles Kings and, the other night in Boston, the Bruins scored nine goals against him. This is not a record, but the light is on so much you need sunglasses in the crease when this happens. When you get nine goals scored against you in one night, you ought to be able to describe a goal right down to the mole on its neck.

On the other hand, maybe Gary's problem is that he, too, has no idea what one looks like. And therefore can't stop it.

Goals, Gary says, are like viruses. You can't see them, but when you get hit by them you know they're there. Plenty of goals have been scored in the NHL by guys trying to stop them. Many a goal has caromed off the skate—or the eye—of a defenseman trying to block it. As a result, a goalie can't trust anybody. He has 11 men to watch—12 if the opposite goalie's out of the net for a late-period flurry. I say 12, because a goalie can't even rely on himself. Many a goalie has carried in a goal himself by mistake.

Like me, Gary takes goals on blind faith—with the accent on blind. "In the first place, you're screened off from most goals," he says. "You can hear the puck coming but you can't always see it."

A puck, of course, is just a giant tiddlywink. It is designed for stealth, just one inch high, three inches across, and the color of skate shoes. The game is almost incomprehensible on TV, like a fox hunt on skates, in that you can't see the quarry.

"Fully half of the goals are scored in scrambles in front of the net, or on deflections or on funny bounces," says Simmons, in an opinion shared by the starting goalie, Rogie Vachon.

The other night, I sat near center ice at the Forum and dutifully tried to watch the puck as the Kings and the Penguins played. I was determined to see a goal.

I felt as if I were on a snipe hunt. The score was 3–2 late in the third period. According to the scoreboard, that is. You couldn't prove it by me.

With about two minutes left, I sneaked a look at my program to see which of the bewildering series of lines was on the ice. A great roar went up. The light went on. Next to me the official scorer, John Bealey, was shouting into a telephone. "Score by No. 19! Assist by 17 and 7!" He turned to me. "Did you see that?! A breakaway by Butch Goring! He deaked the goalie right out of his skates! A great goal!"

I took his word for it. I sighed, and just put it down with the others in my book, *My Life at Center Ice, Or, Great Goals I Never Saw.*

THE HALL OF WHAT?

APRIL 6, 1978

SALISBURY, NORTH CAROLINA—A Hall of Fame is something Ty Cobb belongs to. Red Grange. Jim Brown. Ben Hogan.

It's for guys with great coordination, with all their hair and teeth, who can see swell without glasses, who can catch a falling object with one hand or block a 280-pound lineman, hit the curve, block a shot, make a $50,000 putt.

Halls of Fame are not for myopic writers, guys who say "Huh?" a lot when you talk softly, who typewrite with one finger and get gas when they eat too fast.

So, what in the world is this unworthy traveler doing in a Hall of Fame? What am I doing in a Hall of Fame if Maury Wills or Enos Slaughter can't get in one?

I'll be cussed if I know, but the National Sportscasters and Sportswriters Association inducted me into the same august company as Babe Ruth, Ty Cobb, and the Galloping Ghost this week, and they'll have to explain it to you, I can't. I feel like Rabbit Maranville. Or that guy who played third base with Tinker and Evers and Chance.

You know, when a guy makes the real Hall of Fame at Cooperstown or Canton or Pinehurst, he usually can tell you how he got there—his home runs, his catches, passes, drives, 9-irons or free throw percentage.

But, what did I do—out-adjective the next guy? Did I split fewer infinitives than anybody else? Avoid hitting into the double negative? The pros talk about "playing with pain." Did I write with pain, shrug off the hangovers better than anyone else and hit that space bar with desire?

Did I go with the pitch better, take what the defense gave me? Go for that extra yardage with adverbs hanging all over me?

I do hold the major league vodka one game, one season, one

Series, and Super Bowl records. I tied the record for most nights on Bourbon Street, and tied with many for most dawns viewed through the bottom of a glass with a cherry in it. But that's not Hall of Fame stuff in my profession. That just makes you a journeyman.

Maybe it was my expertise? Uh-uh. I've been covering horse races for 25 years and I still can't tell a colt from a filly except under very special circumstances.

Auto racing? If they took the steering wheel out, I couldn't tell the front from the back of one of those Indy cars. I have no idea what a magneto is, and I'd never drive anything you had to climb in the windows to start up.

In basketball, I wouldn't know a moving pick from a moving picture. And the differences between a "high post" and a "low post," I leave to the post office.

In football, I could never figure out why every game had to start with a run off tackle, particularly when it always lost two yards or made no gain. But coaches look at me pityingly when I ask why. And give me an answer studded with obscure definitions of defenses that make me feel as if I asked Einstein to explain the expanding universe.

Baseball? I'll tell you what. I wouldn't know a balk from a hole in the ground. Walt Alston used to draw me pictures, and I still didn't get it. The infield fly rule is about as simple as calligraphy. It might as well be a Japanese naval code.

Prize fighting? All right, I can tell a right cross from a left jab. But I always think the other guy from the one the judges pick won the fight. Anyway, Joe Louis and Ray Robinson were the last fighters I would cross the street to see.

Golf? I can't break 90. To tell the truth, I can't break 100. If it weren't for "gimmes," I probably couldn't break 200.

So what does that leave—writing?

I never wrote a line like "Outlined against the blue-gray October sky, the Four Horsemen rode again. They formed the crest of a Midwest cyclone, etc." I'm no Grantland Rice. I never thought up "Murderer's Row" for the Yankees. I thought that I thought up "Louisville Lip" for the former Cassius Clay but John Hall convinced me he beat me to it. Frankly, it's not worth fighting over.

You know who's in this Hall of Fame? Ring Lardner, for one. If he were alive today, he'd resign. He'd figure, there goes the neighborhood. I got a nerve being in the same county with Ring Lardner, never mind the same shrine.

Dan Parker is in it. Red Smith. Ted Husing. Dizzy Dean, the only guy to make two Halls of Fame, our and theirs. Red Barber is there. John Kieran. Graham McNamee. I tell you, there are some guys there who wouldn't even have a drink with me.

But, then, you see, times change. Guys who bat .286 get candy bars named after them today. Utility outfielders get $60,000 a year. Regulars start at a million.

I'm a prime example of inflation, is what I am. I'm in a Hall of Fame with guys whose typewriters I couldn't carry. But that's nothing. Look who's been sleeping in Lincoln's bed lately.

They even had my old pal, John Wayne, lined up to do the induction. But, it turned out, Duke had a more pressing appointment at Massachusetts General Hospital. Tennessee Ernie Ford and Andy Griffith came riding to the rescue, in the best traditions of a John Wayne movie. The Indians lost, as usual.

It made me very proud, if very mystified. I felt like a guy who had wandered into the wrong party, who showed up at the fox hunt ball wearing brown shoes, and everybody was too polite to throw him out.

It reminds me of the long road that began when either John Carter or Dr. Ed McKenzie called me from North Carolina 15 years ago to say that I had been selected by the ballot of the NSSA for its finalist award. "NSSA?! Salisbury?!" I protested. "I never heard of them!" "That's all right," was their soothing response. "They never heard of you, either."

And now, here I am immortalized in stone forever, horned-rimmed glasses and all, in this funny little Gone-with-the-Wind town in the Confederacy. It reminds me of the time when Bill Cosby, the comedian, was asked to describe my writing style at a Friars dinner. "Well," he said, "he's a cross between Eleanor Roosevelt and Hilo Hattie."

Shucks, I was proud even to be noticed. And I'm proud to be in the Hall of Fame, too. Just think, me and Joe DiMaggio!

LAWS OF
MURRAY

NOVEMBER 23, 1978

Murphy's Law, that all-time axiom on the inevitability of error in human endeavor, was first postulated by a systems engineer at a testing lab at Edwards Air Force Base some years ago and is the takeoff point for a book, *Murphy's Law and Other Reasons Why Things Go Wrong!* by Arthur Bloch and published in its fifth printing by Price/Stern/Sloan, the chuckle merchants of the paper chase.

The law has been refined down to "Whatever can go wrong, will," and Bloch has followed up with a collection of "laws" from various other Pythagoreans or modern theorem-makers. His basic theme is the acceptance of despair or, as they say on Mad Avenue, "The bottom line is, it won't work."

O'Brien's Law is "Murphy was an optimist." Jerry Brown's Law of Lowered Expectations has many parts: "Everything tastes more or less like chicken, and sounds more or less like Beethoven," and, "If aspirin won't cure it, you're beyond modern medical science."

There are others, "To make a bus come, light a cigarette," "To make the phone ring, go to the bathroom." Also, "Nothing is hard for the man who doesn't have to do it himself."

Murray's Variants of the Murphy-Bloch laws are not quite as universal and are most applicable in the arena.

Nothing is ever so bad it can't be made worse by firing the coach.

A free agent is anything but.

If you can smile when everything about you is going wrong, join the San Francisco 49ers.

Things always get worse just before they get impossible.

Nothing is ever accomplished by reason—look at Woody Hayes.

You can fool all of the people all of the time—if you own the network.

The "Peter Principle" that everything keeps rising until it reaches its level of incompetence is best illustrated by the Minnesota Vikings in the Super Bowl.

Anger is always a proper substitute for logic.

If everything else fails, throw it away.

The old Army game, "If it moves, salute it, if it doesn't move, paint it!" is changed to, "If it moves, salute it. If it doesn't move, it must be the Rams and Atlanta."

Whatever can go to New York, will. Whatever can't will go to Philadelphia.

The wrong Ram quarterback is the one that's in there.

Any two TV programs you like will go on opposite each other.

Hockey is a game played by six good skaters and the home team.

Hockey is the only game that can be played equally well with the lights out. There's more to hockey than meets the eye—at least I hope so.

I'm consistent, you're stubborn.

Rhetoric is the art of being wrong out loud.

You're taking yourself too seriously in the company when you forget it's not your money.

Money isn't everything, look at the California Angels.

When you think everything is hopeless, just remember Yogi Berra.

Cars with the lucky pieces hanging off the rearview mirror will always seem to star in bad accidents.

The guy with the coat slung over his shoulder without his arms in the sleeves in movies is up to no good.

Just remember Nixon not only admitted he was wrong, he set out to prove it. Never tape anything but your mouth. Or your assistant's. Never record your mistakes no matter how proud of them you may be at the time.

The way to make a line move faster is to join the other one.

All things considered, it's better to have Earl Campbell.

The race is not always to the swift, look at Jack Nicklaus.

Never envy the big star of the show, that turkey you're eating thought he had a no-cut contract.

And a Happy Thanksgiving to all of you, and if you can't remember which side your bread is buttered on, don't worry— it's the side that hits the floor.

If you have any complaints, send them to Murphy. Or Arthur Bloch.

THE SAME OLD SONG

JANUARY 16, 1979

MIAMI—All right, it's Super Week again and here I am by sunny Biscayne Bay and I'm fed up. I didn't come 3,000 miles to watch another 1920 Purdue-Iowa game or the Rock Island Red Bugs in a semipro game against the Holy Name Society. Accordingly, I have drafted a letter to the commissioner of all football in the interest of sports fans everywhere.

"Dear Pete Rozelle:

"Well, Pete, here we are at Super Bowl XIII, the sports equivalent of a four-act German opera for pure excitement. Frankly, Pete, I've had it up to here with the not-so-Super Bowls.

"Oh, I don't want you to get the idea I'm one of those guys from an acid-rock paper who drinks up all your drinks, eats up all your food, does a solo on the lobby chandelier the night before the game and then writes *War and Peace* on what a phony hype it all is.

"I don't mind the hype, Pete. Just give me a game.

"The trouble with the game is, it's predictable as the weather in Alaska. As monotonous as a sermon. It usually looks like two woolly mammoths slugging it out in a tar pit.

"Pete, just ask yourself when one of the plays in a Super Bowl went into the anecdotal lore of the game. I mean, like Roy Riegels running the wrong way, a Doyle Nave last-minute pass, a Dream Backfield, a Four Horsemen. Shucks, you haven't even had a coach slugging a player.

"It's not a game, it's a computer match. Dull, usually one-sided, devoid of surprises, even controversy which is the life-blood of sports. When's the last time you heard anybody discussing a Super Bowl game 24 hours after it was played? One hour, for all of that.

43

"Naw, it's just like an exhibition game in August. This thing has not produced one memorable thrill in its existence.

"I think I know what the trouble is, Pete. A coach doesn't want to be embarrassed in this thing. Lord knows the Minnesota Vikings have come close but I mean *really* embarrassed—73–0, like.

"You see, when the stakes are too high, everybody tenses up. So, you go out there and play George Allen football. I mean, two cracks at the line, a swing pass behind the line, a punt—and wait for the other guy to make mistakes.

"Play it by the book, in other words. Like a baseball manager who bunts and gives the hitters the 'take' sign.

"Pete, I've noticed something with the bowls that don't mean anything. You look at the scores of the Bluebonnet Bowl, the Peach Bowl, the Frijole or Rhododendron Bowls. Nobody cares who wins. Nobody is going to come up to you 20 years from now and say, 'How could you let the Big 10 win that Bowl?' The Rose Bowl, maybe. A guy runs the wrong way in the Rose Bowl and he's 'Wrong Way Riegels' all his life.

"But in three other bowls they let it all hang out. The scores are 40–28, or 35–34 (as the so-what Cotton Bowl was this year) or 35–28. They throw the ball around, they try flea-flickers, double reverses, wild card backfield sets. Because they know it's only show biz. A TV show. Woody Hayes even thought he could bop a kid in the Adam's apple because it was, after all, only the Gator Bowl. That's not to be confused with something that really *counts*, I mean, Woody probably wouldn't pop a guy in the Michigan game. He wouldn't open up that much.

"Now, what I want you to do, Pete, is call in the contenders in this Super Bowl and say, 'Hey, I'm the Lord High Commissioner of this thing, right? All right, as of Super Bowl XIII there's going to be some changes made.' I want to see the bomb thrown on first down. Any coach who sends in, or quarterback who calls, a run off tackle on the first play of the game gets an automatic fine or is barred from future Super Bowls.

"No field goal may be kicked under 45 yards. Any team that has a fourth-and-one inside the other team's territory, even if it's the 49-yard line, must go for it.

"There'll be absolutely no falling down on the ball by the quarterback just because there's only a minute to go and he's got four downs to use up the clock. The minute a quarterback falls on the ball, we give the ball immediately to the other team.

"If a guy fumbles the ball, I don't care whether his knee was down or not. You've got to hang onto the ball. None of this whistling it dead, Pete. What they're whistling dead is the game. When you come down from a tackle, you have to have the ball with you. This is particularly true of the end zone. No ball, no touchdown.

"No team is allowed more than five punts a game. A team that has the ball and a two-touchdown lead with eight minutes or less to go must pass the ball two out of three plays anyway. No such thing as killing the clock in any form will be tolerated. If a team one touchdown behind has the ball on the other team's 35-yard line when the game ends, give them another two minutes or, if they've run out of time-outs during a drive in the last two minutes give them a couple more.

"Pete, a football coach knows he only has to hold the line about a total of nine minutes of action in a football game. And, in the Super Bowl, everybody tries not to lose, really. It's like a guy in golf going for the fat part of the green, a jockey taking the safe route on the outside.

"I'm just trying to help, Pete. Do it the way you've been doing it and you're going to get one of those 12–9 games decided by some immigrant who used to make only a dollar an hour with his feet stomping grapes before the great field goal boom hit the country.

"If you don't do any of these things in Super Bowl XIII, Pete, do me one favor anyway. Wake me when it's over. I gotta write."

THE JOY OF SEEING

FEBRUARY 13, 1979

I guess this story should really go to the *Reader's Digest*, you know, one of those "I Was Joe's Pancreas" stories they run now and then. But I guess I owe someone an explanation as to where I was during Super Bowl XIII. I was not on the binoculars, that's for sure.

Do me a favor, will you? Look out that living room window of yours, the one that points across the street to the street sign, a sign that says, maybe, "Washington Street."

See it real good, do you?

What if that sign looked as it if said, "W-A-X-Q-*-H-V-X-P"? Supposing it suddenly looked to you as if it were in Sanskrit or some other foreign language?

Supposing you couldn't see it at all?

Now, just imagine you are in a hotel room in Miami Beach and one afternoon you look across the street and see a complex of shops and restaurants and store fronts and there is this sign over the complex reading "Bal Harbour Plaza."

Supposing the next day you looked across the street and suddenly that sign over the complex looked as if it said "Bel Shazzar's Court," or even "Mene Mene, Tekel Uparsin"?

That's just about what happened to me on Super Bowl week. I arrived on the premises sporting a cataract in my right eye. By midweek, the left eye had joined the fun. All I could see out of my left eye was a sandstorm. Not in Miami, just in my eye.

By Saturday morning, I was going through the hotel lobby by Braille. Saturday is an off-day for most journalists Super Bowl week. The players are sequestered. The interviews are over, and everyone is marking time for the great Super Sunday.

With a bunch of writers, I decided to go to Gulfstream Park, the racetrack, for the day. I got to the racetrack. I felt like having a sandwich. I ordered an egg salad sandwich. Now, I don't know about you, but to me, an egg salad sandwich is about the whitest thing you can have on a white plate with a white napkin underneath it. Except this one looked as if it were growing red worms.

I either had the worst case of DT's in history, or my eye was filling with blood. I quickly found the track publicity man who took me to the track doctor. He squinted into the eye for a while and confessed he was unable to detect anything untoward and recommended that I go to a nearby emergency hospital.

I was chauffeured there where I sat for about 2½ to 3 hours amidst a whole waiting room of people who had fallen off skateboards, or had incipient heart attacks or had otherwise ruined their Saturday afternoon, too.

I was finally ushered into the presence of a doctor in a green smock who stared into my eyes with a flashlight, waved his fingers at me, and then said my vision was all right. I think this was the same guy who told the captain of the Titanic full speed ahead.

I won't bore you with a whole lot of details, but what I had was a detached retina. Now a detached retina is something that happens to preliminary prizefighters—not guys who make their livings hitting typewriters instead of floors.

You talk about Super Bowls. This detached retina was having one helluva second half. And, it had the ball on the one-foot line by the time I came back from the emergency room and found my pal, Dr. John Perry, in the hotel lobby. John is a former Rams doctor, and he quickly found me one of the finest eye surgeons in the hemisphere. Dr. David Sime. They also forbade me to fly home, and headed me for the O.R. on the double. I was finally off the Titanic and into a life boat.

People tell me I missed the greatest Super Bowl in history in the Orange Bowl that afternoon. Not in my book I didn't. The greatest Super Bowl in my history was being played in the operating room at Mercy Hospital in Miami that day. I won't say I was in deep trouble, but Jimmy the Greek said that if you took me that afternoon, you got 40 points.

I'll tell you one thing: it was the most thrilling four quarters of my life. Now, I'm sure Roger Staubach had his troubles that afternoon. But believe me, nothing Mean Joe Greene could do is half as frightening as looking at a needle come down toward your eye all afternoon. I would like to see even Hollywood Henderson go one-on-one in that situation.

For a lot of reasons, I could only have a local anesthetic. I won't say I was excited, but when my blood pressure hit 260, somebody there must have thought they had discovered a slow leak in the Red Sea.

As retinal tears go, mine was major league—four tears. Origin unsure, but probably due to a fall in Hawaii late last year.

The postoperative problem of what to do with a patch on one eye and a cataract on the other becomes critical. In a hospital, there is very little you can do except lie flat on your back and stare at the ceiling. With my one good eye I was allowed occasionally to watch a television set that was too far away to give me a very clear idea of what was going on. It was a little like watching a snowstorm through a keyhole.

I had to experiment. I quickly found American movies were ill-suited for the purpose. For instance, in an American western, what would appear to be two mountain lions fighting in the top of a tall tree would often prove to be a stagecoach driving out of town with a schoolmarm in it. Action pictures could have been anything. Runaway Rorschach tests.

I came to love Public Broadcasting Service features. For one thing, they were all English-made. And they seemed to consist of four hours of inaction, entire "dramas" consisting of two people walking in the center of the room, one with a box of chocolates, and taking a stand not two feet apart.

One of them, the one eating the chocolates, would be the Queen of England. The other one would be Disraeli or somebody, and they would stand there for four hours and just jabber. It was ideal for me. I never had to move my eyes, just my ears. I became a big fan of drawing room dramas.

Action dramas were no fun at all, particularly war dramas. I could not tell the Gestapo from Errol Flynn, I couldn't tell a Japanese admiral from John Wayne. In fact, I could not tell whether I was looking at World War II or the War of the Roses.

Football games were a disaster. I watched the Pro Bowl game. I became very depressed when Howard Cosell kept telling me it was an apathetic, dull and uninteresting game in which even the spectators yawned, because it looked to me like the wildest kind of mayhem. I was constantly surprised that the quarterback got the pass off. I counted 56 sacks in the game and was amazed to discover that some of those "sacks" resulted in long bomb completions.

I also counted 17 apparent decapitations of quarterbacks, only to discover later the quarterback didn't even lose his helmet.

Well, to sum up, Super Bowl XIII had all the thrills for me of being caught in a cave-in. I felt like Floyd Collins. It was the first Super Bowl I had missed, and when I miss 'em, I don't fool. I'm even beginning to think longingly back to the good old days of the Minnesota Viking's Super Bowls. At least I could see them.

It is my notion now that Super Bowls, like tall office buildings, should skip the 13th floor. We should have gone direct from Super Bowl XII to Super Bowl XIV with no stopping between.

In the meantime, if you can see and read that street sign on the corner, don't worry about little things like the mortgage, your job, or even Super Bowls or the Rams. The minute you can't read that street sign, take my word for it, everything else just becomes red blotches on the horizon. Everything else is chicken liver. So the Dallas Cowboys lost the Super Bowl! Big deal. There's one of those every year. Eyes come only two to a customer.

TRANSLATING THE QUOTES

MARCH 4, 1979

Every year at this time, as one of our many services to our fine subscribers, we supply a "buyer beware" section in the best traditions of *Consumer Guide* and Ralph Nader.

What we are interested in is not exploding gas tanks or overbooking on Appalachian Airlines but the most insidious form of double-entry bookkeeping—the manager's quotes.

This is the all-purpose statement guaranteed not only to fill the seats, and sell season tickets, but to persuade those who should know better, the players themselves, that they are not only better than they are but probably better than the 1938 Newark Bears, who would probably have beat them by 20 games.

Here are some examples. First is what the manager says, followed by what he thinks:

"That new kid we got has got a great arm."—*"Too bad we had to pay for the rest of him to get it. To think they put arms on him and took them off the Venus de Milo."*

"Our bullpen is stronger than ever this year."—*"And a good thing, because we haven't got a starting pitcher who is a cinch to last through the national anthem."*

"Old Slugger is having some problems, but we're going to send him to a specialist."—*"Yeah, Dr. Freud. Old Slugger's problem is not from the neck down, it's from the eyes up. They should put him in the whirlpool bath upside-down."*

"This guy reminds me of a young Ruth."—*"Or a young Alice."*

"Why didn't we go into the free-agent market? Because we didn't need to."—*"Yeah, to hear the front office tell it, what would I do with a Dave Parker, Pete Rose, Jim Rice, Reggie Jackson, Rod Carew? Come to think of it, at that, even Joe DiMaggio couldn't help this bunch of clowns."*

"Our infield is the best in the league."—*"It's got this red clay and crushed brick and nice green grass and manicured foul lines. It's the guys standing on it who are not so hot."*

"This team can go for the seats with the best of them."—*"Or haven't you seen our shortstop with a double-play ball? He's broken more seats than the 1927 Yankees. Only his are behind first base, not the center-field wall. Our center fielder has even hit the upper-deck seats. He seems to think the cutoff man is the one selling hot dogs."*

"The Yankees are only human."—*"And Man O' War was just a horse, and a lion is just a cat."*

"All Reggie Jackson can do is hit."—*"And all Rembrandt could do was paint. All Secretariat could do was run."*

"My guy throws harder than Feller."—*"And Feller is only 60."*

"Our bench is much improved."—*"We painted it. The guys sitting on it are just as bad as ever."*

"We don't bow down to anybody."—*"How can we? Have you seen the bellies on these guys? I don't see how they can tie their shoes. My outfield looks like three side orders of mashed potatoes with hats on. The only thing they hit regularly is the hash browns. Their idea of a diet is only one beer for breakfast."*

"I don't believe in curfews."—*"The only way to get these guys in the room before 2 A.M. is to put a belly dancer in it."*

"My third baseman is the equal of any in the league. He has as good a range as anyone."—*"For cooking lasagna, that is. He stands so still in the field the pigeons think he's a statue. They're going to have a tougher time telling when he dies than Calvin Coolidge. Even his lips haven't moved in seven years. He couldn't stop an uphill putt, and his throws to first should have stamps—two-cent stamps. They could get there faster by boat, and more accurately dropped in a bottle."*

"This team specializes in extra-base hits."—*"Believe it! This is the only team in the league that could turn a routine ground ball into a double, a pop fly into a triple, and a sacrifice bunt into an inside-the-park home run. If there was a way to turn a foul tip into a single, they'd never get anybody out. They're easier to score on than Iowa State."*

"We'll play long ball with anybody."—*"We've got the pitching staff for it. These guys give up so many long balls, the team emblem should be a gopher. Their idea of a good pitch is a triple. The only thing the catcher ever gets his hands on is a wild pitch."*

"If all else fails, we'll outthink the rest of the league."—*"Oh sure! I've got 20 guys who can't even read a menu, two guys who have trouble with a boulevard stop sign, and one guy it took two months to learn the steal sign and when I flashed it to him, he went out and held up a gas station. I got one guy we don't know if he can talk or not, and a catcher who thought the infield fly rule applied to insects, signed a million-dollar contract without knowing how many zeros were in one, and, when they asked him for his autobiography, he said he drove a Lincoln and his wife drove a Chrysler. He orders by pointing. Anyway, if you could beat the Yankees by outthinking them, Harvard would be playing in Fenway Park instead of the Red Sox."*

IF YOU'RE EXPECTING ONE-LINERS

JULY 1, 1979

OK, hang the drum slowly, professor. Muffle the cymbals. Kill the laugh track. You might say that Old Blue Eye is back. But that's as funny as this is going to get.

I feel I owe my friends an explanation as to where I've been all these weeks. Believe me, I would rather have been in a press box.

I lost an old friend the other day. He was blue-eyed, impish, he cried a lot with me, laughed a lot with me, saw a great many things with me. I don't know why he left me. Boredom, perhaps.

We read a lot of books together, we did a lot of crossword puzzles together, we saw films together. He had a pretty exciting life. He saw Babe Ruth hit a home run when we were both 12 years old. He saw Willie Mays steal second base, he saw Maury Wills steal his 104th base. He saw Rocky Marciano get up. I thought he led a pretty good life.

One night a long time ago he saw this pretty lady who laughed a lot, played the piano and he couldn't look away from her. Later he looked on as I married this pretty lady. He saw her through 34 years. He loved to see her laugh, he loved to see her happy.

You see, the friend I lost was my eye. My good eye. The other eye, the right one, we've been carrying for years. We just let him tag along like Don Quixote's nag. It's been a long time since he could read the number on a halfback or tell whether a ball was fair or foul or even which fighter was down.

So, one blue eye is missing and the other misses a lot.

So my best friend left me, at least temporarily, in a twilight world where it's always 8 o'clock on a summer night.

He stole away like a thief in the night and he took a lot with him. But not everything. He left a lot of memories. He couldn't take those with him. He just took the future with him and the present. He couldn't take the past.

I don't know why he had to go. I thought we were pals. I thought the things we did together we enjoyed doing together. Sure, we cried together. There were things to cry about.

But it was a long, good relationship, a happy one. It went all the way back to the days when we arranged all the marbles in a circle in the dirt in the lots in Connecticut. We played one o'cat baseball. We saw curveballs together, trying to hit them or catch them. We looked through a catcher's mask together. We were partners in every sense of the word.

He recorded the happy moments, the miracle of children, the beauty of a Pacific sunset, snow-capped mountains, faces on Christmas morning. He allowed me to hit fly balls to young sons in uniforms two sizes too large, to see a pretty daughter march in halftime parades. He allowed me to see most of the major sports events of our time. I suppose I should be grateful that he didn't drift away when I was 12 or 15 or 29 but stuck around over 50 years until we had a vault of memories. Still, I'm only human. I'd like to see again, if possible, Rocky Marciano with his nose bleeding, behind on points and the other guy coming.

I guess I would like to see a Reggie Jackson with the count 3 and 2 and the Series on the line, guessing fastball. I guess I'd like to see Rod Carew with men on first and second and no place to put him, and the pitcher wishing he were standing in the rain someplace, reluctant to let go of the ball.

I'd like to see Stan Musial crouched around a curveball one more time. I'd like to see Don Drysdale trying not to laugh as a young hitter came up there with both feet in the bucket.

I'd like to see Sandy Koufax just once more facing Willie Mays with a no-hitter on the line. I'd like to see Maury Wills with a big lead against a pitcher with a good move. I'd like to see Roberto Clemente with the ball and a guy trying to go from first to third. I'd like to see Pete Rose sliding into home head-first.

I'd like once more to see Henry Aaron standing there with

that quiet bat, a study in deadliness. I'd like to see Bob Gibson scowling at a hitter as if he had some nerve just to pick up a bat. I'd like to see Elroy Hirsch going out for a long one from Bob Waterfield, Johnny Unitas in high-cuts picking apart a zone defense. I'd like to see Casey Stengel walking to the mound on his gnarled old legs to take the pitcher out, beckoning his gnarled old finger behind his back.

I'd like to see Sugar Ray Robinson or Muhammad Ali giving a recital, a ballet, not a fight. Also, to be sure, I'd like to see a sky full of stars, moonlight on the water, and yes, the tips of a royal flush peaking out as I fan out a poker hand, and yes, a straight two-foot putt.

Come to think of it, I'm lucky. I saw all of those things. I see them yet.

RECRUITING SALES TALK

DECEMBER 30, 1979

(Headline: "FBI, NCAA Investigate Transcript Tampering for In-eligible Athletes. Mail Fraud, Bribery and Bogus Credits Charged. Suspensions Levied.")

We take you now to the main offices of the educational ser-vice firm of Lye, Forge, Cheatum & Suborn, specialists in lower education with branches in the 11 Western states and Hawaii. The walls are done in tasteful antique, the carpeting is lush and charts on the wall read: "This is an apple. If I had another apple, I would have two apples. If you want to sell apples, learn this. If you want to play football, see us." There are pictures titled, "See Jane Run," and copies of Batman comics on the coffee tables.

The letterhead on the stationery reads: "If it talks, we can get it into Harvard. If it can't, we'll get it into the Big Lie confer-ence and the Sunbonnet-Festive Bowl. If it's over 6'10", keep it on a leash."

As we look in, Matty Goniffmacher, the firm's demon sales specialist, is on the phone.

"Hullo, who's this? Coach Bum Rush?! Coach, how are you? What can I do for ya? How's that fullback, Orange Utan I sent ya? Ate up the league? I told ya! What!? Oh, you mean literally? Coach, I told you to keep his face mask on at all times even in his sleep! Oh, he ate that, too? Well, I never said it would be easy. I promised you the Rose Bowl, not a rose garden.

"What can I do for you next year? Name it! We got five guys out recruiting right now. The equator is their territory. We got a team in the Himalayas. How would you like to have the Abominable Snowman for your goal-line offense? I've got a Kodiak bear that would think the Pittsburgh Steelers were a berry patch. We found him carrying a Peterbilt truck along the Alcan Highway—eating an ice cream cone with the other paw.

"Whaddaya mean, how do I get 'em eligible? You're talking to a man who could get King Kong into Princeton. *Cum laude.* All you got to do is take the horns off and I'll get a steer into the Big 10. I could get a real bear into the Chicago secondary. Did you know the entire backfield at Moronia State sleeps in a tree all winter? I got a quarterback who'll go No. 1 in the draft and the only letters in the alphabet he reads are X's and O's. We keep a note pinned on him on campus at all times. 'If found, return to the athletic department, at once. Do not attempt to feed.'

"Now what's your problem? You've got a 9.2 halfback who goes 250 pounds and could sidestep raindrops? Tell me, does he have these little spots on him? Oh?! Well, is he human? You're not sure. Well, try this: Put a girl in front of him. If he tries to run up the Empire State building with her, we've got a lot of work to do. If he takes her to Studio 54 and plies her with liquor, you've got yourself a football player.

"Who cares if he can't read? I got some All-Americans who can't even peel their own bananas. I got a tight end in a Louisiana school they'll make a rug out of if he ever gets caught out in hunting season.

"Let me ask you, you got anybody on the coaching staff can read or write? OK, here's what you do. I send you a true-false exam marked 'Cornseed College Mid-Year Full Credit Exam on Modern Fundamentals of Football.' Sample questions: 'If Farmer Jones had two apples, how many apples would Farmer Jones have?' Or 'If a train going 200 miles an hour goes 200 miles, how many miles will it have gone?' If the guy knows the answers to those, I can get him on the Academic All-American. If he doesn't, well, we have extension courses in Advanced Sandbox, and Varsity Clay Modeling.

"We have extension courses from Saskatoon University. No, that's not in Saskatchewan. It's Saskatoon, Arkansas. The extension course is in a pool hall in Pacoima where the classes are conducted by a guy named Slick, who holds degrees from Attica, Leavenworth and the 23rd Precinct, where he underwent a series of multiple-choice questions many times from the robbery squad. He always passed. Got 1 to 10.

"Have one of your coaches fill out the answers and let the player make his X where it says signature. No, no! Don't mail it in! I mean, the government has enough to do these days, eh? I mean, it's our patriotic duty not to load up the federal agents with having to serve subpoenas, hold hearings or tie up manpower investigating mail fraud. So, whatever you do, don't put a U.S. stamp on it. Let's keep this between us; let's keep the government out of it. Government's getting too damned big anyway, right?

"You have a what?! A 3.9 scholar with an IQ in the 160's? Can run the 40 in 4.4, throw the football 80 yards and hit a squirrel in the eye with it. So what's the problem? Oh. He wants to go to school out West. Listen I got two guys in the Big 8 who'll send a plane for him right now. And he can keep it.

"What? He wants to be a what?! A doctor! A surgeon!?

"Listen, old buddy, you send that kid to Muhlenberg or Susquehanna or Amherst. You know how much lab time he'll get in the big-time football factories? Zilch. He won't even be able to prescribe an aspirin.

"No, old man, if you've got some whisky-drinking, women-chasing graduates of a Birmingham jail, or Altoona pool hall, you send them to yours truly. You got a guy who can remove a tumor, straighten a spine, bypass a heart or read an X-ray or hospital chart, you don't need to waste his time reading Green Bay zones. Not with my help, you don't. I've got enough on my conscience as it is. We supply hospitals with customers, not cardiologists. I can get a diploma for a guy with the IQ of a polar bear. In fact I can get one for a polar bear.

"But do you realize what will happen if you start coming around with guys who can spell and hold a book right-side up? You'll put 5,000 coaches out of work! Some staffs have three guys with nothing else to do but find dummy storefront extension courses for cretins who can play linebacker even if they can't write it, who can see an eye chart but can't read it, and who had to be recruited with a rope.

"But I draw the line at ruining doctors. Or inventors or engineers or scientists, generally. I have nightmares thinking what might have happened if Edison could catch a football in a crowd, or the Wright Brothers spent their nights inventing the single wing. What if Louis Pasteur were a placekicker? No, I don't mind the FBI being after me, but I draw the line at tampering with a guy studying cancer research. You can turn him into a bartender with a limp if you want to but don't look at me. I mean there are some things a man won't do, even to beat Michigan."

ONE MAN'S OPINION

APRIL 18, 1980

As workers, baseball players are hardly to be compared with the girls in the Triangle shirtwaist factory fire—no matter what you hear from Marvin Miller.

Cesar Chavez would laugh at them. Samuel Gompers would be astonished. Lenin would probably stand them alongside a barn to be shot. Roosevelt would call them "economic royalists." South African gold miners would just love to be their butlers. Guys who catch hot rivets for a living would like to swap for new baseballs.

You can't beat the hours. Guys used to have to run railroads to make a million dollars a year. An occupation in which the average annual salary is $130,000 should not have a union, it should have a security guard. J. P. Morgan should have belonged to a union if these guys do.

Still, they are the only assets of an industry, the game of baseball, which contributes nothing to the gross national product except popcorn sales. And their skills are not transferable. The ability to hit, catch or throw a curveball is a one-purpose utility. It's the only way in the world most of these guys could become millionaires. Some guys make more money than they can count to.

So, they're lucky baseball is around to keep them in minks and Rollses. They should be grateful for the spadework done by generations of promoters, reporters, announcers, technicians, contractors, and so forth, who made it all possible. They're not of course. They're grateful to a man who had nothing to do with it, Marvin Miller, the only labor leader in history to represent a company of millionaires.

It's not considered a part of journalistic wisdom to oppose legitimate aspirations of the working man, particularly when he is forced to the dire extreme of striking for his rights. And

I personally come from a long line of working men, but the only strikes worth walking out for were for more money or for better working conditions—neither of which is at issue here.

What is at issue is whether or not baseball is entitled to extract indemnity for an aggrieved club when one of its stars is signed as a free agent by another club.

This is not a proper subject for a strike. It's a court decision, as Marvin Miller must well know. The swollen-salary free-agent market, which has made millionaires out of right fielders, is not a labor triumph, anyway. It was brought about by a legal decision by a man the owners themselves had hired as an arbitrator.

The craven way baseball players have gone about their strike is hardly in the best traditions of the United Mine Workers, anyway. They struck during the exhibition season, a period in which players receive only meal money and expenses. They proposed to stage the real strike sometime at the end of May, at which time I expect the vote will be somewhat less unanimous than a 767–1 announced for March.

By then, a million-dollars-a-year player will be earning $6,170 a day. A 10-day strike will cost him the price of a new Bentley. Those kinds of economics can turn even Samuel Gompers into a company man. They will give new meaning to Jean-Jacques Rousseau's war cry, "Workers of the world, unite! You have nothing to lose but your chains!" which will now become "Baseball players of the world, unite! You have nothing to lose but a half a million dollars—or your wife's new Rolls!"

The dangers in a strike of any service industry is, the public may find it can do without those services. Great newspapers have been sunk by strikes, and great restaurants closed. Baseball would seem to be flirting with extinction.

I can tell you one thing: In a strike, I would a whole lot rather be Marvin Miller than Pete Rose. The ability to be a labor negotiator is—well, negotiable. The ability to hit a curveball is not in great demand on Wall Street.

INSTANT CELEBRITY

MAY 9, 1980

Quick now! For a short lesson in civics—a course titled "Whatever Became Of The Late Great State Of America?"— who was the woman who really won the division of the Boston Marathon that Rosie Ruiz didn't win?

Of course you don't remember. The poor dear is about to become just a trivia answer like, who played third base in the Tinker-to-Evers-to-Chance combination, or, who was the pitcher Roger Maris got his 61st home run off, and, what are the odds against the royal flush in poker?

Pay attention now. I'm only gonna give the answer once, and this may be the only place you'll ever read the young lady's name, and, if you're ever on "The Price Is Right," this answer may be worth a year's supply of a new wonder detergent or a one-week vacation in the Holiday Inn Bratislava. Repeat after me—the winner was JACQUELINE GAREAU—that's G-A-R-E-A-U.

OK, now, forget her. That's the last time her name comes up in the general conversation. She's just the pitcher who, the third baseman who. She's about as important to history now as Paul Revere's horse.

Rosie Ruiz has gone into the language. She has become a part of American folklore like Steve Brodie, Wrong Way Corrigan, Annie Oakley, Calamity Jane, Billy the Kid, Pretty Boy Floyd, Bonnie and Clyde, heroes or heroines for all the wrong reasons—or maybe the right ones. In sports, it's known as the New York Mets Syndrome—worst is best, least is most, fraud is remunerative.

Before you go to feeling sorry for Rosie Ruiz, consider that, in the past week alone, she has starred in a Conrad cartoon, a Buchwald column, 11 Johnny Carson jokes, 227 newspaper editorials, and about 700 talk show topics around the country.

Look at it this way: she made the Boston Marathon. When I was a kid in New England, the Boston Marathon was just a funky event run between games of a day-night Patriots Day doubleheader at Fenway Park or Braves Field, and populated largely by dotty old Harvard profs or goofballs from Japan with kerchiefs knotted about their heads. And the papers outside of Boston never bothered to tell you who won, because, well, like, who cared?

Everyone cares about Rosie. She's the new America's sweetheart. Ms. Walter Mitty. Psychiatrists say she's all of us. Every guy who ever cribbed on an exam, lied about his war record—or even made believe he was Caruso in the shower—knows what she was going through. Remember the guy—Stringfellow, I believe, was his name—who got on "This Is Your Life" some years ago to tell how he practically captured Berlin and drove Hitler to suicide all by himself? Turned out the closest he ever came to Hitler was Salt Lake City, but that's Show Biz. I had a friend once beg me to write to the Carnegie Foundation telling how he had rescued orphans from a nonexistent fire because he wanted to impress his girlfriend.

Don't worry about Rosie. She'll fall into the hands of some manipulative agent who knows a pat hand when he sees one. She'll do a book, maybe a movie. She'll be a bloody celebrity, God help her. I'll bet the people she works with are already in awe of her. I plan to get her autograph myself.

They'll get some psychoanalyst to explain it was all due to the fact her mother didn't understand her—or understood her all too well, it doesn't matter—psychiatry cuts both ways if it has to and it's all our fault anyway. If Rosie Ruiz wants to win the Boston Marathon without running the full course, why, it's a free country, isn't it? That's what America is all about. I'm afraid it is. Besides, she's "anti-establishment" and that's the thing to be in this year of our Lord, right?

Well, as a guy who used to cheat on his golf score—put down fives where eights would have been closer to the truth, none on the mark, but closer—I'm hardly in a position to be waggling a finger. But, I want the same privilege as Rosie. I want to get into a column only in the last two paragraphs, leave the rest blank. I want to step out on the 17th green of the U.S. Open and announce coolly, "I'm four-under to here." Maybe Ali can have a proxy to fight the first 13 rounds against Larry Holmes for him, whereupon he steps in for the last two. Until all that happens, I'm going to root for the Establishment for a change. I always did root for the underdog, and the Big E is getting to be a 14-point underdog in this world. Besides, in this case, the establishment is Jacqueline Gareau, better known as *"who?!"*

A CAR TO REMEMBER

APRIL 22, 1980

I guess the United States of America has turned out more motor cars than anyone else on earth, most of them highly forgettable hunks of chrome and steel about as stylish as a housecoat on a fat lady, about as dashing as a plow. Detroit never could get the hang of class and fashion, and kept turning out things like the 1953 DeSoto and some models that seemed to be trying to duplicate the camel.

The most obscene efforts were those monsters of the 1950s with the huge fins on the back. They were positively hideous, and seemed often to be driven by little old ladies in blue hair who had about as much chance of parking them as they had of docking the Berengaria.

Detroit thought they were just swell, although connoisseurs of the automobile as an art form covered their eyes and acted as if someone had just brought home from an auction a statue with a clock in its belly.

One trouble was, Detroit changed the styling a little every year, not so much to make it better as to make it different. Sometimes, the effect was like ketchup on ice cream, but the American consumer wanted everybody to know his, by God, car was a 1937, not a 1934. This conspicuous consumption did in the Packard, a graceful, partly hand-tooled car which had hit upon a design uniquely its own. Trouble was, you couldn't tell a 1930 Packard from a 1935 except by the serial number. So, people bought lesser cars and Packard drifted out of the business.

Some car companies even thought things like safety and engineering and comfort sold cars—but they soon got disabused. Another trouble was, the carmakers hired European carriage builders in the early days, and these guys thought cars were just going to be automotive surreys with a fringe on top, or stagecoaches with horns. They seemed to think they should design them so horses could pull them when the oil ran out.

The auto show was the big social event of the year when you were a kid in those depression-locked years of the '30s, and I'll never forget the time the one and only truly classic American car made its appearance. I believe it was 1936 and the car was the Cord, the brainchild of a flamboyant huckster from the Middle West, Errett Lobban Cord, the head of the then-Auburn Motorcar Company.

It was a gorgeous thing, the Cord, the nearest thing to a yacht you would find in that roomful of barges. It had pipes coming out from the sides, and it made the throaty purring sound of a mighty cat when its instant ignition was turned on. The car was made with loving care, only a couple of thousand were ever turned out, and, out in Hollywood, every cowboy star or actress married to royalty promptly turned in their Duesenbergs (which Cord also made) for the new Cord cars. It was only fitting. They were not made to carry eggs to the market, they were sleek racing machines, and deserving of the finest ownership.

E. L. Cord didn't put his masterpiece in a showroom with a ribbon around it, he put it on a racetrack in Atlantic City where it drove a 24-hour endurance test at an average speed of 103 mph. Cord's Cord was not just another pretty grille, it was a top performer.

This week, at Riverside, another Cord will be on the track—not the car, the scion. Chris Cord is the grandson of the late E. L. and a chip off the old stock block, as it were. E. L. would have understood him perfectly. Chris shuffles papers through the week at his office in Beverly Hills so he can go racing on weekends. Some weeks its Le Mans or Watkins Glen, but this week it's Riverside, where he'll be piloting in the five-hour enduro there.

During the week, you would see young Cord in an old Cord, a gorgous black-and-silver chassis, circa 1938, the only authentic classic car ever turned out in this country.

Chris Cord can't pilot an E. L. Cord at Riverside this week in the Times Grand Prix event because the conditions call for a production car (Chris will drive a Chevy Monza) and a Cord hasn't been in production since the Germans were in Paris.

What happened? So, why didn't the Cord drive the Cadillacs

and the Rollses and even the Mercedes right off the road? Chris Cord believes it was a combination of circumstances. "It wasn't the price," he says. "The Cord cost only about $3,000 originally." It couldn't really be mass-produced. "It was a turbo-charged beauty 20 years ahead of its time," boasts Chris. It was turned out by automotive watchmakers or their equivalent. Its lines were as clean and uncluttered as a diamond. Just standing still, it looked as if it were going at mach one.

It got lost in the postwar clutter of Firebirds, Sunbirds, DeSotos, Raymond Loewy-Studebakers, and the like. If anyone had told you that the German Mercedes would survive the war but the American Cord wouldn't, you would have wanted to certify it. But the hand-crafted pride of E. L. Cord couldn't compete with the assembly-line iron from Detroit. The Ford had only one letter different, but the economics were quite different; the custom-car business was flooded over by the output from the Rouge.

Still, it's nice to have a Cord on the track at the *Times*-Toyota Grand Prix of Endurance Sunday. Too bad the grandson of the original car can't be out there, too. It's all our cultural loss.

ALL-TIME GREATEST NAME

JULY 1, 1980

There have been lots of great names in baseball history. Napoleon Lajoie (pronounced "Lash-oh-way"), Grover Cleveland Alexander, the only guy in the game with either three first names or three last names, "Germany" Schaefer, "Dummy" Hoy, "Ping" Bodie, Sibby Sisti. And Cletus Elwood Poffenberger and William Adolph Wambsganss weren't bad.

But, for sheer unadulterated alliteration, the all-time baseball name belongs to Van Lingle Mungo. You can't even say it, you've got to sing it. It sounds like something a guy would be singing from the rigging of a banana boat coming into port, or like the rumblings of a steel band. It's part calypso, part hog-call. The consonants just tinkle along like a runaway calliope.

A tunesmith was so taken with the sound of it, he wrote a whole song around it, making Van Mungo the only big league player I know of other than Joe DiMaggio to get a song written about him.

There will be a lot of big stars at the annual Old-timers Game at Dodger Stadium this Sunday. DiMag will be there. Willie Mays, Sandy Koufax, Duke Snider and Henry Aaron will, too. But, the really big excitement will be the presence of the man whose name is a song. Van Lingle Mungo.

The reasons are quite personal. You see, whenever I come across the name Van Lingle Mungo, immediately I'm 40 years younger. In fact, it's a hot day in the '30s and I'm seated in the bleachers in a ballpark in Hartford, Connecticut. The mighty Hartford Senators are playing a July 4 doubleheader against the dreaded, despised, treacherous New Haven Profs for the Eastern League first-half championship.

Justice is triumphing because, on the mound for the home nine is the invincible Van Lingle Mungo, the best pitcher ever to throw in that league, the possessor of an unhittable fastball and a curve that swoops over the plate like a diving pelican. He strikes out 12 of the villainous New Havens that day, including their vaunted superstar from Yale, the footballer-turned-base-ball player, Bruce Caldwell, three times. Hartford wins the pennant by 11½ games. There is joy in Mudville and the sun is shining bright in Bulkeley Stadium.

Why is it the heroes of our youth are always more mythic, larger than life, than those we acquire later in life? Aren't you sure that senators and presidents and ministers were better when you were a boy? Don't you secretly think Dempsey and Louis were really the *last* heavyweight champions? Weren't Gable and Cagney *stars?* And players in films today just actors? Weren't the winters colder, summers hotter, days longer, nights darker, then? Hasn't the world shrunk since you grew up?

So it was with Van Mungo and me. He and Jimmie Foxx, the slugger, were genuine, 14-karat legit bubble gum card carriers' heroes. No one has quite made it since.

Van Mungo didn't make the Hall of Fame. His lifetime record was a so-so 120-won, 115-lost. You say "so-so" until you understand Van Lingle took his fastball and smoking curve onto one of the most pathetic of major league rosters. The Brooklyn Dodgers of the '30s were known journalistically as "The Daffiness Boys," "The Flatbush Follies" and other riotus epithets. Mungo lost a no-hit game once with two outs in the ninth when the second baseman dropped a pop fly. "The *scorer* ruled it a hit because the sun got in his eyes," Mungo recalls.

Mungo twice won 18 games with this collection of comedians and twice won 16 games. The club was mired in the second division throughout that decade, but Mungo was a workhorse, usually pitching well over 300 innings. He usually led the league in games started—38 one season 37 another—and finished 22 of them each year. He led the league in strikeouts one year (1936) when the club finished next to last.

The Dodgers of the era had a lot of players nicknamed "Rabbit," to give you an idea of their power and, even in their bandbox ballpark, the team leader in homers in 1936 had exactly four. Mel Ott, by himself, hit more home runs than Van Mungo's Dodgers.

No less an authority than Billy Herman, a Hall of Fame second baseman who batted against the likes of Dizzy Dean,

Bob Feller, Lefty Gomez, Lefty Grove and Lon Warneke, says, "I think Van Lingle Mungo was possibly the fastest pitcher I ever saw."

I talked to the fastest pitcher Herman ever saw by phone down at his farm in Pageland, South Carolina, where he said he was sitting on his porch watching the bulldozers turn his old farm into condominiums. He remembered the old Hartford Senators well, he said, if not the kid in the bleachers.

"We had a better team down there than the one I went to in Brooklyn," he recalls. "I always thought they called them 'Dodgers' in Brooklyn because of the way they dodged fly balls. Only, sometimes, they didn't. Sometimes the balls hit them in the head."

Van Mungo says he never expected to have songs written about him like *Sweet Sue* or *Sweet Adeline*. "But I got out of baseball because of ulcers. I got five of them. I got 'em in service during the war, but the Army didn't buy that. They just said I ought to of chewed my food better."

Did he wish he had been traded to a contending club? "Well, I would have liked that. In my prime, that is. I went to the Giants late, after the war. You see, I always got to pitch against the big boys. I always got Dean, Hubbell, Vander Meer, Warneke and Schumacher. Those fellows. I pitched the game that knocked the Giants out of the pennant in 1934 after their manager, Bill Terry, had asked, 'Is Brooklyn still in the league?' Beat 'em, 5–1. They clocked my fastball at 109 miles an hour in those days. I tell you, it sang on the way to the plate."

Naturally, Van Lingle Mungo is the only pitcher in the history of the game whose name and fastball were both hummers.

IT WASN'T TOO BAD

AUGUST 5, 1980

Well, now that I'm out of it, I can tell you the real truth about Russia.

And the real truth is—it's not so bad.

Oh, three and a half weeks in Moscow doesn't entitle you to write *Behind Kremlin Walls* or *Me and Marx, The Russia Nobody Knows*. But I can give you a few first-hand impressions.

First of all, it's a handsome city. Oh, it's not Palm Springs. Or even Palm Beach. But it is surrounded by the swift-flowing Moscow River down which course gay excursion boats, and the barges of commerce, and the waters at night reflect the Red stars over the Kremlin, and when you walk along the banks you can almost hear the balalaikas play.

It is an historic city, dotted with the picturesque Orthodox churches built by wealthy private families in the days of the tsars. It is a city of movement. People stream down the streets like a human river in Moscow, and everyone seems to have a purpose. There are no loiterers (the drunks, children and dissidents were floated out of town for the Olympic party, but those left always proceeded as if they were 10 minutes late wherever they were going). They are not a scruffy lot as you might see along the Champs Élyseés in Paris or Carnaby Street in London.

The fashions may not be the latest, but the clothes are clean. There are no sweat shirts or patched jeans, and nobody going to work in shorts and a tank shirt with chest hair hanging out of it. Actually, the scruffiest lot in this town were the journalists. Muscovites' eyes popped to see gray-haired men in shorts jogging through Red Square of a morning.

I did not see a single piece of graffiti in my stay. The subway is clean with marble platforms, swift-moving escalators that haul passengers as much as three stories down or up. Muscovites are proud of their subway and do not scribble obscenities on the marble.

The city is raked more or less constantly by a brisk, almost gale-force wind. The clearest memory I have of night sounds is the whipping of flags on the hotel porte-cochere roof under my window. The wind, which I suppose blows off the steppes, keeps the temperature in the cool 70s, where it stayed the whole Olympics, except for one merciless humid day when the Irishman John Treacy passed out after 9,800 meters in the 10,000, and even the Finn, Lasse Viren, had to stagger home. Even on an August day you could use a sweater, and on an August night, a coat.

The hotel Rossiya, where the press stayed, is the world's biggest, and, if not the best, is certainly comfortable enough, with large airy rooms and lace-curtained windows. The chambermaids are efficient, hard working and appear to work 24-hour shifts. They look at you without interest, but, then, you are just another dirty sheet to them.

The natives are neither friendly nor unfriendly, just unsmiling. (The high-spirited Aussies used to have contests to see who could wring a smile out of the straphangers in the Metro. No one won.) In 24 days, the only two persons to wave at the passing buses of writers, officials, or even athletes, were both small children.

The communication facilities were first-rate, including the wildest kind of modernity for Russia, direct phone dialing anywhere in the Western world, an innovation which startled old Russia hands, used to waiting 30 minutes to two days for calls to go through.

This is a city rich in history. On the road to the new airport you can see the statue to the tank traps that stopped Hitler's Wehrmacht on a road so close to the heart of Moscow that the German officers could see Red Square clearly through binoculars. The homes where old Bolsheviks plotted the return of Lenin while dodging the tsar's Okruna are preserved in some quarters.

The Games were magnificent. In two weeks, only one event got off late—a relay race was delayed three minutes one night. Every other event honored the announced time. It was a vintage Olympics because of the pole vault and high jump records, and the world's first 28-foot long jump. (I discount

Beamon's freak 29−2¹/₂ at Mexico.) American journalists were gnashing their teeth in the pole vault because the crossbar, at first, was not put up beyond 19 feet and, when it was, the pole vaulter was too tired to cross over it.

The 80 gold medals were not the victory Moscow was looking for. It wanted the hearts and minds of the 5,500 journalists, officials and observers. The rulers wanted the Soviet Union on page one for something besides troop movements. They wanted to win this Battle of Moscow, too.

But the press of the world was harder to fool than Hitler's generals. The Russians got for their pains—and it must have been almost physical pain for the censors—stories hinting at Russians cheating in the field events, Russian security overkill and victory stand snubs by dozens of their guest countries. The Olympic Games did not change Russia, and vice versa, and the Iron Curtain wasn't breached, just relocated temporarily.

It proved that police states can run Olympics efficiently. But Mussolini could have told them that. Or Hitler. If it wasn't as bad as visitors feared, neither was it Paris in the spring, Athens in the fall or even Zurich in the winter. The Russians think they made points with the world, and maybe they did. Olympic Games, like indecisive battles, take years to sort out and catalog. But the Russians think they made the club and that their performance will minister to group esteem in the Soviet Union. But, as for Mother Russia generally, you have to feel, along with Leon Trotsky, that it's a great place to visit— but I wouldn't want to die there.

BO, YOU HAVE COMPANY

DECEMBER 28, 1980

I never thought I'd live to see the day I'd say this but, after 35 years of happy married life, a new girl has entered my life.

You should see her. Got these great big blue eyes. Flirts with you shamelessly. Hair of silk gold. Never needs any makeup, eye shadow, toe paint or perfume—she's got her own. You could get rich selling it.

I have fallen hopelessly in love with her despite the vast differences in our ages. Look, some girls just like older men, I keep telling myself. My God, I bought her a fur coat for Christmas! No fool like an old fool, they say.

She has these pretty chubby legs. The kind that don't need high heels. She's a perfect "10."

She can't cook. She can't sew or dance, either. She can't even speak English. Still, my friends don't come to me and say they can't for the life of them see what I can see in her. They can see it, all right. Most of them wish they had one, too.

Because of the big difference in our ages—let's just say it's over 50 years, it isn't even a May-December thing, it's a March-December thing—I thought I might have to dye my hair for her or leave my shirt open to the waist and go around with all these gold chains like a wine clerk or a Fijian cannibal, or in loafers with no socks on.

But I don't even have to let my hair grow or get pink eyeglasses. She likes me just the way I am, old and nearsighted. She doesn't want to go anywhere at night. She's a real old-fashioned gal. The kind that married dear old dad, actually. And really, she couldn't care less about Gucci's. She drinks milk. She likes me and not my '76 Mercury or the fact I can introduce her to Joe Namath or get her Rams tickets.

I don't know why I'm telling you all this. I guess it's because I want you to see it here first and not in the *National Enquirer* or

New York Star: "Sportswriter Loses Head to Nymph ¹/₁₀th His Age."

I guess it comes to every guy around my age. His youth is slipping away. So is his hair. He says "Eh?" a lot and always thinks the light's bad. Then, suddenly this pretty smile, this well-turned ankle shows up in his life, and he's 20 again.

That's what happened to me. I never saw such little hands and feet and ears in my life. Well, maybe once before. Her mother had them, too. When I say she's a perfect "10," I mean she's 10–10–10. She's just the right size for cuddling, 2'2". Besides, I walked her mother and grandmother down the aisle.

Whattaya mean saying, you old goat, why you're old enough to be her grandfather? *I am her grandfather!*

Ladies and gentlemen, meet Danica Erin Skeoch (pronounced "Skee-oh"), the only person who has come between me and Monday Night Football. I mean, I will even turn off the Rams to take her for a stroll. I'd rather watch her than Bo Derek. Or Lynn Swann.

This was our first Christmas together, and we've got a lot to do. This year it was the fur coat and muff but, next year, it might be a basketball or the autobiography of Ty Cobb. She's getting old. She's almost one.

We've got a lot of catching up to do. I've got to teach her to keep her left up, never to bet the washy horse in the paddock. I want to take her to her first bullfight, her first prizefight, her first hockey fight. I took her mother, but it didn't catch.

But she'll probably want to hear about the Noor-Citation races. I'll have to teach her never to take points with the Rams or that team with the funny little horns on the helmets will break her heart. I'll have to teach her to listen to Scully and learn the game properly, that over-under is a sucker bet. I'll teach her that slot machines are not made for her, and that the Bally Co. or whoever wouldn't put all that money into them if they gave away money.

I'll tell her to stand on 18, that a flush is no good in seven-card, deuces wild, but bet the house in straight stud. Never draw to a non-pair or bet into a pair showing in five-card. Never bet with a guy on a boat with his own deck.

I'll have to tell her about fillies in the springtime, European fighters and guys who say, "Are these good?" I'll tell her never to let Shoemaker get off at odds over 4–1, and to always bet the home team in Philadelphia when they got mounted cops in the outfield and machine guns on the roof. In fact, always bet the home team anywhere with that.

She looks to me like she could go to her left pretty well and she can hit—she broke a plate with a spoon, and she's not even a year old. She might be drafted as a future by the Steelers. She's got speed. Caught her going across the living room floor in a 4-flat—on all fours. She doesn't like to lose—as you will find out if you take a piece of candy from her. She's No. 1 in anybody's draft.

Well, you can see how she turned my head and got me to dreaming again. One of the great prospects of our time. And here she is, the little home wrecker, right here. See what I mean.

WE JUST HAVE IT TOO GOOD

JANUARY 6, 1981

Since we are in a period of headlong conservation and runaway restoration—"Save the Whales," "Save our Seals," "Save the Brown Derby"—we would like to form today our own urgent society which we might title "Save our Seal Beach," or "Keep Santa Barbara Rich," or "Leave San Diego the Way it Is." It might also be called "What's the Matter with Wyoming?"

The problem, you see, is the Rose Bowl. It's insidious. Subversive. It is plotting the destruction of California as we know and love it.

You see, California, 364 days a year, has its share of problems. It's too hot, it's too wet, it has smog, fog, fires, wind.

But not New Year's. New Year's Day dawns bright and clear every year. It looks like a stage setting for a Jeannette MacDonald–Nelson Eddy musical. Lush, sunny. Snow in the mountains. Orange blossoms blinking in the sun.

There have been 67 Rose Bowls. And the weather has been perfect for about 64 of them. In fact, even allowing for rain, a case could be made for the 1942 Rose Bowl to have been the worse, weather-wise, in the history of the event. And that one was played in Durham, North Carolina.

The trouble is, NBC televises this fantasy land into 80 million homes around the country, many of which have driveways full of snow or trees hung with icicles or are in places where oranges will never grow and palm trees never root.

And the people there look up and see guys sitting bare to the waist at a football game and girls in shorts dancing on the sidelines and cheerleaders removing their sweaters and sweating through their routines. And the viewers look outside and it's Duluth out there and they say "What in the world am I doing here?! Mama, call Cross-Country Van Lines, pack the dishes and tell the postman to forward our mail to Long Beach."

You see, what the Rose Bowl teaches you is, you don't have to have snow shovels and oil furnaces and earmuffs and mittens to live in January. All you need are shorts, a pair of Adidas and, maybe, a small foreign car.

And, so, someday, California is going to be so full of people, it's going to slide into the ocean. It's got more people in it than some countries; in fact, than most countries.

Clearly, some action must be taken. Our society, accordingly, has some plans afoot to neutralize the Rose Bowl menace. Since we can't transfer it permanently to Durham—that was a wartime emergency measure because they thought the Japanese might attack the Duke-Oregon State game if it were held out here.

We could, of course, persuade the Japanese to attack again. But they're well over that sort of thing. Too busy making cars, don't you see.

The nice thing about transferring it to Durham is that, after the game, nobody particularly wants to move to Durham.

But the society has a few other plans. Since we can't change the weather, we will merely juggle the appearances. After all, we are the masters of make believe out here, and one of our committeemen, Pasadena's David Bryant, is a charter member, ever since he found that he not only couldn't get to the Rose Bowl because of the traffic, he couldn't even get to the liquor store.

Bryant thinks that, for attendance at the Rose Bowl, it should be mandatory to wear ski masks, mittens and ear flaps, and tickets should be sold only to people with runny noses, chronic sneezes or who are skilled at looking miserable.

Tickets should not be sold to anybody with a tan. NBC should be forbidden to zero in on anyone not wearing a shirt, even if it's Cheryl Tiegs.

Sunglasses will be confiscated on the spot. We will have to blot out the magnificent backdrop of the San Gabriel Mountains, unless they are on fire. We will get an opaque netting to put over the top of the Rose Bowl. We will get a snow machine from MGM to blow frosted cornflakes across the field when the band comes on.

The band will have to learn how to keep its teeth chattering. The claps and the foot-stomping are a nice touch, but we may have to have the announcer explain that this is to ward off chilblains and not to show enthusiasm.

We will never let on that the wind chill factor is in the 90s. We can paint a thunderstorm on the ceiling, or bring in the sound track from the movie *Rain*.

Never mind showing them the Rose Parade. We don't want to leave them with the impression we live in a place where you can grow roses in January, for heaven's sake. Show them the traffic jam instead and say "Boy, I bet you don't have this in downtown Columbus today."

Of course, we could always move the game to Durham—and then not tell them it's Durham.

There are a few other refinements we are working on. Like having Leonid Brezhnev as grand marshal of the Rose Parade. We could play the game at night—say at 2 in the morning when you won't have to fake the chattering teeth.

In other words, emphasize the negative. Your committee is working tirelessly in your behalf in this matter. We have banned movie actors and entertainers because people keep thinking if they come out here they're going to run into Bob Hope in the supermarket or sit under the hair dryer next to Nancy Reagan.

The only other thing we can do is start inviting Harvard and Washington and Jefferson again so nobody will watch anyway.

IT'S SEEN AND NOT HEARD

FEBRUARY 13, 1981

Many years ago in New Haven a detective sergeant friend of mine named Leo Reynolds, a vice cop and a hockey fan, used to say to me over coffee and doughnuts at the Arena coffee shop, "A hockey game without fights is like a meal without wine, a dance without music, a cruise without moonlight.

"If you want to see ice skating," he said, "go see Sonja Henie. If you want to see hockey, go see Eddie Shore." Eddie Shore, at the period, was a homicidal maniac on ice, passing out skull fractures. In other words, whenever Leo went to see a hockey game without high-sticking, poke-checking, slashing or skull-fracturing, he would scorn it."They left out the music," he would complain. "If I want to see *Nutcracker Suite,* I'll go to the Schubert."

Fred Shero, when he was coach of the famed—and feared—Broad Street Bullies, the 1973–74 Philadelphia Flyers, summed up the creed succinctly when he said, "If you can't beat 'em in an alley, you can't beat 'em on the ice." His captain, Bobby Clarke, capsulized nosebleed hockey: "You take the direct route to the puck and you arrive in ill humor."

Hockey is the Bloody Mary of sports. You could get killed playing hockey. Several people have. You put a mix on the ice of 10 people carrying sticks, most with hair-trigger tempers, crashing into one another at speeds of 40 mph, and you're not surprised there aren't two complete sets of teeth in the whole league.

There are two ways to play hockey: you can knock the puck off a player—or you can knock the player off the puck.

The people who love the game for its own sake—and there

must be 12 of them, at least—decry this kind of mayhem on the ice. There are probably some auto race fans who don't like to see accidents, too, fight fans who detest knockouts. Some baseball fans like pitchers' battles, and some people like basketball without elbows. But that's not the place to invest your money.

The National Hockey League once a year gives its public a look at drawing-room hockey, the game as art, the bloodless bullfight—the annual All-Star Game. The latest one was at the Forum the other night.

It wasn't exactly a bore. It would have had to improve to be that. Before it started, the hockey writer, Gordon Edes, predicted "We're going to see a baseball fan's delight tonight—a double no-hitter."

To begin with, the contest is between something called the Prince of Wales conference and the Clarence Campbell Conference. Right there, you know it's not Dempsey-Tunney or Notre Dame–Army.

I won't say the players didn't have a stake in it, but when someone asked if it could go into overtime one veteran hockey writer shook his head. "If the game goes into the final minute tied," he advised, "look for the players to part like the Red Sea in front of whoever has the puck and escort him to a goal."

There were only two minor penalties, and those in the first couple of minutes. Some rookies probably didn't get the message right away.

The game was over in an unseemly two hours. Nobody threw a glove on the ice all night. As detective Reynolds might sneer, "Give it to Tchaikovsky." Holiday on Ice.

Still, it was hockey as it was meant to be played, chivalrous, fluid, graceful. Peggy Fleming could have played in it. Randy Gardner or Tai Babilonia. Dick Button could have narrated it. It looked like a Currier and Ives print.

No, I'm afraid they're going to need those helmets in the game still. The penalty boxes are not yet ready to be cobwebbed. You don't want to be able to see a hockey game so much as to hear it. What makes the Stanley cup such an historic vase is, it's full of blood.

Hockey heroes are not guys who can do a double Lutz or a camel or a sitz-spin. They're guys who take you into the corners and mug you for the puck. The oldest guy in the All-Star game Tuesday was only 30. And there was only one that old. That's not because skating is so hard on the knees and lower back. That's because boards are.

Hockey is not yet ready to become ice dancing. It's still a game where you take your teeth out to play. An All-Star game looks like 40 guys bucking for the Lady Byng Award, guys who would go around lighting each other's cigarettes.

A regular-season game, and these same guys play like they came home and found the other guys hiding in their bedroom closet. They play it that way for the same reason moviemakers put burning cars in the scripts. The public'll pay to see it.

IT DOESN'T SUIT THEM

JUNE 9, 1981

Ordinarily, I'm inclined to let baseball, as an industry, shift for itself. I have enough problems without worrying about Bowie Kuhn's. But I do admit to having this recurring nightmare. In it, the Chicago White Sox get in the World Series. And I have a horror of them being seen all over the world in those—y-e-e-ch!—uniforms.

I mean, have you ever seen a major league athletic team look any sicklier? They look like a bunch of guys who just left a hotel fire or got dressed in the dark in somebody else's clothes.

I mean, their shirts hang out, their pants flop over their calves, they have this open meshwork in their shirts. They look as if they're on their way to a game of one o'cat in a vacant lot. They're the most undignified suits this side of a Borneo headhunters tribe. You can't really tell if they just came to the park in their pajamas, or if they're seriously suited up for a game.

They make everybody look fat. They put Greg Luzinski on the cover of a magazine in a Chicago White Sox uniform the other day and set the sport back about 90 years.

Even the gender these costumes suggest is uncertain. You don't know whether you've wandered into a ballgame or the road company of *Charley's Aunt.*

There are certain things which should be immutable in nature. Bankers and prime ministers should have oak-paneled offices. Queens should wear big floppy hats to the races. Circus aerialists should wear pink tights.

And ballplayers should wear baseball uniforms. And baseball uniforms should be like tuxedos—the same today as they were 50, 75, 100 years ago.

Can you imagine Ty Cobb wearing one of those pantsuits the White Sox think is fashionable? He'd kill somebody first. Can you imagine Joe DiMaggio or Willie Mays having to wear one of these sloppy outfits? I tell you, they're downright undignified. It's demeaning.

Personally, I'm a traditionalist. I can't even cotton to—to coin a word—those doubleknit jobs that have taken over the industry. A baseball uniform should button up the way Babe Ruth's did. I remember the first time I saw a zipper on a baseball suit I knew the game was going to hell.

The greatest uniforms in the history of the game were the ones worn by the St. Louis Cardinals. They had that great bat across the shirt front with the two red birds on either end, and those great socks with the rings of red and black and white. The Cardinals were pleasing to watch. Plus, the old Gas House Gang always added dirt to the ensemble. I honestly think those uniforms moved a player up a few notches in class. You *felt* like a major leaguer in the cardinal and white.

The most famous uniforms, I suppose, were the vaunted Yankee pinstripes but, sartorially, they never did much for me. I didn't like either one—the Yankees *or* the uniform. The Yanks were the first to put numbers on their backs, but they are among the last to hold out against putting their names on. In a way, it's a waste of time. The Yankees are highly recognizable anyway. What's annoying is when a team like the Milwaukee Brewers doesn't put names on the back of its uniforms, although, I must admit, in most cases, even that wouldn't be much of a help.

The second-worst uniforms in the history of baseball were those designed by Charlie Finley for his Oakland A's. When they came out in those green and white and gold creations, you were surprised their noses didn't light up. They looked like a collection of large white rabbits. They were one of the great teams in baseball for half a decade, but who could take them seriously in those abominations? It hurt just to look at them.

No, the old gray flannels were good enough for Shoeless Joe Jackson and Three-Fingered Mordecai Brown and they're good enough for the modern-day Chicago White Sox. The White Sox have a bigger disgrace than the 1919 Black Sox in these negligees.

I see where the new owners of the White Sox have ordered a contest to create a new design for the team uniform. I have a suggestion for them: get a 1936 newspaper, carefully cut out a picture of the center fielder for the New York Yankees,

No. 5 on your program. That would be Joe DiMaggio—with his hat on straight, his shoelaces tied and his shoes shined. Submit that to your contest board. That's what a ballplayer should look like. Always.

SOME NIGHTS I STAY UP THROUGH THE NEWS

DECEMBER 31, 1981

I woke up Tuesday morning and went to look in the mirror. The guy in there was having a birthday, I won't tell you which one. Suffice it to say, he's much older than I.

I check on him every ten years or so. I can't seem to get rid of him. He keeps getting older while it's well known I'm growing younger. I'm somewhere between 30 and 35. He's God-knows-what.

He's got these pouches under his eyes. His skin is kind of blotchy. God knows, my skin is clear.

He's always getting heartburn while it's well known I can eat a taco, chili relleno and polish it off with a flagon of Dos Equis and not even belch. His hair is getting gray around the edges while mine is as black as Rudolph Valentino's. He's always trying to get me to go to bed early, but I fool him. I stay up clear through the 11 o'clock news some nights.

He uses wood for an approach shot to a green. I, on the other hand, choke down on a wedge. He creaks when he walks. I cross the room like a panther. I notice he's put on a lot of weight, but I can still get into my graduation suit. He can't even putt. Me, I'm deadly at 40 feet.

I keep young. You never hear me, when Ron Cey boots a ball at third, say, "Pie Traynor would've got two!" When a guy makes a leaping catch in the outfield, I never say, "DiMaggio would have been waiting for it." I don't look at Larry Holmes and say, "Dempsey would have killed him." The guy in the mirror sticks to the past. I don't. I have to throttle him to keep him from saying to Tony Dorsett, "You're not a patch on Red Grange, kid." You date yourself with that kind of talk. This guy actually boasts he saw Babe Ruth hit a home run once. Personally, I like to ask people if there really was a Babe Ruth or is he, like Santa Claus, a grownups' lie.

He's always complaining that the nights are darker than they used to be and he wonders why everybody has started to whisper and not talk up like they used to. He plays TV so loud you can hardly hear yourself drink. Personally, I can hear snow falling. Or a cat crossing a rug. Upstairs.

He listens to Lawrence Welk. He wears ties. I'm into disco, myself. I wear gold chains, and none of my shirts button.

He's always going through the dictionary. I could write one. I remember every word ever written. He's always wondering how to spell "obsolescent." I can spell it in German.

He tries to tell me to be my age. I tell him to shut up and get me a motorcycle for Christmas. He tells me not to be in a hurry to take the Christmas tree down, it may be the last one I'll ever have. With a friend like that who needs enemies? His teeth are bothering him. I eat corn just to annoy him.

I caught him reading the obituary page once and I yelled at him, "If I ever catch you reading that page again, you'll be in it!"

My friends, Bill and Katie Huber, of the Ventura Hubers, have sent me a birthday card for him culled from an old Ann Landers or Dear Abby column. It's perfect for him:

"You know you're getting old," it reads, "when the following happens:

"1—Almost everything hurts—what doesn't hurt doesn't work anymore.

"2—It feels like the morning after the night before—but you haven't been anywhere.

"3—All the names in your little black book end in 'M.D.'

"4—You look forward to a dull evening.

"5—Your knees buckle, but your belt won't.

"6—You're 17 around the neck, 42 around the waist, and 126 around the golf course.

"7—You sink your teeth into a steak. And they stay there.

"8—You try to straighten the wrinkles in your stockings— and find out you're not wearing any.

"9—A little old lady has to help you across the street. She's your wife."

Well, those are his problems. To tell you the truth, he keeps me young. Whatever he tells me to do, I do the opposite. If he says, go to bed, I go up to the Sunset Strip. If he says, write nice about Cincinnati—or Seattle, or Santa Clara—I tear into them. If this old geezer thinks he owns me, he's got another think coming.

LET'S BE HONEST ABOUT THE MASTERS

APRIL 9, 1982

No one knows quite how the Masters golf tournament became a "major." The little world of golf looked up one morning and there it was on the doorstep marked, "Important. Refrigerate After Opening. Store With the British Open, the American Open and PGA. Keep Out of Reach of Children."

I suspect the golf historian, Herbert Warren Wind, had as much to do with it as anybody. The presence of the incomparable Bobby Jones as inventor, founder and resident dreamer of the tournament, which was otherwise stuck away in a little hillbilly corner of Tobacco Road in North Georgia, didn't hurt.

Herb and Jones grew up an era when amateur golf was king. Gentlemen didn't play a game for money, and the Masters was conceived as a showcase for amateurs, with only a smattering of the most socially acceptable pros invited to play.

Nevertheless, an amateur never won it and, I dare say, never will, a fact of some annoyance to Master Jones, the only amateur in history ever to beat the pros at their own game.

The amateur influence thus declined. Jones finally concluded, regretfully, that none of those weekend players the stock brokers from Long Island, dentists from Cucamonga, auto salesmen from San Francisco were going to be able to match shots with the flower of the American golf tour. So he began to invite tour winners.

They had sort of wanted to keep the Masters as a kind of inside party in Golf. You know, one of those parties the big rich keep from the view of the masses. But, it became part of locker room lore and first-tee mystique, and the media came sniffing around, positive it was missing something as, indeed, it was. It

89

was a pure golf party. No Hollywood hoopla. No pro-am. It was like a Skull and Bones dinner at Yale.

TV was beguiled. It yearned to get its cameras into those secret places. The Masters finally let them all in. But on the Masters' terms. It didn't need media hype. Its millionaires no more needed their pictures in the papers then the Mafia dons. They preferred running the tournament as they ran the country: in the dark.

Nothing whets media appetites like being told they are not wanted. They eagerly accepted the Masters' conditions, and relinquished control over the show to a large exent. Any other event, and they might have insisted it be played at night, that timeouts be arranged for commercials, rules modified, the sort of things they did to football, baseball and boxing. But when they threatened to withdraw their cameras from the Masters unless proprietors relented, the Masters said, "Good!"

They said the tournament would not outlast Bobby Jones. It did. They said it wouldn't outlast Cliff Roberts, the crusty New York financier, confidant of presidents, who blew his brains out on the 13th green one night three years ago, but it did.

The Masters, somewhat reluctantly, has become a fixture on the American sports scene. Augusta has grown from a one-hotel, one-restaurant, one Confederate-statue town to a metropolis for a week. It belongs to the ages now. Also to Channel 2.

But, it retains one part of the whimsy it has had since the day Jones founded it in 1934. A former nursery, the 365-acre course is studded with exotic shrubs brought to it for centuries from all corners of the world. So, Jones named his holes after them. The first hole, for example, is the Tea Olive hole. The second, is the Pink Dogwood. The third is the Flowering Peach. And so on.

This, it seems to some of us, is like nicknaming Dracula, "Cuddles." The Little Red Riding Hoods who wander onto it with a golf stick should know that under that sleeping cap is not grandma but a full-grown and hungry wolf.

Accordingly, a friend and fellow hacker, Dynamite Page and I have decided to rename Augusta National's hell holes after a more appropriate set of guideposts—movie titles. Hole No. 1 is no longer the Tea Olive, it's the *I Wake Up Screaming* hole. Hole 2 is not Pink Dogwood, it's the *Kiss The Blood Off My Hands*.

Hole 3, Flowering Peach on the card, is the *Chainsaw Massacre* hole. Hole 4 is *Murder, My Sweet.* Hole 5 is *Each Dawn I Die.* Holes 6 is *Circle of Deceit* or *Ring of Fear.* Holes 7 through 12 are *Five Graves To Cairo* and/or *Rocky Horror Show.* Hole 13 is *Wuthering Heights,* and 14 is *The Curse of the Cat People.* Hole 15 is *Magnificent Obsession.* Hole 16 is *The House of Frankenstein.* Hole 17 is *Death in the Afternoon.* And 18 is *The Creature From the Black Lagoon,* or, more properly, *The Creature That Ate Tom Weiskopf.* It seems much more fitting somehow to label it this way rather than to have somebody done in by a flowering crab-apple plant or a yellow jasmine bush.

BREEDING COUNTS BUT DOESN'T ADD UP

JULY 22, 1982

Once, in a burst of ardor, Lady Astor proposed to the great George Bernard Shaw that they have an offspring. "Just think," she said, "It could have your brains and my looks." "Yes," retorted Shaw, "But what if it had my looks and your brains?"

It sometimes seems to me as if horse breeders make Lady Astor look like a pessimist. They are so slavishly devoted to the primacy of genes and heritage—it's called "pedigree"—that they make the House of Lords look like a truck drivers' picnic, Burke's Peerage look like the Yellow Pages, the Social Register about as fashionable as a police blotter.

It's the last stand of royalty in the world, with more inbreeding and state marriages than in the Hapsburg and Bourbon empires combined. It's no wonder so many horses are bleeders. The crowned heads of Europe were hemophiliacs.

It is the conceit of breeders that royalty will always stare down commoners in the stretch, that one horse can look at another on the way to the wire and say, in effect, "Look, peasant, I'm better than you are because my father and mother were," and the peasant will wilt.

History—human and equine—tells us otherwise. But if you checked the public prints this week, you will have noticed that a syndicate of horse breeders paid $4.25 million for a yearling colt. Why? Because his father is Nijinsky II, who won the English version of racing's Triple Crown in 1970. His grandfather was Northern Dancer, who won the Kentucky Derby and Preakness in 1964, running what was then the fastest Kentucky Derby ever.

The Kentucky yearling sales are the biggest crapshoot in the world. Guys at auctions are all Lady Astors. Breed the best to the best and you get the best, they believe.

It just ain't so. You can find royally bred animals, half and full brothers to classic winners, filling out cards in Juarez or Latonia Downs any day.

You know how many Kentucky Derby winners have sired Kentucky Derby winners in the 108 runnings of that classic? Ten. The last winner to sire a winner was Determine, who won in 1954.

Know how many Preakness winners sired Preakness winners in 107 runnings? Seven. Know how many Belmont winners sired Belmont winners in 114 years? Nine.

Seattle Slew, who won the Triple Crown, no less, in 1977, was a $17,500 purchase at the yearling sale. It's hard to get a plow horse for that these days. Carry Back, who won the Derby and Preakness in 1961, cost his owner, Jack Price, only $400 in stud fee. (Northern Dancer will command $125,000—if you can get in his book, that is.)

None of this deters the guys who hit the auction ring with syndicate millions, whether they are Irish bookmakers or Saudi sheiks. They buy horses like William R. Hearst bought fine art. Or philatelists buy stamps.

Race horses have only one function in life. They race. And they're ill-equipped for that. They are the fragilest of God's creatures. Their legs, asked to hold up 1,200 pounds of massive musculature, could hardly hold up a spider. Their bones are as brittle as dry twigs.

But, horse bidding has come to have a life all its own. It's almost as if the race track isn't a necessary part of it anymore. It's like a bunch of people trading in gold stock when there isn't any gold, or in commodity futures without any commodity.

The big bucks, the "safe" bucks, are in stud syndication. It's a separate poker game. A sire gets a sure $100,000 every time he goes to that post, and that makes him a better investment than a horse who might break a leg or hit a fence and have to be destroyed running for that amount.

Tax writeoffs make it even more attractive. The only problem is, they're killing the geese that lay the golden eggs. Or, at least, they're removing them from production. No one pays to see stud services. No one bets on them. Great horses are removed from the track as soon as they have won enough to get a star in their stud book. The public is cheated. The sport is cheated.

But, the opportunity to play God is too great to resist. Like Lady Astor, the breeder dreams of The Perfect Horse. They forget that there have been 40 presidents of the U.S., and only one of them was the son of a president—John Quincy Adams, the sixth president, and son of the second. And he died in 1848. Napoleon had no progeny that won battles. Famous men rarely duplicated themselves, not Caesar, Lincoln or Washington. Not even in the days of divine accession.

In horse racing, a lowly sire like Prospector, an honest enough plodder, produced 1982's triumphant horse, Conquistador Cielo. Genes are transmittable, but not always in the order in which you may want. As George Bernard Shaw wisely suspected.

THE SPORT THAT TIME LEAVES ALONE

MARCH 16, 1986

(Since our hero will be winging his way to spring training camps in Florida as this goes to press, he has requested permission to reprise a column he wrote earlier on the eve of a baseball season, a salute to baseball, a hymn to yesterday. He says you don't have to read it if you don't want to.)

I like songs like *Girl of My Dreams.* I like books by Charles Dickens.

I like country roads and moonlight, homemade fudge and ocean sunsets.

I like Christmas carols and Easter parades, jelly beans and black-eyed peas.

I like pumpkins on Halloween, turkey on Thanksgiving, and church on Sundays.

I like old photographs and paper planes, potato salad on picnics and umbrellas on the beach.

I like trolley cars and old trains, cowboy movies and college musicals.

I like Fourth of July fireworks, campaign speeches and cotton candy, Ferris wheels and merry-go-rounds.

I like kids on Christmas morning, boys fishing and puppies in the yard.

I like political conventions, not primaries. I like pictures you can understand hanging on the wall—landscapes, not pipe-fittings; museums, not junkyards; the *Mona Lisa,* not graffiti.

I like love stories and happy endings, Norman Rockwell and grand opera. I like diamond rings and high heels, men who smoke cigars and wear hats. I don't like lawsuits, lockouts, liars and loopholes.

So, I'm glad baseball is opening again.

You see, I also like home runs and double steals, strikeouts and tight infields. I like hot dogs and seventh-inning stretches, pennant races and magic numbers, doubleheaders and double plays.

I like Fenway Park and office pools, Casey Stengel stories— and even pitching changes.

I like the home team, the "crucial" series, *Take Me Out to the Ball Game,* bugle calls and bobblehead dolls, bedsheet banners and squeeze bunts.

I like, "Three strikes, yer out!" I like, "Four balls, yer on!" I like sacrifice flies and the hit-and-run, nine innings a game and the game's never over till the final out.

I like Johnny Bench and Joe Morgan. Pete Rose going head-first into third. I liked Casey Stengel and Bill Veeck, the *Sporting News* and Walter O'Malley. Our crowd.

I like Bat Night, the national anthem, organ music, Ty Cobb's spikes, Babe Ruth's bat, Cooperstown, 3-and-2 counts, even exploding scoreboards.

I like Vin Scully, Harry Caray, Joe Garagiola and that Shakespearean announcer in Yankee Stadium. I like George Steinbrenner and Peter O'Malley. I like every coach who ever hit a fungo. I like fungoes.

I like Stan the Man and Leo the Lip, the Big Train and Ol' Diz. I like the Iron Horse, and Lefty, the Babe, and Old Teddy Ballgame, the Thumper.

I like players like Country Slaughter and Junior Gilliam, Maury Wills and Bad Henry. The wonderful Willie, Double-X, and Jackie R.

I like to read *The Boys of Summer* or other things by Roger Angell or even play-by-plays. I like the minor leagues and the sports pages and postgame interviews. I like umpires. I like leather-lunged fans because they care. I even like boos because booing is a form of caring.

I like to look down on a field of green and white, a summertime land of Oz, a place to dream. I've never been unhappy in a ballpark.

I like to look down and see the same geometry my grandfather saw. I hate change.

I like one o'cat in the sandlots, bubblegum cards in the schoolyard, batting practice and trade rumors. I even like artificial grass.

I like baseball. Because it's always 1910. I like 1910. It was a better time.

I may grow up some day.

I hope not.

JUST ONCE, I'D LIKE TO SEE . . .

Well, it's that time of the year again, chestnuts roasting on an open fire, rump a pum pum, jingle bells, all that jazz. I think I'll send along a letter to my old friend St. Nick and see what falls down the chiminey for me.

Dear Santa,

Listen, old sport, I really don't need any soap on a rope or ties with a picture of Maui on them this year. In fact, I got one Christmas present already. There was this guy playing for Miami who scored a touchdown and, when he went into his funky dance and spiked the ball, he sprained a ligament or something. Way to go, Santa! It's a nice start, but if you're making a list and checking it twice, here are some other things I'd like to find under the Christmas tree.

—If it could be arranged, I'd like to see a World Series where it's the bottom of the ninth, the visiting team is ahead by two runs, but the bases are loaded and there's two out. What I would like is for the batter to hit a high fly to center field. The runners go and are crossing the plate as the center fielder puts up his glove to make a nonchalant one-handed catch. You guessed it! He drops the ball! I want it to pop right out of his mitt and just lie there. He has just nonchalanted away the world championship. I ask this not for myself but for an old-time ballplayer friend of mine who gets tears in his eyes every time he sees a guy one-hand a routine fly ball and he cries out, "John McGraw would have him on a bus to Peoria by morning!"

—Just once, when one of those tennis brats throws a tantrum, I would like to have the guy sitting in a chair be the ex-light-heavyweight champion of Brazil or the Third Fleet or something and have him come down and say to the player, 'What was that you called me again?' And then, he'd unload the best one-two he's thrown since he won the Olympics in Helsinki. A punch to the snoot can do wonders for a guy's manners. All I ask is the incident be caught by a camera as it will be the most popular piece of film since *Bambi*.

—You know those guys who throw their arms in the air and do a little dance over their fallen victim, the quarterback they've just sacked, or the receiver they tossed out of bounds into a snowbank? Well, I would like for them to go home and have a fight with their wives. If possible, I'd like to have tapes of it to play when I'm feeling down.

—The next time two heavyweight contenders get in a phony publicity scuffle at the contract-signing ceremony, arrange for one of them to break a knuckle on a microphone. If a bystander gets hurt in the scuffle, have him turn out to be the son of the godfather of the local Mafia.

—The next time a school gets caught cheating in recruiting or staging phantom classes for athletes, don't tell them they can't play in the Rose Bowl or the NCAA tournament the next few years. Tell them they can't have a team at all for the next two years. You'll only have to do that once.

—Put a time clock on golfers lining up a putt or studying an approach. Let no golfer ever walk ahead of his ball. If he does, penalize him a stroke for offsides when he walks up to a green from a ball 100 or even 40 yards out. Give him three minutes to get the ball in the hole from any point on the green.

—Let baseball have split seasons and wild cards and mini-playoffs, it might just as well get under the red light the same as all those other sports. Integrity's nice, but it gets lousy Nielsens.

And, if you can't give me any of those things, you old humbug, how about a new Cadillac? Or, give the Rams back Jack Reynolds, Vince Ferragamo, Bob Brudzinski and Fred Dryer, and all is forgiven.

WHO LET LAWYERS IN THE BALLPARK?

AUGUST 4, 1981

Baseball is not crabbed old men sitting around a negotiating table serenading each other with the stilted prose of "where-ases" and "In consideration of the specifications thereto" and "Parties of the second part hereinafter referred to as the bargaining committee of the employees of said major league clubs."

Baseball is Willie Mays scuttling out after a long one with his back to home plate and that peculiar sideways gait of his, clutching his glove in a pouch at his waist as his hat flies off. Baseball is Willie Mays robbing Vic Wertz of a three-base hit and the World Series.

Baseball is not some London insurance man in a frock coat dangling a policy that will cost his company more than a ship sinking.

Baseball is DiMag waiting at the plate in that classic straight-up stance of his for a Bob Feller fastball.

Baseball is not labor lawyers and contract negotiators and federal mediators.

Baseball is Musial crouched at the plate like a leopard on a limb, guessing curve, but coiled for the heater if it comes. Baseball is Koufax staring down the barrel where Mickey Mantle waits, waggling the biggest bat you've ever seen.

Baseball isn't codicils and writs and preliminary injunctions.

Baseball is Pete Rose going in headfirst with the winning run. Baseball is Clemente settling under a high one and turning slightly sideways so he can get set to throw out the runner trying to go home on the out.

Baseball is not cold men with agate eyes fighting over balance sheets and player pools and player depreciation.

Baseball is Rod Carew with the pitcher in a hole and left fielder shading too far to his left, leaving a tiny pocket to drop an extra-base hit down the left-field foul line.

Baseball is Babe Ruth pointing, Ty Cobb sliding. It's Whitey Ford loading one up for Campanella with the Series on the line. It's Lou Gehrig standing in Yankee Stadium for the last time, trying not to cry as he tells the world how lucky he was to be a Yankee.

Baseball players are not migrant workers, they don't pick grapes for a living. They don't find work out of waterfront shapeups, they don't sew dresses in dingy factory lofts. They're custodians of little boys' dreams. Little boys of all ages from 8 to 80.

Baseball has to do with our youth. We're all 25 years younger when we take our seats, hot dogs in hand, shouting "Play ball!" and it's like the day again when our fathers took us to our first doubleheader at the old ball grounds out of town where the open trollies dumped off loads of fans in straw hats and sleeve garters. Baseball is *The Boys of Summer,* and we're all the boys of summer.

Baseball is "Why didn't he bunt?" or "Why didn't he start Drysdale?" or "Why didn't he walk 'im?" or "Why didn't they pinch hit for 'im?" Baseball is controversy, lovely controversy. Not the controversy of "parties of the first part" or "in consideration whereof." A strike in baseball is a belt-high fastball, not a national catastrophe.

Baseball is the Big Six, Big Train, Shoeless Joe. It's Grover Alexander with blood-shot eyes striking out Lazzeri with the bases loaded. Baseball is "Alston, you're a bum!" and "Call yerself an umpire, do you Shag?"

Baseball is not pompous rich men exercising their arrogance. Baseball is coddled by society like an over-protected child. Baseball owes this society. It is the beneficiary of millions in free advertising, and in exemptions from the basic laws of the Republic. Baseball is a temple into which the money-changers should not have been allowed to creep.

Baseball is wondrous eccentrics, Dizzy and Rube, and Billy Loes and Casey Stengel hobbling out to the mound on lumpy

101

legs, a creature out of a Black Forest tree house, a Rumplestilt-skin in pinstripes. Baseball is our exemption from the clangorous world of commerce, the burning blocks, the seamy streets, the other world where there never are any clear-cut winners, only degrees of losers.

There's a new record out, sung by the troubadour, Terry Cashman, and it's called "Willie, Mickey and the Duke," and it's pure baseball, there isn't a dollar sign in it. The way it should be. Oliver Wendell Holmes himself said baseball was a sport, not a business. It's not Wall Street, it's Dream Street. It's three hours on a desert island for the guy who has to go home to a peeling tenement and a six o'clock alarm when it's over. It's the great escape, our uncommon denominator. So, get the lawyers out, leave the little boys in.

How dare they trifle with it?

NO BOSOX
TEA PARTY

JULY 13, 1980

The trouble with the Boston Red Sox is that relic they keep in left field. Overage, overweight, can't move, can't throw, it just stands there. Can't even catch and is easy to hit a ball over.

Carl Yastrzemski? Shoot, no! Carl is only 41. The relic I refer to is 67. It was born the year the Titanic sank. Carl only weighs 180. This relic weighs 20 tons. Carl is one of the best fielders in the business. This relic has dents all over it from getting hit by fly balls.

The relic I refer to, of course, is The Great Wall Of Boston, The Left-Field Fence, The Tombstone of the Red Sox. It has done more to bury their pennant chances year in and year out than the generations of scatter-arm shortstops, banjo hitters, crooked-arm pitchers and even the unfriendly press. The Wall is the biggest enemy to Boston since the Redcoats.

The Wall was built in 1912. Its peculiar configuration was necessitated by the proximity of city streets. In those days, you didn't dare condemn public property for the use of private enterprise, especially not for a baseball team.

The Wall thus had some great years. Its greatest victim was none other than Theodore S. Williams himself, Teddy Ballgame, just the greatest slugger the town had ever seen. But, great as he was, no telling what records Ted could have set if the Wall were in right field.

The Red Sox managed one measly pennant in that era, in 1946. The Wall otherwise stopped them cold. Their next greatest hitter was Carl Yastrzemski. A left-hander, too. Then came Freddie Lynn. A left-hander, too. With the right-field fence two zip codes away, they looked at the seductive left-field fence—and became inside-out hitters. That's like teaching Dempsey to jab.

It is one of the ironies of history that the only two pennant-deciding games ever played in American League history were played in Fenway Park. And the Wall won both of them. In 1948 Lou Boudreau, shortstop and manager of the Cleveland Indians, hit two home runs, and had two other hits, over and onto the Wall—and that was the old ballgame and the old pennant, Cleveland, 8–3. In 1978 the light-hitting Bucky Dent won the pennant for the Yankees with a banjo home run that cleared the 314-foot wall by half a foot. Lynn and Yaz had hit 375-foot shots in the same game. To right field. They were caught.

For the Red Sox, it's like shooting craps in a hat. Somebody else's hat. You would think they would want to tear down the Wall and dance on its grave. But you might as well want to tear down Faneuil Hall. Or dynamite Plymouth Rock. Boston would organize another tea party if you tried to touch so much as a dent in its old gray head. Paul Revere would mount up again.

Last year, Fred Lynn hit .386 in Boston—and .276 on the road. Jim Rice hit .369 in Boston—and .283 away. Yaz hit .302 in Fenway—and .238 away. Butch Hobson hit .312 in Boston—and .215 away. Carlton Fisk hit .320 in Boston—and .216 away. Home runs? Lynn had 28 at home, 11 away. Rice had 27 at home, 12 away. Yaz had 15 at Fenway, 6 elsewhere.

You probably noticed Fred Lynn hit a home run for the only runs scored by the American League in last Tuesday's All-Star Game. It must have been a pleasure to be able to swing through a ball for a change. In Fenway, don't bet he wouldn't have tried to slice an inside-out single off the Wall in that situation.

The moral? Don't bet on the Sox to win the pennant until they tear up Lansdowne Street and get the Wall out of their lineup. The Wall has done more damage to the Red Sox than Harry Frazee. Only the Berlin Wall has caused more misery to the home team, to the good guys.

RED-BLOODED RUNNERS

NOVEMBER 24, 1977

The most pampered individuals in the world today are not daughters of the Texas big rich, debutantes, princesses, kings, crown princes, or even oil sheiks. They're sports heroes. They are coddled, catered to, waited on, provided for and fawned over from the first day they break two clocks, hit three home runs, throw four touchdown passes, or score 98% from the free-throw line.

But it's not only the ones who can read and write and even talk who get most of the pampering. That honor goes to a breed of sports heroes who don't have to answer telephones, reach decisions, hire agents or even feed themselves—thoroughbred racehorses. They are bona fide tantrum-throwing, breath-holding *enfants terribles* of the worst sort.

They never have to do anything real horses have to do—pull a plow, cut a cow, ride in a battle, lead a parade. They work about two minutes a week. The rest of the time they sleep and eat. They also sulk, jump shadows, bite, kick and get all lathered up when they're called upon to do something. They got the nervous system of a guy with terminal DTs. They are playboys. They squander other peoples' money. Like, the bettors.

Standardbred horses, on the other hand, are taught to pull a wagon. They're not pampered, they are allowed to graze, they're not chauffeured by some 98-pound 18-year-old, but usually by some 200-pound grandfather. They're not even allowed to run freely but are hobbled and must go about in a mannered gait like a belle in a hoopskirt. They could be hitched up to a harrow tomorrow.

They even run at night. They are descendants of horses who pulled buckboards, stagecoaches, surreys, and ice wagons. They are close-coupled, squat. They look more like truck drivers than gigolos. They are red-blooded, not blue, outcrossed, not inbred.

Dream Maker, the U.S. champion standardbred pacer, defends his reputation in the $100,000 American Pacing Classic at Hollywood Park Friday night. But if he had been a thoroughbred, he would probably be on a psychiatrist's couch today.

Last July, six months after the Canadian construction magnate, Antonio Chiaravalle, had bought him (for $80,000, or about what a good thoroughbred would command at stud), he was shipped to Roosevelt Raceway to compete in the second leg of the U.S. Pacing championship and, after a grueling, 17-hour trip from the farm near Toronto, the driver drove the van under an overpass on a Long Island parkway. Or, rather, he tried to drive the van under the overpass. It wouldn't fit, and, suddenly, Dream Maker was penned in a vice of torn metal in a stall in a truck box pulled halfway off its bed. Dream Maker's chains broke, his nose bled, and he was like a miner in a cave-in. They had to call in a special police team to cut him loose.

A thoroughbred might have cast himself in his stall, but Dream Maker was yawning when they cut him out. Two days later, he finished second, a dirty nose, to Armbro Ranger in the second leg of the championship series.

On another trip, from Detroit to the farm in Caledonia, Canada, Dream Maker's van hit a blizzard. It got worse, until the driver had to abandon horse and trailer. For two days, Dream Maker and another horse stabled alongside in the truck, were stranded in 16 feet of snow.

Imagine Secretariat stranded in 16 feet of snow for two days! They would have called out the Marines. Dream Maker paid no more attention to it than an Eskimo.

Owners treat thoroughbreds like Rembrandts. Seattle Slew had armed guards on his trips West. He has his own vet, trainer, groom, press agent, and jockey wherever he goes. Dream Maker's people put the horse in the charge of a 22-year-old woman who looks more like Dorothy Hamill than David Harum. Judy Boone drives and trains the horse out here. Dream Maker has had three different jockeys, or drivers, in his pacing championship legs. They just check the yellow pages.

Nor are standardbreds retired to stud as soon as they win a stakes or so. Dream Maker has raced 71 times, won 25 with 12 seconds and nine thirds, but he is expected to keep doing his chores around the farm for three or four more years (he's only four) before he's permitted to date.

I mean, it's all right for those lowlife thoroughbreds to run around with loose women and live like sultans, but a good standardbred has work to do and wagons to pull. So, shut up and run.

TRIBUTE TO ABE

JANUARY 21, 1969

When Abe Saperstein died a few years ago, there was a brief, almost laconic obituary released over the wires. Abe would have had it any other way.

It was not that Abe was immodest, although nobody ever caught him making anonymous donations to anything respectable. It was just that Abe would gnash his teeth at any loss of opportunity to publicize his own unique public monument—the Harlem Globetrotters.

The Harlem Globetrotters are, to put it simply, the most extraordinary athletic team in the history of games. The 1927 Yankees, the 1930 Notre Dame eleven, the Australian Davis Cup squads—no group, no dynasty approaches the Globies either in durability, skill or drawing power. Part minstrel and part sport, part of their fascination is that no one ever figured out how good they are.

They have been in more fixed matches than a mob fighter. They go around the country, no, the world, with their own sparmates, but their charm is, underneath that veneer of buffoonery exists some of the world's greatest athletic talent.

Wilt Chamberlain came out of the Globies to swallow basketball, Bob Gibson came out to surround baseball. The Harlem Globetrotters squelched riots in Germany, revolutions in South America. They shot baskets with Castro, joked with kings. They have had audiences with three Popes. Their trademark is the smile.

They are a throwback to the days when we had such offenses to the American conscience as "Negro leagues" and "barnstorming troupes," when our greatest performers graced our shabbiest stages.

Abe Saperstein founded this gaudy group when he found them on the playgrounds of Chicago in 1927, school dropouts who put down their shoeshine boxes to perform feats with basketballs that magicians do with handkerchiefs.

Abe reveled in the title, "The Jewish Abraham Lincoln," and, while no one ever got the best of him in a contract fight, he once packed his team off to London at his own expense to raise $400,000 for Prince Philip's favorite charity. The Globetrotters have helped heal the sick, mend the maimed, straighten the misshapen—moral and physical—of nearly every country on earth. They were a bigger attraction in Moscow than those roller-skating bears, or the biers of despots.

They were as powerful a lever at toppling prejudice as the Constitutional Amendment. Using them as a base, Abe (and Bill Veeck) came within one swipe of a pen in 1941 of buying the Philadelphia Phillies and fielding an all-Negro lineup. Baseball took five more years to integrate, and then only a drop at a time, but it was Saperstein who showed up in the Cleveland dugout with Satchel Paige one historic night when integration was achieved.

Twenty years ago, you could have bought the team by paying off the mortgage on the bus. The Globies wore out a bus every six months. And you could have won 11 or 12 NBA championships in a row. Today, thanks in part to the Globies, black youngsters take in more money in basketball than the entire cash crop their grandfathers picked in their lifetimes.

The Globetrotters no longer could sweep the court with an all-star NBA team, perhaps not even with a second division club. But neither can Bill Russell drop-kick a basket.

The Globies take on a team of movie stars (Don Adams, Jim Brown, Bill Cosby, Jack Lemmon) for the benefit of brain-damaged children of the Dubnoff School and the Teach Foundation Saturday night at the Forum. They will get laughs for kids who have forgotten even how to smile. And if you haven't seen Meadowlark Lemon play basketball, why, turn in your season tickets. Also, I like to think you'll be paying tribute to a departed little round man Satch Paige once introduced as "Abraham Lincolnstein."

GOLF IS TO FOOTBALL AS PALM SPRINGS IS TO PITTSBURGH

JANUARY 11, 1979

PALM DESERT—The cultural shock is the worst. Going from NFL playoff games, bowl games, nosebleeds, black eyes and separated shoulders to a game where the worst thing that can happen to you is a ball out of bounds is almost too hard to take. It's like going from the Gulag Archipelago to Miami Beach, from a Siberian prison camp to Waikiki.

Golf is a game where a "late hit" means a slice, not a fracture. It's where "rough" does not refer to Mean Joe Greene but high grass. Where hardly anybody ever needs crutches and the bleeding is all internal.

The game is played at a walk and the most terrifying thing a golfer ever sees is a downhill putt. He doesn't need 20 yards of plastic to protect his rib cage or a mouthpiece or face cage. No one has ever seen a golfer carried off the field. No neurosurgeons are needed at ringside. The turf is not artificial and hard as a throw rug on a boulder.

A golfer's idea of trauma is a scalped lie or a ball buried in sand. A "catastrophe" is a 7 on a par 5. You don't need a helmet like a fighter pilot; you don't have to wait in a "pocket" of 250-pound blockers while two tons of blitzing backs and linemen try to tear your head off. You don't need cutmen, plaster casts, canes or wheelchairs. You bleed where nobody can see it.

You don't have to be 7 feet tall or 300 pounds fat. You don't have to run fast, hit hard, or knock anybody down. You get to keep all your teeth and ears and eyes. It's hard to fracture your thumb on a putt. The holes are not guarded by guys named

110

"Too Tall" or "The Animal" or "Mean Joe." They're guarded by little palm trees you can hit over or sand traps you can miss.

When a football player says, "Something terrible happened to me yesterday," he says it through a body cast where only his eyes and mouth are showing and you say, "I can tell." When a golfer says, "Something terrible happened to me," he means two over par. A "cut" is a score that isn't in the low 60s and ties, not a 20-stitcher over the eye or a tear in the mouth. The worst thing that can happen to you is, you might have to take your shoe off to hit a ball out of a water hazard.

Listen now as the first day's co-leader comes into the press tent. Bob Murphy is in roughly the same physical condition as an Irish bartender. He could match bellies with Jackie Gleason. He would probably die on the Chicago Bears 10-yard line. Here he is, the first day's co-champion.

He has made $882,491 in his career without ever having a concussion or bruised ribs and will probably never need a knee operation. He spends his life in the kind of sylvan retreats you imagine Eden looked like. Birds sing, the sun shines, a guy carries his clubs for him. There's no heavy lifting. He can make 50 grand this week without hammering a nail, sawing a plank, climbing a rigging or knocking down Jack Lambert.

Here comes John Mahaffey, golf's new Golden Boy. Look at him now as he comes in the press tent. He looks a little like the Rams' Pat Haden. Except he has not broken his thumb on Randy White's helmet or Harvey Martin's armor. He hasn't got a mark on him. His ear is not bleeding or cauliflowered, his eyes are clear, his speech is not slurred. He's not big enough to make a defensive halfback at 5'9", 150. He's not fast, he probably can't hit a good curve, or throw one, but he made $153,520 on golf courses last year.

People are in awe because he shot a 66 on the "difficult" Tamarisk golf course. To anyone who has climbed Everest, Tamarisk is about as "difficult" as porch steps.

John is a star but when he finishes a golf tournament, it does not take a week for the bones to mend, the bruises to heal, the blood to clot. He will not be "washed up" at 35. In fact, not at 45. You can play tournament golf till you're 60, if you're Sam Snead. You can win tournaments in your 50s if you're Julius Boros. The greatest golfer out here, Jack Nicklaus, will be 38 in a week. And he's probably not even at his peak.

There's no disabled list in golf. It's like finding money. The parent who gives his child a football, boxing gloves, hockey stick or vaulting pole should be taken into psychiatry. These are the luckiest guys in sport. Johnny Bench, who gets his thumbs, knuckles and wrists broken by foul balls for a living and spends summer afternoons on his knees like a charwoman, plays in this thing for a ribbon or a medal or a tea tray. His pro, Hubert Green, is playing for the $50,000—or even the $500 every pro who makes the cut gets.

Pros in other sports get what Churchill promised the British people—blood, sweat and tears. Pro golfers don't even sweat. They just hit a little white ball with scientifically perfect instruments onto a manicured lawn that looks like what you'd imagine a French king's grounds looked like in 1760. They go through life with a suntan, wearing fashion-model clothes picked for them and laid out by style coordinators.

Roger Staubach just got a lousy break in life. Lynn Swann gets headaches for a living. You think Raymond Floyd has ever been on a stretcher in his whole life? You think Jack Nicklaus has made $3,349,393 in his life without ever breathing hard? You think he's ever going to be able to tell it's going to rain by the feeling in his knees? Arnold Palmer's going to be 50 years old this year. You think anybody in this year's Super Bowl is going to be in one 20 years from now?

If they are, they're probably going to be carried there. Golfers are the luckiest guys this side of Louis XIV. Anybody who made any money easier than this would be prosecuted.

NO GRUNDGES IN THE KUMQUAT BOWL

JANUARY 4, 1978

I think if there's one thing to be learned from the spate of New Year's bowl games, it's that the established rivalries do not make the best games.

It was the off-Broadway productions that stopped the show—the Fiesta Bowl, the Sun Bowl, the Astro-Bluebonnet, Gator, Kumquat, Papaya, or Seedless Raisins that provided the liveliest entertainment.

It all began with the Gator Bowl. The score was an interesting 34–3 in favor of Pittsburgh over Clemson, but the Pitt quarter-back completed 23 passes for 387 yards and four touchdowns, and a performance like that you remember like Gielgud's Hamlet or Bernhardt's Camille, or Spencer Tracy playing a priest—an artist at work.

We moved then to El Paso where a semi-secret tournament featuring Stanford and LSU was being put on. It was a rodeo. LSU finished the game with 375 yards on offense and Stanford had 372. LSU had a runner named Charles Alexander who ripped for 197 yards in 30 carries and Stanford had a passer, Guy Benjamin, who completed 23 out of 36.

Then, the Trojans took on the Texas Aggies in the Astrodome, spotted them two touchdowns and won the game—get this!—47–28. It was great good fun—50, count 'em! Fifty first downs! SC made 400 yards rushing, A & M made 500. It had about as much defense as an Irish picnic. But who cared?

I think there's a reason for all this: first of all, the stakes are limited in these games. These are not games for national championships, these are lighthearted romps for good teams that had so-so seasons. They don't scout each other as minutely as the major bowl contenders. I mean, the Big 10 and the Pac-8 swap film as early as November 20 some years, and nothing the other team does surprises the opponent.

The lesser-bowl teams just blow up the football and go out and play. It's like a street game, or like Yale-Harvard used to be before computers, films, recruiting and all the other modern devices that changed football from a game to a business.

The pros? Humbug! A Rams-Minnesota game is a ritualized gavotte, as predictable as a revival of *Rio Rita*. I have a colleague, Mal Florence, who refers to this type of football as "grundgy." The NFL has a high percentage of "grundges," guys who grind out yardage by the inch, win football games by a field goal or a point-after. It's like watching a guy lay brick, or listening to paint dry. A bore.

The grundgiest games in the world are between two veteran teams who get to the Super Bowl determined not to make a mistake. The Rams and the Vikings could play by numbers— or by phone. The Rams could announce a "45-P" and the Vike defense could counter with "30-Red" and the computer could flash "two-yard loss."

They use great runners as decoys, they warn their passers that, any time you put the ball in the air 50 or more times in the NFL, you lose. They spend weeks putting the grundge in the game.

But, when Stanford arrives in El Paso, or LSU does, they decide to have some fun. I mean, who cares if you lose the Sun Bowl? Are USC alums going to turn in their pompons if they lose the, for crying out loud, Bluebonnet Bowl? But if they lose to UCLA—now, *that's* serious!

It's just too bad we couldn't have a season full of these kinds of games. Get rid of those four-quarter arm wrestles. We saw the Washington Huskies shock Michigan out of its standard game plan of 21 first downs for two touchdowns and a 14–6 win. Michigan found out it could be just as exciting as Saturday night on the waterfront itself.

But, they'll go back to the films and grundge it out, and to the coach's first commandment—defense wins football games.

Well, it doesn't win the Gator Bowl, or the Bluebonnet, or the

Sun—or the Peach Bowl (47 first downs, 477 passing yards). It only wins the Rams-Vikings, Washington Redskins–Green Bay games and other certified grundge matches. In fact, I liked it even better when we were kids and used to choose up sides 10 seconds before the game. Let me tell you, there wasn't a "grundge" on the field! Nobody followed orders. We were all *stars,* baby! And was it fun!

A TRANSIENT BUSINESS

FEBRUARY 10, 1980

May it please the court, in the matter of the Los Angeles Coliseum Commission versus the National Football League, I would respectfully ask permission to look at the record.

Now, we have here a yellowed clipping dated 1869 and it attests that, in that year of Our Lord, a man felicitously named Harry Wright formed the first professional sports team of any kind in this country, a baseball team called the Red Stockings. Mr. Wright boldly affixed the city name, Cincinnati, to the players' uniform blouses. There is no record he ever asked anyone's permission.

The Red Stockings became a smashing success barnstorming around the country, and soon other entrepreneurs got into the act. They formed teams called the White Stockings of Chicago, Athletics of Philadelphia, Olympics of Washington, Haymakers of Troy, Mutuals of New York, Kekiongas of Fort Wayne, and Forests of Cleveland. They sewed the city names on their uniforms. No one gave them permission to do so. They just moved in and began rearranging the furniture.

The association of baseball teams became the National Association of Professional Baseball Players and it began setting rules for admission. For one thing, they ruled that no member could be admitted unless his team represented a city over 75,000 in population. Towns under 75,000 just bowed and took the disenfranchisement.

In 1901, an ex-sportswriter, Byron Bancroft (Ban) Johnson, formed a rival league, the American Baseball League. He got no federal, state, county or city charter. He just located franchises where he chose—Milwaukee, Boston, Detroit, Buffalo, St. Paul. Oh, he did jerk the franchise out of St. Paul and move it to the more lucrative south side of Chicago where it became the White Stockings. He canceled Buffalo altogether. He didn't seek anyone's authority save his own, but, then, inexplicably, he sought the permission of the rival National League so he could "expand" into Washington, Baltimore and Philadelphia. That was like General Motors asking Ford if it could open an agency in Peoria. The National League ignored him. So he put in his franchises anyway.

The next season the manager of the Baltimore franchise, the feisty John McGraw, jumped to New York to the National League team there. So Ban Johnson jerked the franchise out of Baltimore and moved it to New York, where it ultimately became the Yankees. Neither Baltimore nor New York got any say in the matter.

That was baseball . . .

In August of 1920, on the running boards of cars in an agency in Canton, Ohio, George Halas and five cronies started the National Football League. They awarded franchises to 12 cities. Membership fee was put at $100 per team. No one ever paid it.

Greatly to their surprise, Akron, Chicago, Buffalo, Green Bay, Canton, Dayton, Rock Island, Cleveland, Rochester, Detroit, Columbus and Cincinnati found themselves charter members of a new professional sports league. They "owned" a bunch of football players. Which meant they were entitled to pay to see them. No one thought there was anything odd about this.

A dog kennel bankrolled the team in Marion, Ohio. A shirt-starching factory in Decatur owned the Chicago Bears. Only in Green Bay did the townspeople get in the act. When the Packers were about to go bust, the local merchants ponied up $2,500 for a nonprofit corporation to run the team, the only bona fide instance ever of true community involvement.

The National Football League went in and out of more towns faster than the Jesse James Gang. "Metropolises" like Pottsville, Pennsylvania, Evansville, Kenosha, Racine and Hammond, Indiana, got teams. So did Hartford, Toledo, Duluth, and Providence. Tim Mara and Billy Gibson, a fight manager, got New York all to themselves (save for the occasional Brooklyn franchise, which didn't last long) for $500. The guys who "sold" it to them had no more right to do that than to sell them the Brooklyn Bridge.

Both football and baseball had a ready-made plan for the emergence of rival leagues, thereinafter termed "outlaw."

They waited till they went broke and then cannibalized them. Baseball got an additional bonanza. The "outlaw" Federal League sued the established league after going belly up (at a loss of $10 million) in 1916. When the case got to the Supreme Court six years later Justice Oliver Wendell Holmes ruled baseball was not a business but a sport. No one knows yet where he got that piece of law; probably from Caligula.

Pro football was so contemptuous of the rights of the fans that, in 1936, when the Boston Redskins won the Eastern title, owner George Preston Marshall not only played the championship game in New York but at the same time moved the franchise to Washington. Washington didn't know whether to say "Thanks" or "Why us?" It wasn't consulted.

Baseball stayed put till 1952, when the Boston Braves drew 281,278 fans for 77 home games. They left town in the dead of night and didn't stop running till they reached Milwaukee. They left there the same way for Atlanta 14 years later. No plebiscite gave them the right to do either.

The St. Louis Browns moved to Baltimore in 1954 after seasons in which they drew as many as 80,000 fans total for the year. Baltimore didn't want the Browns. Nobody wanted the Browns. The Philadelphia Athletics began their way West through Kansas City to Oakland and, at last reports, were beginning to head back by way of Denver. They may yet wind up back in Altoona.

In 1958, the great California gold strike took place. The 58ers—the Brooklyn Dodgers and the New York Giants—moved to California. It was their own idea. In fact, the Dodgers had to survive a massive, hostile, adversary general election to get to stay there. And, of course, the Rams came from Cleveland in 1946, even though they had to overcome the resistance of the colleges who were tenants in the Coliseum and a press which was sympathetic to the colleges.

The moral is: franchises move, even to localities where they're not particularly wanted.

Which brings us to 1980 and Al Davis, an owner in an old tradition, who now wants to move the Oakland Raiders to Los Angeles. And why not? It stays open clear till 2 o'clock in the morning, most nights, and has an area population of 8 million people with nothing to do when the sun goes down or the surf's not up. Oakland, on the other hand, is one of the few, if not only, California communities to suffer a population drop in the past 15 years (going from 367,000 to 331,000).

The NFL is in a snit. It wants Al Davis to keep doing business in that little corner store. Al says it's a question of Macy's telling Gimbel's. Where to locate, that is.

The NFL left Los Angeles just lying there. That's like leaving a diamond necklace in the washroom of a waterfront saloon in Marseilles. Al Davis knows if he doesn't pick it up, the next guy will.

Can the NFL stop him? it's doubtful. Oliver Wendell Holmes is dead, and the courts have shown a stubborn disinclination lately to go partners with the NFL in the business of shredding the U.S. Constitution.

No one has ever told the lords of sports they just couldn't take over a territory, sew its name on their shirt, and start doing business as though they owned the place. Why start now? Why shouldn't Al Davis be able to do what every sports promoter has been able to do from Harry Wright to Walter O'Malley? Why is it up to the courts to enforce professional sports' own rules when they've never been able to or interested enough to try? Since they operate so far outside the Constitution anyway, and always have, there is no such thing as an "outlaw." They're all outlaws.

FROM RUSSIA WITH LOVE OR ... I'LL NEVER SMILE AGAIN

JULY 16, 1980

MOSCOW—All things considered, I'd rather be in Philadelphia.

Or Pittsburgh? Cincinnati? Tell Cincinnati, I'm sorry. I'll make it up to them. Give my regards to Broadway. Also to downtown Dubuque.

Tell President Carter: Having a swell time, wish you were here.

Here we are, representing the United States of America, the last of the 3-foot high jumpers, the 6-foot pole vaulters, 30-second sprinters, two-day marathoners, guys who couldn't snatch-and-jerk the Sunday Times. If the local populace doesn't know the American team is not coming, they must get a jolt when they see us coming. I can just hear the old man, "Ivan, you're not going to believe this but the American Olympians are here and they're an average of 55 years old, alcoholic, wear bifocals, hearing aids, and they smoke in bed and complain of gas in the stomach. If I didn't know better, I'd swear they were a bunch of commissars. Except they take more baths."

I am certainly thankful to the IOC for transporting me to this little bit of heaven off Red Square. These are certainly the happiest cast of people I have ever seen in my life. You know they're happy because they don't have to show it. I mean, you know how they put on these plastic smiles in Hollywood and on Broadway and in Palm Springs and Palm Beach? Pretend they're having a good time?

Well, these people don't bother to put on any fronts. It goes without saying they're the happiest people on earth, so they don't have to show it. The last smile I saw was the stewardess getting off the plane in Stockholm.

Of course, it may be that smiles are just another shortage in this glorious workers' paradise. There are, after all, certain things you have to give up to insure the Revolution. You have to watch these things. It starts with a smile, you know, then a laugh—and the next thing you know they think the government's funny.

Smiles are subversive. You picture the guy at customs, frowning at you as you spread open your suitcase, showing the toilet tissue, peanut butter jars, Kleenex, soap, and little pieces of paper with "Help!" scrawled on them in case you get caught smiling and thrown in a tower dungeon, and the customs officer frowns and says "Any contraband? Copies of the *London Times, Playboy*, dope, smiles, laughs and snickers?"

It may be that smiling requires a special permit or that you can only buy them in the stores marked for foreigners' use only. You have to queue up for everything else in the proletarian Eden. Maybe you get to smile only every other Thursday between the hours of two and four. In the morning. Maybe now that the dissidents and the refuseniks and the subversives who are apt to burst right out laughing have been removed from the city and put out of the way—much the way titled families used to lock the idiot sons in the attic when company called—the KGB's main function is to keep an eye on the smilers.

You picture them pouncing on some luckless straphanger and hustling him off to the Lubianka bawling "You are accused of the nasty, decadent bourgeois trick of smiling. You were seen smiling at the haircuts of the Supreme Soviet Presidium and smothering a laugh only the other day! How do you plead?" And the poor fellow would cry "Nyet, comrade! Actually, I *like* Comrade Kosygin's mohawk! I did *not* say Comrade Brezhnev's hair looked out of place without a bone in it. Comrade, I have not smiled since 1972! Although, of course, I am quite happy!"

Apparently, there are no circumstances under which a smile can, so to speak, be countenanced by the regime except under the most extreme of provocations. For example, if you hear from Afghanistan that your son Laventry's wounds are not so serious as at first believed, or if you are told that the stuff in the store windows at GUM is also available inside. Under such extreme circumstances, apparently, a smile is permitted, not to exceed one millimeter at each corner of the mouth so as not to annoy the people sitting next to you whose turn to smile won't come up till 1988.

You can queue up, I presume, at the Ministry in Charge of Emotions (they have a bureau for everything in this country) and present a case for an extra ration of smiles—say, you just found out your mother-in-law got an apartment of her own, or you've been reading *Pravda* editorials which can be harder on your laugh centers than someone tickling you in the ribs with a boa feather.

Obviously, most people cannot stand the long lines at the smile desk or they turn away in disgust when they find out it's not the chicken line (in Moscow, you get in any two-block long line you see because the only thing the country doesn't have a shortage of is lines) because I haven't seen a genuine 32-tooth smile since I got here.

As I say, I know the people are happy. It's just that their faces don't know it yet. They're well-clothed. At least one out of two of them have these leisure suits with shoulder boards on them and I'm told they come free from the government. In fact, with each suit they throw in a genuine repeating rifle in guaranteed working order. Robert Hall should have thought of it. These suits are the rage here.

Smiling is not central, I guess, to building a super state of the people. Smiling is for exploited masses, although I must say the old women sweeping the streets with birch brooms do not exactly look as if they were going to burst into calypso at any minute. Smiling is just not in the five-year plan but I did get the ghost of one out of an Iron Curtain photographer colleague when he asked somewhat maliciously about the boat people of Cuba and I told him, deadpan, that actually they were trying for Murmansk but ran aground in Florida.

The real problem with Russia is you forget how to smile. I have made up a list of instructions to myself when I return home. "Pull down on the left corner of your mouth, pull up on the right corner. Show your teeth. Try to think of something pleasant like lifting off from Sheremetievo airport in a westerly direction or having all the ice cream you can eat and not having to wait in line for it. Breathe normally and let your eyes begin to crinkle. Practice in front of mirror till it comes as natural as to a cheerleader."

Only trouble is, I'm afraid one of the government agents will find it and accuse me of trying to undermine a form of government where the people are so happy they can afford to frown all the time.

Portraits

MAN WITHOUT A FUNNYBONE

FEBRUARY 26, 1967

Arnold (Red) Auerbach was born in Brooklyn of Jewish parents, ate Chinese food, drank Coke for breakfast, collected letter openers, lived like a monk apart from his wife nine months of the year and saw absolutely nothing funny about life.

Which was a pity because, by some standards, his life was hilarious.

He directed all his life drive to winning an annual professional basketball championship which is the athletic version of collecting letter openers. And he's not the least bit defensive about it. "I didn't have to be a basketball coach, you know," he said. "My father had a dry cleaning business."

"Red's sense of humor stood him in good stead," a friend observed. "He didn't have any."

Red saw his career as one long walk through enemy territory armed only with purity of heart. It's set forth in poker-faced detail in his new book *Winning The Hard Way—Basketball's Greatest Coach Tells His Story*, which you can get for $5.95.

There are those who say Red's success can be summed up in two words—"Bill Russell," that he insured himself of instant immortality the day he signed the majestic San Francisco center to a $19,500 contract.

If so, Red's life has been a study in wasted motion. Since then he has 1) racked up an all-time league high of $17,000 in fines; 2) socked the owner of the St. Louis Hawks in the jaw; 3) walked his team off the court; 4) loosened more teeth than sugar slugging private citizens; and 5) publicly condemned the league, the league president, the officials, press, rival owners, his own owner and every institution short of the Congress of the United States with equal fervor and conviction. He had all the social graces of the Bowery Boys.

On the plus side, he 1) quietly brought the first Negro into the NBA; 2) fumingly held up a game in Yugoslavia one night until the hosts came up with an American flag to go with the Communist ones on the rafters (on the same trip he blasted the U.S. ambassador to Egypt for not greeting the team—"President Johnson and Dean Rusk saw us off, why can't this creep phone us up? I have to say we got some real phonies in the diplomatic service." His Excellency was glad to get back to people who merely stoned the Embassy after a word from Red).

He led the league in lawsuits. People holding their jaws were constantly showing up at the desk sergeant's demanding a warrant. He got a technical foul the afternoon they gave him a ceremony for his 1,000th win. He got kicked out of the game at the All-Star contest in San Francisco when he came out of retirement for one night. When his first struggling franchise hit Boston, the regal Bill Cunningham, Back Bay's oracle, phoned him up to say, "Tell me a funny story and I'll do a column on your team." "I'm a coach, not a comic, " growled Red, and hung up.

His first book, *Basketball For the Player, the Fan, and the Coach*, contained some of the most practical advice this side of *How to Rob a Bank*. You had to think the YMCA didn't have *this* in mind when they invented the game: 1) "grabbing or pulling the pants or shirt of an opponent can be very aggravating"; 2) "place the scorer's and timer's table near *your* bench"; 3) "when the other team is given possession of the ball, don't throw the ball directly to an opponent. The ball should be thrown rather slowly to the official. This will give your men time to get set on defense"; 4) "if the opposing team has a high scorer, keep reminding the other players of their uselessness."

He had a strict policy against socializing with any of the Celtics' wives during the season—and this included Mrs. Auerbach, who lived in Washington in season while Mr. Auerbach lived in Boston. He got home for Christmas *once* in 20 years. His daughters not only didn't believe in Santa Claus, they were a little suspicious of that fable about Dad.

Red played the game of life as if it were sudden-death overtime. The Celtics under Auerbach didn't laugh much. But they cried a lot. They were as emotional as *Aida*.

The betting was heavy there wouldn't be a sniffle in the room when Red retired but William Felton Russell, himself, arose to say: "When I took this job somebody said, 'What did you take it for? You got nothing to gain. You got to follow Red Auerbach.'

"I don't think I'm going to be another Red Auerbach. Personally, I think you're the greatest basketball coach that ever lived. You know, over the years . . . I heard a lot of coaches and writers say the only thing that made you a great coach was Bill Russell. It helped. But that's not what did it.

"Now, this is kind of embarrassing, but I'll go so far, Red, as to say this: I like you. And I'll admit there aren't very many men that I like. But you I do. For a number of reasons. First of all, I've always been able to respect you. I don't think you're a genius, just an extraordinarily intelligent man. We'll be friends until one of us dies. And I don't want too many friends, Red."

I know some men who have to make do with a lot less epitaph than that.

IDOL WHOSE TIME IS PAST

OCTOBER 5, 1975

If you've never seen McCormack sing, Tracy act, Astaire dance, Toscanini conduct or Dillinger steal, you may want to tune in Channel 4 over the weekend. You wouldn't want to miss another vanishing piece of art—Willie Mays playing.

It'll be your last chance. Incredible as it seems, Willie Mays is middle-aged. I didn't think that was possible. I thought he'd go through life age 20, playing stickball, giggling, his hat falling off, playing pepper with Leo Durocher, looking bug-eyed at a cowboy-and-Indian movie on TV, cracking gum, catching fly balls with his back to home plate and throwing out sprinters from the outfield by 20 feet.

A man gets sad late in life when he goes out and looks at a tree he planted and it's 80 feet high and he can't even climb it anymore. And there must be some guy who works the subways or lays pipe or runs Wall Street or opens cab doors at hotels who measures time by memories of the old Polo Grounds or Ebbets Field or Yankee Stadium, and he remembers the first day Willie came up. And you tell him Willie Mays is 42 years old and batting .211, and it's like you kicked him in the stomach. Next, he'll be reading obituaries of guys he went to school with.

We all thought Willie Mays would just get younger. He was one of those touched individuals for whom time seemed to run backward. He was one of those guys in this life you smiled just thinking about him. You might have hated New York, the Giants, the rest of the team, the manager, or the owner. But you couldn't hate Willie Mays. It was like hating a kid in a baby carriage, or Skippy, or Charlie Chaplin in his tramp costume on the lam from the cops. Willie Mays was everybody's pal when he was in uniform and you were in the seats with a beer and a hot dog. Willie was Mr. Feelgood. Other people got old. Willie stayed 20.

Other guys could do things better. Aaron could hit farther, Clemente could throw longer, Wills could run faster. But nobody could catch better and, if you wanted one guy for four things, Willie was your man, Casey Stengel used to say. If he ain't in the Hall of Fame first crack, they should burn it.

But why you should skip the football games and the billfishing tournaments and lion hunts this weekend is not to watch a graying old-timer creak through his last games, the throes of a career. Not to watch McCormack with laryngitis, Tracy blowing his lines, Astaire with the gout, Toscanini going deaf, or Dillinger sinking to the sidewalk.

You see, Willie Mays is one of the greatest big-game, late-inning players I've seen. You never got Willie Mays out in the ninth inning. Ask Eddie Roebuck, who had to pitch to Willie with the bases loaded and one out and a 4−2 lead in the decisive pennant playoff game in 1962. Willie hit it right back through him and, when the dust cleared, the Giants had a 6−4 victory and the pennant. Ask Ralph Terry, who had a 1−0 lead, two out, and a man on first in the ninth inning of the final game of the '62 World Series and Willie Mays up. Willie banged a long double to right. Runner Matty Alou should have scored, but was held up at third, or the Giants surely would have won.

You just don't get Willie Mays out in the twilight of a game.

When I was 42 years old I commenced to have trouble tying my shoelaces. I had to watch what I ate and my hair started to come off in my comb. I had trouble sleeping and I noticed I drove the car five miles an hour slower. The nights seemed darker than when I was young. I went home from parties earlier.

Still, you could put the con on the old man who had taken over your body for short bursts. You could stay up all night or drink at lunch once in awhile. You could come off the bench and feel the outfielders of time backing up a step or the pitcher looking nervously at the bench.

I'd like it to happen to Willie this weekend. I'd like him to have one more Series. Give him the bat one more ninth inning with runners in scoring position and the game on the line. Give him one more three-base hit to turn into an out with his glove. Give him one more runner who can't slide under the throw.

Don't let Willie Mays go out 42 years old and batting .211. For a lot of us, let him go out 20 years old again, and going into his home run trot while a stadium goes crazy and guys who monger iron or drive cabs or fix flats or park other people's cars the rest of the year stand up one more time and say, "Way to go, Willie!" Let's put off tomorrow at least one more week.

CATCHIN' UP
WITH SATCH

AUGUST 11, 1974

The grand old game of baseball and its chroniclers almost needed smelling salts not long ago when one pitcher worked in 13 straight games.

What would they say of one who pitched in 169 straight games?

Everyone gasps at the fact Hoyt Wilhelm pitched in 1,070 games lifetime.

What would they do over someone who lost track after 3,000?

So, Walter Johnson struck out 3,503 batters in his career. What about a guy who struck out that many in three years? The same guy who went around the country with a sign: "Guaranteed to strike out the first nine home town batters or your money back?"

The modern ballplayer complains about the arduousness of travel. His longest trip is 4½ hours by jet. He travels in air-conditioned comfort, dines on steak and lobster. If he's a star, he makes upwards of 200 grand a year. Even if he's not, he stays at the best hotels, gets chauffeured everywhere. When he retires, his pension can reach $2,500 a month and more.

What if I told you a greater pitcher than any of them worked for less money a day than these guys get in meal money? That he went around in a three-wheeled bus, air-conditioned only when someone broke a window?

You look at the record book and it says that Leroy Paige, a right-handed pitcher, won 28 major league games, struck out 290 major league batters, and had an earned-run average of 3.2. What the record book doesn't tell you is that Paige was almost as old as baseball when he did these things. A dubious birth certificate shows he was 48 his last full season in the major leagues. I say "dubious" because there are those who remember walking to school with Satchel Paige in the year it says he was born.

There are those who say the Paige page in baseball history shouldn't count, that the big league is the standard of prowess in baseball, and the fact Satchel didn't get in one till he was at least 42 or at most 48 is unfortunate but beside the point.

The argument carried some weight in the days when ball-players in "Negro leagues" might be said to be "unproven." In the light of what's happened since, the only thing that might be said to be unproven about them was how much better they were than the white ones.

Just imagine Henry Aaron, Willie Mays, Roberto Clemente, Bob Gibson, Reggie Jackson, Rod Carew and Richie Allen in one league, and we rest our case. The weight of the evidence is that Satchel Paige did what he did in a *bigger* league. Besides, every time he hooked up with a barnstorming, white big-league team he usually struck out 17 or so in a game.

I caught up with this patriarch of the pitch the other day at lunch. Satch is in Hollywood because they're going to make a movie of his life for TV. Jim Hawkins, an actor-producer, is going to make it for Johnny Carson–Paramount Productions for CBS.

I asked the venerable right-hander what he thought of Mike Marshall pitching in 100 or so games a year. "I was in 169 straight," snorted Satchel. "Won all of them. In 1953. They had turned me loose from Cleveland and from St. Louis that year. They had took me in the big leagues when I hadn't started a game in 15 years and I pitched two shutouts. I got old but my arm stayed 19."

What did he think of today's hitters? "Josh Gibson was the greatest hitter who ever lived. He couldn't play in those ball-parks with the roof on 'em. He would have hit 'em through the roof."

What about all the base stealing? Satch looked hurt. "All that throwin' over to first base!" he snorted. "Ask anybody did I ever throw over to first base. I never did throw over there. I jes' stepped back off the mound. They had to scramble back to first base. They were the ones got tired. Let them get tired, don't you go to doin' it."

Would he like to be pitching today? "Ain't seen nothin' changed. The plate's the same. The ball's the same. You got to pitch strikes is all. They used to plant two bats six inches apart and I'd throw it between 'em. Across the label. Mr. Ted Williams wouldn't hit nothin' but strikes. These players today will hit anything."

Satchel, who views the world with the suspicion it might bunt on him with a man on third at any time, has a head-high fastball for anyone who expects his movie to come out *Stepin Fetchit at the Old Ballgame.*

"If anyone had told me in the 1920s that coloreds would play in the big leagues, I would have said you're out of your mind. They didn't want no coloreds then. Had to eat out of the back door. But I don't be mad. I jes' pity 'em. If they had it to do all over again, I don't believe they would.

"At the same time, we ain't all that far. If I get on a plane and there are four seats and I sit in one of 'em, won't nobody sit there less'n they have to. They'll circle the plane 15 times before they'll finally sit there. Shows how bad a condition we're in. And I'm talkin' about right now. Today. 'Course, I'd be lyin' if I didn't say they get real different when they find out who I am."

Satch is cussed if he'll go around wearin' a sign saying, "I ain't no nigger, I'm Satchel Paige." So, he hopes the movie will show it's not only Mike Marshall, Walter Johnson and Hoyt Wilhelm who still have to catch up with him, it's all of us.

A WOMAN OF THE CENTURY

NOVEMBER 17, 1974

I interviewed the Rose Queen the other day. She was like all the rest. Shock of frosted curly hair. Bright blue eyes. Nice teeth. Great smile. Sensational legs. Nothing unusual. With Rose Queens, you've seen one, you've seen 'em all.

Only this one was the Rose Queen of 1908.

She was also the Wimbledon champion. Of 1905. Billie Jean King should look so good 70 years from now. I should look so good right now.

May Sutton Bundy won't give her age. Which is the privilege of all young ladies over 20—which she sure is. She won her first tennis tournament in 1900. She won her last one last year. In between, she won a lot more. She also raised four kids, a houseful of grandchildren and great-grandchildren, and a lot of football players and tennis players. Daughter Dorothy won the Australian championship and barely lost the U.S. championship to Anita Lizana in 1937.

May Sutton Bundy is as much a part of California history as Governor Pico. She was the first, and maybe the best, of a long line of California tennis champions that extended through Helen Wills, Alice Marble, Little Mo Connolly and Billie Jean King—to say nothing of Maurice McLoughlin, Little Bill Johnston, Donald Budge, Ted Schroeder, Jack Kramer and Pancho Gonzales.

She lives by herself near Santa Monica Canyon in a vine-covered cottage reminiscent of another, more graceful day in the life of this state.

It was like walking into a history book. Artificial flowers, faded pictures from the turn of the century, and more antique silverware than they have in the kitchen at Buckingham Palace, all attesting to tennis victories over the most famous faces in the

135

history books—Mary K. Browne, Molla Bjurstedt Mallory, Dorothy Douglass Chambers, Hazel Hotchkiss Wightman.

The Wimbledon Cup is there from 1905 and 1907 victories—when she was not only the first American to win it, but the first to enter it. Although English-born, May was the first "colonial" to win the "all-England championships" in those days. King George V looked on.

On the wall is a painting of Father, who was a captain in Her Majesty's Navy, a veteran of the Crimean War and the harbormaster at Plymouth, England, before he brought his family, including his mop-haired tomboy, May, 6, to Pasadena to retire. Father is in full uniform, epaulets, sword, and more medals than Mark Spitz.

Captain Adolphus Sutton's little daughter May is today somewhere between 29 and 90 by the calendar, but not a day over 18 in her heart. There were no ear trumpets, eye glasses, or old dance cards in sight. Just a deck of cards and a Bible. She was on her way to a bridge party when I found her. I suspect she was No. 1 seed.

It's hard to imagine that this lively, lovely lady was an international sports champion when Teddy Roosevelt was still vice president, Victoria was queen, and that she was making triumphal trans-Atlantic crossings seven years before the Titanic.

Unless she was two when she won the California State championship at the turn of the century, she must be nearing 90. She still drives her own car, makes her own meals, and plays her own hand. She doesn't live among her cats and dream of the old days.

May Sutton Bundy preceded even Hollywood to California. She was a celebrity long before Charlie Chaplin, Mary Pickford or Cecil B. DeMille. In her way, she was a gaslight women's libber. She dropped school for tennis at an early age. ("All they taught was Latin and Greek, which was good for reading prescriptions and not much else.") She won the U.S. Women's singles and doubles at Germantown, Pennsylvania, in 1904.

She married young. Husband Tom Bundy was a top tennis player, good enough to have played Davis Cup, and often carry even the storied Bill Larned to five sets. But he also went to the net in playing the stock market, which finally lobbed him to death, although the Bundys, before their divorce, pioneered Brentwood real estate (Bundy Drive is named after them) and once sold a corner of La Brea and Wilshire for $400,000, or $380,000 more than they paid for it.

Mrs. Bundy won the Pacific Southwest Tournament (or its equivalent) in 1900, and came back to win it in 1928 on a dare. She's more interested in tomorrow than yesterday but she speaks of Tilden, Larned, Beals Wright and Molla Mallory as if they were going to show up on center court any minute and spin for serve.

She has seen good days and bad, and in the end, you can't always tell which was which, she says. After divorce, she never remarried, and still refers to her late husband as "Mr. Bundy." (He died in 1942.)

But she feels women's movements should not be restricted to walks down the boardwalk at Atlantic City.

"I think it is working out to be a more fair world, thanks to the women's movements," she says. "I can't see where a world that was 75 percent for the men and 25 percent for women should continue. I think both sexes will find much more happiness if that moves more to 50–50."

She thinks marriage as an institution must be preserved, however, if society is to. "A promiscuous way of living is not the biblical way of life, which is the right way," she insists. "It wasn't the way God intended people to live but he's been very patient about it." Her recipe for a long, active life, for winning hands and silver trophies? "Everybody should spend one hour a week in church."

What Thorpe was to track, Grange to football, or Ruth to baseball, May Sutton Bundy was to tennis. I felt as if I had spent an hour in another, better world.

This remarkable lady will be on the dais at the "Champions of Yesterday and Today" banquet for the Multiple Sclerosis Society at the Beverly Wilshire Tuesday night. I expect all those great champions from Bobby Feller to Bobby Riggs, Oscar Robertson to Gayle Sayers will really get to their feet to salute the nearest thing to a queen—at least, of sport—we have ever had in this country.

HE EARNED HIS WAY

FEBRUARY 19, 1975

It's all very well for George C. Scott to turn down an Oscar, Marlon Brando to send a squaw to pick his up. It's perfectly all right for Bill Russell to turn down the Basketball Hall of Fame. A man can turn down a Nobel Prize if he wants to.

The thing is, you can fall out of bed with a dunk shot. If you're 7 feet tall, the rest is easy.

Playing General Patton is no big thing if you were a kid who could imitate the teacher in grade school—or do Jimmy Cagney going to the electric chair at the amateur nights. How tough is it to take all your clothes off and tango, or to stuff your cheeks with cotton and mumble a lot?

But, when you're the first black player in the history of the Masters golf tournament to make the field, what do you say? "I haven't a thing to wear?" "Shove it, whitey?" "Where were you when I needed you?" "Too late, fellows, who needs you?"

You don't fall out of bed with a golf swing. Nature doesn't have a helluva lot to do with it. You can't put on a moustache and powder your hair and go around shooting 69s. You don't script birdies. There's no director to club you all the way around.

If you're black, there's a basketball hoop on every street corner. But you got to go hunt up a golf course and lug somebody else's 50-pound bag around in the hot sun for a quarter a loop to get close to that game.

Robert Lee Elder is the first black golfer ever to get invited to the Masters. It wasn't one of those black-tie embossed RSVP invitations, "The Tournament Committee of the Masters requests the pleasure of your company, regrets only." Lee Elder had to shoot his way into this party. Nobody sent a car for him. He isn't exactly, like, the guest of honor. If he didn't show up, they'd start without him.

A lot of people who couldn't shoot bogey golf themselves thought Lee should tell them he preferred staying in the back of the bus. It's pretty easy to turn down something you, so to speak, inherited. Getting into the Hall of Fame for a jump shot you were born with is like honoring a bird because he can fly. Giving an Academy Award to a guy for reading what Billy Wilder wrote or doing what Frank Capra told him to do is like giving a testimonial to a guy for growing red hair.

But, let me tell you about Lee Elder. Lee Elder wasn't born 7 feet tall, or able to run the 100 in 9.2. I don't think he can even dance. What Lee Elder was born with was a lot of patience, determination, guts and willpower. You can't play golf without all four of these. You can't punch a 3-foot putt in the mouth. A ball out of bounds doesn't care how angry you get at it. You put a ball into the hole with your brains, not your height, or your speed, or your strength. It doesn't matter to a golf ball how fast you can run, or how high you can jump.

Lee Elder learned his trade at Tenison Park in East Dallas where golf was not a game, it was a racket. Jesse James never made as much money with a shooting iron as some of those people did there with a 9-iron.

Lee lifted bags for some of the greatest highwaymen this side of a police blotter or a post office bulletin. Titanic Thompson, who could play you with either hand—or shoot you with either hand—stole here.

Titanic once shot a man who tried to take the winnings Titanic had spent 36 holes stealing. Lee packed for him. He became a good caddy because he knew the short way to the hole and played for guys who damned well wanted to know it.

In 1952, Lloyd Mangrum picked him to pack for him in the U.S. Open at Norwood in Dallas. To those of us who knew Lloydie, he was damned particular about who he chose to lug his sticks.

Lee came to Los Angeles where he became a partner of Joe Louis. Playing for big money has never scared Lee Elder since.

You don't get a lot of help from God in building a golf swing. Guys have perfected one with a withered arm, a gimpy leg, a half of one eye. Man isn't too big a help, either. You can't legislate your way to a win in the U.S. Open.

Lee Elder's swing wasn't made in heaven, it was made in Houston. Or on Western Avenue. It was made by moonlight, or in the rain, or any other time the course was closed to the rest of humanity.

When he made the Masters (they changed the rules a few years ago to take the tournament out of the hands of a bunch of auto dealers and into the hands of golfers and let poor winners automatically qualify), he wasn't interested in making the *Atlantic Monthly* or *Harper's* or getting a hats-off review from the *New Republic*.

Lee was more interested in *Sports Illustrated*. When you spend half your life trying to qualify for $5,000 black tournaments or Soda Pop opens at 6 o'clock in the morning on the week of the tournament, no amount of guys wearing beads and waving pamphlets are going to keep you out of a $229,549 tournament.

Lee Elder's soapbox is the first tee. His sermon is a first at Monsanto, an appearance at the Masters, a playoff with Nicklaus. I don't know of any rhetoric that could be more penetrating or more meaningful. A 69 is plenty of militancy for whitey in this game.

To refuse Augusta, would to me be as silly as a man on a plantation in 1863 saying at the Emancipation Proclamation, "Thanks, but I'm going to stay right where I am, Mr. Lincoln, and sulk."

HE DARED STAND ALONE

APRIL 4, 1975

Don't bang the drums slowly. Don't muffle the caissons, or lead a riderless horse. Strike up the band. Let the trumpets roll. Never mind the 21-gun salute, just bring a plate of fudge. Raise your glasses in a toast if you must—but fill them with malted milk.

John Wooden is not going out as a great general or field leader. This is not Old Blood and Guts or Old Hickory, this is Mr. Chips saying goodby.

John Wooden never wanted to be thought of as a fiery leader. Life to him was a one-room schoolhouse with pictures of George Washington, Christ and a pair of crossed flags. Outside, the pumpkins ripening under a harvest moon. A pedagogue is all he ever wanted to be or remembered as. A simple country teacher.

His precepts were right off a wall motto. His idols were gentle Hoosier poets, not the purple-prose artists of the sports pages. A reserve guard stumbled out of a pregame meeting once to mumble in some shock to a frat brother, "Our game plan is by Edgar A. Guest, and our front line seems to be made up of Faith, Hope and Charity."

John Wooden, someone once said, was "the only basketball coach from the Old Testament." Others preferred to think of him as New Testament—"St. John," who walked to work across Santa Monica Bay.

His lifestyle was embodied in a cornerstone of philosophy which he called the "Pyramid of Success," which looked like a collection of Horatio Alger titles. They were real easy to follow—if you lived in a convent.

His basketball was 20th century, but his life lessons were B.C. "Dare to be Daniel! Dare to stand alone!" He spouted more poems than Lord Byron. Most of his thoughts for the day had a strong odor of new-mown hay about them or sycamores in the candlelight, and sometimes the ghetto kids from New York, more used to subway graffiti than "The Old Oaken Bucket" or "Moonlight Along The Wabash," wished he'd stick to setting picks.

Critics contend that it was easy to put your faith in the Bible when your center was between 7 and 8 feet tall and as agile as an acrobat, but that you would have to turn to more recent works when your whole team could come to the games in a single Volkswagen. Wooden went out and won NCAA championships with nothing more than 6'5" centers and the Book of Leviticus.

In the world of modern sport, piety in a coach is as suspect as piety in a faro dealer. The fabric of recruitment is as corrupt as a military junta, and it was hard to believe anyone in it could not sooner or later be found in possession of 30 pieces of silver he couldn't account for.

Every time John Wooden hinted at retirement in recent years, the scribes—to say nothing of the Pharisees—nodded sagely and said, "Aha! Now comes the NCAA investigation!" So, Wooden would get tight-lipped—and stay on for another two years.

An act like this might have been hard to maintain at a little church school in the middle of the Dakotas. At UCLA, a campus surrounded by Gomorrah by the Sea, it was believed impossible. No one believed the mysteries of zone defense could be equated with Deuteronomy, but Wooden quietly went his winning way with the Bible in one hand and a basketball in the other.

When he came to UCLA, basketball was such a poor relation in intercollegiate sports that the team barely had matching uniforms. It was considered a refuge for guys too little or too timid for football and too slow or too tall for track.

By the time he left, football was becoming the poor relation. One coach fled all the way to Georgia Tech when an alum called him up on the eve of the USC football game and asked him if there was any way he could use his influence to get the old grad *basketball* tickets.

Mentors are in the shortest supply in college athletics. Baseball is a soloist sport, as is most of track, wrestling, or even net sports. But football and basketball belong to the coach. A

Rockne, Howard Jones, an Amos Alonzo Stagg, Adolph Rupp, a Vince Lombardi comes along only once a generation. And so does a John Wooden.

Wooden's monument may not be a gym, an arena, a plaque, or a fading picture on a wall. It may not even be this assortment of champions or his legacies to the pros. It may be a standard of play which made Saturday's Louisville-UCLA and Monday's Kentucky-UCLA games possibly the best pure basketball games ever played at the college level. Wooden went out a winner for the 10th time but the real winner was the game he left behind.

But the campus need not be given over to ribbons of black, or the mournful tread of a dirge. As long as Wooden basketball is played, Wooden will be at UCLA.

Notre Dame didn't sink to intramural football when Rockne left and, while the UCLA teams may not be co-coached by James Whitcomb Riley, or Matthew, Mark, Luke and John with an assist from George Ade anymore, the true believers are like the undergrad who found a coed weeping because coach Wooden had gone off to join the ages. "So what?" he shrugged. "After all, it's only the *three days!*"

DR. J CAME TO PLAY

AUGUST 22, 1975

This town has had more than its share of legends. What do you want, movies? There's Charlie Chaplin, Rudolph Valentino, Cagney, Tracy, Garbo. Politics? Winston Churchill slept here. Both Roosevelts. The arts? Hemingway worked here. Fowler lived here. Caruso sang here. Stravinsky composed here. Even the *Mona Lisa* came here. A Lautrec is in every bathroom in Beverly Hills.

In sports, Cousy dribbled here. Koufax curved here. Dempsey bobbed and weaved here. Babe Ruth hit here. Sammy Baugh threw and Don Hutson caught here. Wyatt Earp died here.

But, even though Kareem Abdul-Jabbar played here, Chamberlain dunked here and Elgin Baylor was employed here, there was been a large gap in the basketball culture of Los Angeles. "The Doctor" has never been here.

Tonight, at the Sports Arena, he makes a house call. Tonight, in a benefit game for the Soulville Foundation, an organization dedicated to getting rocks out of the hands of ghetto kids and replacing them with books, the storied Doctor J, the ultimate basketball player, will make a first-performance-by-the-artist-ever here.

It will be interesting to see if he can be seen by the naked eye. It is said that the good doctor was not born, he sprang full-blown when somebody rubbed his hand across a lamp. He disappears back into the bottle every night.

He has three or four arms, depending on whom you talk to. His eyes can see 360 degrees in any direction, including the one in the back of his head. His arms are so long he has to be careful not to step on them. He is 6'6", stretching to 11 feet when he jumps. He disappears on the way to the basket, and materializes above the rim after everyone has dropped to the ground to see if he hit a trapdoor. His dunk shots go down through the basket and then bounce up back *through* it again.

He is so soft-spoken, only three people in the league know what language he speaks. He can hang in the air so long on a jump shot, they say, he could jump out of a one-story building and take an hour to hit the ground. If he jumped off the Empire State building, he'd hover indefinitely.

All of these things you hear about Julius Winfield Erving Jr., Ph.D. (Doctor of Phenomenons).

Julius Erving sprang into prominence on the storied playgrounds of New York where, according to street lore, he scored 200 or so points a night, grabbed 70 to 90 rebounds, made the ball—or himself—disappear behind his back. His body is one big elastic band, they say, and, according to legend, after he had played 48 minutes against the New York Knicks' Dave Stallworth one night, a spectator asked, "How do you like Julius Erving?" and Stallworth replied, "I'd like to meet him sometime—tell me, what does he look like?"

Dr. J hangs out his shingle with the New York Nets of the ABA, a semi-private organization whose existence is not widely known on the West Coast—or the East, either, for that matter. He earned his nickname for his habit of operating on the basketball floor, of taking apart an opponent as if he were performing a prefrontal lobotomy. He handles a ball as if it were a bubble. With fingers, it is said, 12 to 14 inches long, not counting the nails.

Dr. J did the basketball world a favor by going to the University of Massachusetts. If he had gone to UCLA, or North Carolina State, it was said, there wouldn't be enough money in any state to buy him. He might have had to play in his own league or go on tour as a one-man Globetrotter.

When he finally did come into pro basketball, he was so sought after he wound up signing with three teams and two leagues and a fourth one sued in court claiming it had seen him first. The New York Nets' owner, Ray Boe, bought out all the litigants by scattering millions of dollars in all directions; so Dr. J came close to becoming the first billion-dollar man outside of TV fiction. Boe considers him a $4 million bargain.

It is said that seeing Dr. J shoot baskets is like hearing Horowitz play Chopin or Olivier do Shakespeare. You suddenly realize you've never seen it or heard it before.

Dr. J gets a new set of patients to operate on tonight, too. Abdul-Jabbar and Bill Walton will be in the operating room. There will be several hitherto undiagnosable cases on the other side of the line, too. But Dr. J's former patients are not worried. He'll have them walking in no time, they say.

BASEBALL'S SHOWBOAT

DECEMBER 21, 1975

Bill Veeck (rhyme it with "Aw, heck!") is the kind of a guy who drinks beer from a bottle, eats standing up, wears no man's tie, and loves to throw snowballs at top hats.

He's America's gadfly. He's the kind of a guy you might expect to find in the center-field bleachers. He is, in his own words, a street-corner guy. You might expect to find him shooting craps in an alley, or hustling a mark on a riverboat.

He grew up in Prohibition Chicago where his pals were the great roustabouts on the old Chicago Cubs baseball team, like Hack Wilson, Rabbit Maranville, Pat Malone and Charlie Grimm. Dad was the president of the Cubs. Baseball was in his blood.

Baseball is a game played by dirty-faced little boys on city lots or cow pastures. But it is run professionally by a bunch of bankers, chewing gum heirs, mortgagors, generals, judges and beer barons whose principal interest is in making 10 percent on their money.

Bill Veeck is an ex-marine who lost a leg at Guadalcanal, wears a crew cut, chain-smokes, and thinks baseball should be fun—the rankest kind of heresy in baseball's board rooms, where they think it should be like High Mass, played in library silence amid clouds of incense.

They let Bill in baseball after the war when he bought the Cleveland Indians, as dull a collection of athletes as ever went through the motions. They hadn't won a pennant in 28 years, and couldn't have cared less. They were as passionless as cost accountants, a locker room full of 9-to-5 guys who correctly understood their function in life was to lose gracefully to the Yankees and get on home.

147

Veeck signed the patriarch of baseball, Satchel Paige, and the first American League black player, Larry Doby, and he introduced fireworks, the exploding scoreboard, and passed out corsages and put on so many circus acts that, when a visiting journalist asked one night what the battery was going to be, he got the sour answer, "Barnum and Bailey." Another writer suggested that when they announced the Tigers were in town, the customers didn't know whether they meant the team or the real thing.

Veeck also won a pennant, and set the all-time attendance mark of 2,620,627, a record which stood until the Dodgers moved to Los Angeles a decade later. It is still an American League record.

Veeck got bored. Success makes him restless, and he sold the Indians and bought the St. Louis Browns, a team which had more stockholders than customers. His financial advisers suggested a much better buy would be the Hindenburg.

Veeck sent a midget up to bat, booked animal acts, let the fans pick out the lineups, hired clowns—but nothing could be funnier than the ballclub. Veeck went broke in St. Louis. To say the team finished last was an understatement. Veeck wanted to move the club to Milwaukee, but baseball gave that territory to Lou Perini and the Boston Braves. Veeck wanted to move to Baltimore. And the owners said no. But the minute he sold the club, they OK'd its move to Baltimore.

Veeck bought the Chicago White Sox of 1959, promptly won a pennant, promptly got bored again, then sold the club. In the intervening decade, Veeck recalls, "I set the record for the most unsuccessful offers for a major league baseball team."

This week, William Louis Veeck set the listed world record for *acquiring* major league baseball teams when he rebought the Chicago White Sox. He promptly dealt off the manager, most of the infield, and the leading pitcher. He signed on a manager who hasn't managed since 1960, leading one wag to suggest, "Bill Veeck has turned the clock ahead to 1930."

The man who forced expansion, introduced animated scoreboards and bat and helmet nights, and who pushed for the designated hitter rule ("Why should you have one guy go out there night after night and *prove* he can't hit? I had a whole team like that at St. Louis") is back where he can make waves.

148

The titled heads of the game have probably taken to their storm cellars or headache powders. Actually, it should be the best news for business since Barnum bought Jumbo, or Disney started to draw that talking mouse.

THE PIRATE HAS HEART

FEBRUARY 17, 1976

At first glance, Bob Morgan looks perfect for the part of a pirate, a first-class makeup job worthy of a Lon Chaney. He's only got one leg, and his right eye looks as if it belongs to the loser in a sword fight. Put a parrot on his shoulder, a stocking-cap on his head, and a cutlass in his teeth, and you'd swear he just walked out of page 200 of *Treasure Island.* He looks as if he was born in a rigging. This is Morgan the Pirate, all right.

But Bobby Morgan's infirmities are not courtesy of Pere Westmore or the studio's prop department. They are, unfortunately, not at all make-believe. Bob Morgan became perfect for pirate casting one April day in 1962 when a trainload of logs broke their chain as they were swerving through a location scene in the Arizona mountains for the movie *How the West Was Won.*

The logs burst their fetters and sent Bob Morgan off the train and under the wheels and bouncing along the track. It took them five minutes to find all of him and get him to a hospital to see if they could paste together a reasonable facsimile of the Robert Morgan who had showed up for work that morning.

At that time, Morgan was a handsome, 6'3", 200-pound collar-ad stuntman, who had been one of the best college basketball players in the state, and a golfer of such low handicap that he frequently won successive pro-ams on the California winter tour.

So far as the film companies were concerned, Bob's was just another industrial accident, covered only by state workmen's compensation. It was just another fall for a stuntman, and someone got into the hospital to get Bob to sign a disclaimer that he had not waived compensation before showing up for work that near-fatal day. It's ironic that the investigator found the only parts of Bob Morgan that were in working order that day—his fingers. The rest of him, the evidence showed, was in a coma.

When you look like a matinee idol one day, and a gargoyle the next, the shock to the system is almost total. No one felt sorrier for Bob Morgan than Bob Morgan, at first. And for a while, he hid from sight. He felt cheated by life, to say nothing of the movie industry. He drank.

Then, one day, I happened to be playing down the second hole at Riviera, where the Glen Campbell Open is being played this week, and there I saw a strange apparition, a tall, one-legged, one-eyed player was banging 2-irons to a nearby practice green. He was swiveling around on a round artificial leg. He was grinning. It was Bob Morgan. "Well, I'm alive, ain't I?" he asked cheerfully.

Bob Morgan won the Ben Hogan Award for the athlete who makes the most dramatic comeback from a near-catastrophic illness or accident that year.

All this was 12–14 years ago, and a lot of doctors knew there would be fits of depression, that a new leg and a new swing weren't really workmen's compensation enough. There were endless legal hassles, all of which Bob Morgan lost. People just assumed the defendant companies had sent crates of money. All they sent were crates of subpoenas. Bob Morgan got disability insurance—period.

The other day, I chanced on the set of a pirate movie called *The Blarney Cock*. It's a legit pirate adventure film, and not one of those campy Mel Brooks or Ritz Brothers outrages. James Earl Jones is in it. So is Robert Shaw.

And so is Robert Morgan. There he was, peg-legged and smiling, climbing the rigging. He's given up on the lawsuits, the drawn shades and the bitterness and has come to terms with his new life. He's still falling out of stagecoaches going over cliffs for a living. And he's happy to be back at the old store.

This Morgan the Pirate thinks he's found some buried treasure, too. "Hey, I finally think I'm going to get some action on that swivel leg I patented for golf. The Veterans Administra-

tion is interested in it. For one-legged golf, it may be the greatest invention since the steel shaft. Who knows? Maybe someone
will win a tournament with it one day!"

Well, why not? If you could rule the Spanish Main with one
leg, what's so tough about the Monsanto Open?

BABY-FACE BOMBER

FEBRUARY 22, 1976

Ben Crenshaw has the biggest feet, the babiest face, and the longest swing ever seen on a golfer 5 feet 9 inches tall. He looks like he should be just learning to ride two-wheelers, not win golf tournaments. For the rest of golf, it's a little like getting shot at from a baby carriage.

Most golfers' swings are 380 degrees. Ben's is at least 580. It starts somewhere between his knees and navel on the backswing and goes around three or four times before it hits the ball. Sometimes, Ben himself seems to spin around twice, like a propeller. When he hits the ball, it goes screaming out of there almost into orbit and comes down glowing. The power of the swing is such that Ben has to screw himself into the ground like a post-hole digger to keep himself from flying after the ball. If he ever misses, he won't come down for five minutes.

He looks as if he came direct from a Christmas pageant. The face—cherubic, blue-eyed, pink-cheeked, looks out of place without a halo over it or wings behind. The tour is used to blond hair, but Ben's looks as if it still might have cradle cap. He's 24 years old but looks like someone who just got a new bike for Christmas. But he's already won three tournaments which is, for instance, three more than Arnold Palmer had won at that age and two more than Johnny Miller.

Crenshaw takes a crack at the ball the way Dempsey would hit a chin or Larry Csonka a line. They'd call him Belting Ben if they were still into nicknames. Sometimes, of course, the ball curves foul. And when it does, you need two men and a dog to find it. Not since another Ben—Hogan—has anyone 5'9" driven a ball so far.

Despite the fact he looks like someone you'd like to take to a parade and buy a balloon, Ben came into golf under more pressure to succeed than anyone since Jack Nicklaus—or St. Nicholas. So much was expected of him, you'd think he was found under a burning bush. He had absolutely scattered collegiate golf, winning the NCAA title three years in a row. They spoke of him in Texas as if he changed water into wine on the side.

When people saw where his drives landed, they hung around expecting to see King Kong emerging from the woods. Ben won the first pro tournament he entered. He got his pro card by beating the qualifying school field by 12 strokes.

The way old-timers in Texas talked about him, it seemed unfair to have him wait to go to the Hall of Fame, and unfair to the rest of golf not to have him give shots. Most guys can sort of "feel" their way into the tour. Ben came in on a sedan chair to the sound of trumpets. But the crown came down over his eyes at first.

Ben played golf as if it came wrapped in tinsel. He could have won half a dozen tournaments, but he never hit a commercial shot in his life. He went to the flag, the horizon, first place, not the cut or the top 60. He threw roundhouse rights at the course, never clinched with it. Naturally, a few shots got away in this kind of toe-to-toe exchange, but little Ben shrugged, teed up another ball—and hit it just as hard.

He walked up on a green as if he intended to arrest it. Hands on hips, a confident, almost swaggering, rolling gait of a Texas Ranger on his size 11½ shoes, out roping rustlers.

Ben Crenshaw never crept through a round of golf in his life. He shot an 82 or a 62 with the same boyish enthusiasm. He never ran around tinkering with his swing, or begging for an explanation for a bad round. When the course knocked him down, he got up swinging like Dempsey. He'd come home all beat up—but so would the course.

Ben is the newest rising star of golf. What Palmer was in '55, what Mickey Mantle was in '51, what Dempsey was at Toledo, or O. J. Simpson at his first Rose Bowl, Johnny Bench in his first World Series, Crenshaw is—the hope of an entire sport.

He's not going to win his third tournament in a row at the Glen Campbell L.A. Open today, but when someone observed "that kid's got a great future if he keeps his feet on the ground," the answer came back, "With that swing, he's got to keep his feet on the ground. If he ever doesn't, he'll look like the world's biggest divot. And when they say, 'Crenshaw just landed in a trap,' they'll mean it literally."

THAT'S SHOE BIZ

APRIL 6, 1976

Bob Lanier of the Detroit Pistons is a 25-points-a-night scorer. He frequently grabs 20 or more rebounds a game. He played the most minutes and was the game's MVP in the 1974 All-Star lineup that included Kareem Abdul-Jabbar and Nate Thurmond.

And, yet, the first thing anybody notices about him is his feet. He's got the biggest feet of any creature that wears shoes. If you saw his footprints in the snow, you'd run like hell.

If Bob Lanier played football, he'd have to line up one yard behind the line of scrimmage or be offside. Rumor has it, his shoes are off-loaded at the Detroit River docks by tug. It takes him 20 minutes to unlace them. Even in basketball, he can get a three-second violation while standing on the sidelines.

Bob Lanier is 6'11", 250 pounds, but all anybody wants to talk about are the bottom 25 inches. He was on the CBS post-game show one afternoon, after an outstanding day on the court, and a girl reporter only wanted to try on his shoes. She disappeared into them. Bob Lanier disappeared, too. He threw the shoes against the wall and walked out.

Big Bob never wanted to be Big Foot. He tried to go around pretending everyone wears size 22 or so. Even as a kid, he was never able to go into Thom McAn's and say casually, "Do you have anything in a 21½-X?" He shouted any journalist out of the dressing room who tried to bring up the subject of feet. It was hard not to bring it up. Writers would stare at those toes, which are bigger than most peoples' feet, and start the general questioning "Uh, Bob, how many feet—er, I mean, rebounds, did you have tonight?"

But, this year, a curious thing happened: Lee Williams, the publicity man for the Basketball Hall of Fame, asked to include some pro basketball memorabilia in the bicentennial Freedom

Train, decided to liven the exhibit with something besides the ball Wilt Chamberlain scored 100 points with, or the warm-up jacket worn by Oscar Robertson—and he put in a pair of Bob Lanier's shoes.

They quickly became the most popular exhibit in the car, not to say the train. I mean, let's face it: The bat Babe Ruth hit his 60th home run with looks like any other bat. The Bob Lanier shoes don't look like any other pair of shoes. They look, in fact, like supertankers.

It is not unusual for a person to rail against the thing which makes him or her unique. I can remember Marilyn Monroe loftily preferring to explain her reading of *The Brothers Karamazov*, as if anyone with her dimensions needed a literary reputation.

Golfers on the tour who are great putters hate the reputation. And I can recall Hank Aaron standing around a batting cage and saying resentfully, "I do other things besides hit home runs."

There is evidence Babe Ruth considered the rest of his career downhill when he left the pitcher's mound. Terrible-Tempered Tommy Bolt always wanted to be known as a guy who could see both sides of a question equally. For all I know, W.C. Fields probably wanted to be known as a man of moderation. And Bill Shoemaker used to chin himself on coat racks trying to be 6 feet tall—so he could be driving a truck instead of Swaps.

And so Bob Lanier would probably have preferred to have been known as just another pretty foot.

But, if Bob had any sense of the shoe business, if the late P.T. Barnum had had him, he would probably begin wearing shoes two sizes (or more) too large for him. He would edge them in neon, or loud colors. He would sell advertising on the soles.

When your shoes can rival the Declaration of Independence, the Adams Chronicles, or Lincoln's shawl as a national monument, your feet belong to the world. I would let my toenails grow if I were Bob and, if the Detroit Pistons get in the playoff finals, 20 million people will concentrate not on the scorer's feats, but on the scorer's feet.

COMANECI OLYMPICS

JULY 21, 1976

MONTREAL—An Olympics is 7,000 athletes competing in 200 events. It is as complex as a train wreck.

But, like every other institution, it frequently becomes the lengthened shadow of one man—or one woman.

Lots of guys won medals in the 1912 Olympics. Name two. On the other hand, everybody can name the guy who didn't get any medals—Jim Thorpe. The 1912 Olympics were Jim Thorpe's. The big man who wasn't there if you look at the official results is the only one who was if you know the real history. They took Jim Thorpe's medals away but not his Olympics.

1932? That was Babe Didrikson's—two gold medals in the javelin and hurdles and a heist of her gold in the high jump.

1936 was supposed to be Hitler's Olympics but it was Jesse Owens'. Four gold medals struck a blow for black group esteem that never did subside thereafter. Neither did Jesse's marks, some of which lasted over a generation.

In '48, it was Fanny Blankers-Koen, Dutch hausfrau, mother of two, who, at age 30, won four gold medals—hurdles, 100, 200 and relay. She struck a blow for motherhood, home and hearth.

1968 belonged to Bob Beamon. In one incredible leap, with a style reminiscent of a guy falling out of a tree, he put the long jump record out nearly 2 feet. No one has yet gotten within a foot of him. It was like beating the mile mark by 30 seconds.

The 1972 Olympics belonged to (choose one) Mark Spitz or Olga Korbut. Spitz won all the medals; Olga won all the hearts.

But the Montreal Olympics unfolding now may well belong throughout posterity to a tiny, big-eyed Romanian schoolgirl who has now done three times what no one else had done in Olympic history before—gotten a perfect score in an event

158

ordinarily scored so severely that the computers originally were not even programmed for a "10" or "perfection" score.

Nadia Comaneci may make an "11" next time out on the uneven bars. She should break a leg to bring the competition down to her level. She is Peter Pan on a balance beam, Tinkerbell on a wire, a marionette to delight all ages, part Shirley Temple, part Dresden doll. There is a fairyland aura to her performance. No one real has that incredible muscle control. No body can whirl around a parallel bar like a silk pinwheel like that. Ribbons and ballet slippers twirl in a stunning flash of color and precision like a Himalayan prayer wheel. Her body appears joined together by rubber bands, her feats are a dervish of daring. She is the darling of Montreal and maybe 800 million television addicts.

Is Nadia Comaneci that good—or is everyone just that sentimental? Is anybody really a perfect 10? At the age of 14, how can she earn ordinal rhapsodies from heretofore stern and tight-lipped judges who can see a terminal fault in just a fraction of a hesitation on a vault or exercise?

The story really begins in Munich in 1972. Olga Korbut was not really the best gymnast at the meet. But she was the most adorable. She drew deep-throated roars at the Sportshalle that had not been heard in Deutschland since Hitler hit the bunker. While purists stood by in ill-concealed contempt, Olga captured the hearts first, the minds later, the medals finally.

Her performance was a bit on the flamboyant side but the world fell in love when this 4'10" sprite and refugee from a Disney movie did a backward somersault on the balance beam—a feat so daring it was promptly suggested it be banned. The federation did not want a generation of broken necks from Korbut imitators. The ban attempt failed when Korbut threatened to retire—at the age of 17. Olga didn't need gymnastics but gymnastics needed Olga.

But Olga really took over the Olympics with a failure. She missed the bar on a backward somersault one night, tumbled to the floor. When tears began to course down her cheeks, the spectators would have killed for her. Little Red Riding Hood shouldn't get eaten by the wolf. Little dolls in leotards shouldn't cry.

What Palmer did for golf, Ruth for baseball, Olga Korbut did for women's gymnastics. You can get a ticket for anything in

Montreal if you set your mind—and wallet—to it. You cannot get a ticket to women's gymnastics.

Korbut is old now—a doddering 21. Nadia Comaneci is the Olga Korbut of 1976—5 feet, 88 pounds of such flashing grace and power she looks like a propeller attached to the bar. She is the most famous collection of syllables to come out of Romania since Magda Lupescu, who wasn't much on the balance beam but had her talents.

Nadia flashed to the first perfect score ever in the Olympics gymnastics Sunday, then doubled it the next night. Among those washed away was the divine Olga, who was struggling to 9.7s in other events as Nadia was bringing 18,000 people screaming to their feet as she flew through the air in a blaze of *sukuharas* or flips like an imp out of a blanket, or something shot out of a cannon.

A journalist who has trouble turning over in bed is obviously unqualified to judge how much of her scoring is prowess and how much hero worship. But after hours of sitting watching the competition, I can tell you confidently that, when the Americans, Japanese, West Germans and Czechs marched out of the hall to be replaced by the Romanians, Russians, East Germans and Hungarians, the first team had arrived. These birds flew straight and true and everyone in the group knew he was in the big leagues. These were the Pittsburgh Steelers, the heavyweight champs of this sport. Everything else was Triple A. These were the Reds. They didn't miss bars, fall to the floor, slip on the beam. This was a shower of stars.

In the comic-opera interview that always follows the competitions, Nadia Comaneci, who probably sleeps hanging down and could probably somersault a ledge a pigeon would fall off of, laughingly shrugged off questions as to whether her perfect scores astonished her. "I have done it 19 times," she explained. "It is not really new." She probably was surprised she didn't get a 12. Or, at least, a 10.9.

Comaneci has been in ballet slippers since she could walk. She was taken from her home at an early age and turned over to the state.

Where other people take a stroll through the park, she does back flips. She probably eats in midair.

But a perfect score in gymnastics is not exactly like pitching a perfect game in the big leagues or bowling 300 or shooting a 58. The scoring is subjective, sometimes emotional.

Never mind. Comaneci joins the Beamons, Thorpes, Fanny Blankers-Koens, Owenses, Spitzes and, yes, maybe Korbuts. Her "10s" will make far more Olympic history than all those guys rowing, sword-fighting, canoeing, shooting or horseback riding. So far, it's the "Comaneci Olympics."

WHO IS THIS GUY?

SEPTEMBER 21, 1977

In golf, a headline "Unknown Wins Open" is nothing. Commonplace. In a World Series, you might get a "Rookie Shuts Out Yankees" or "Utility Infielder Runs Wild Against A's." In football, you get "One-Play O'Brien" or Doyle Nave coming off the bench, splinters and all, to win the Rose Bowl.

But tennis is as formful as Burke's Peerage. Finals are foregone conclusions. It's not a victory, it's a coronation.

You look down Wimbledon's rolls and you don't see Orville J. Moody or Lou Graham, no One-Tournament O'Brien, no Pepper Martin. You see the tried and true, the recognizable, the familiar. Tennis is very big on tradition. No nasty shocks, please. They like their finalists as familiar as the butler in that game.

Which is why staid old Wimbledon was rocked to its royal box this summer when an upstart from Long Island became the first 18-year-old ever to reach the men's semifinals there. I mean, here was this stripling strutting around in the round of eight on Centre Court where only names like Bill Tilden, Donald Budge, Henri Cochet, Rod Laver, Jack Kramer and Lew Hoad had appeared before.

John Patrick McEnroe hadn't even shaved yet. In fact, he hadn't even gotten a haircut. He still had his baby curls. The gateman thought he had come to get autographs. The linesmen thought he was the ballboy.

John McEnroe doesn't look an All-England semifinalist. With his forehead band on, he looks as if he's on his way to choir practice, or to be an altar boy. He's the kind of kid who asks the cocktail waitress if she's got milkshakes. He's got these big blue eyes which glow even in the light, like a big cat's in a tree. The sensation of losing to him is a little like getting run over by a baby carriage.

The wire services had a terrible time with his name, the near misses ranging from "McHenry" to "MacMonroe" but no worse than some of the top seeds had with his game. McEnroe ran through veteran players like Egypt's Ismail El Shafei, Germany's Karl Meiler, Rhodesia's Colin Dowdeswell, the U. S.'s Sandy Mayer, and Australia's best player, Phil Dent, before he found himself on Wimbledon's Centre Court for the first time in his life with the world's best player on the other side of the net, Jimmy Connors. "It took a lot of getting used to," John remembers.

For Connors, it was like rallying off the garage door at home. He beat the 18-year-old, 6–3, 6–3, 4–6, 6–4—decisive but not demoralizing.

When McEnroe beat steady Eddie Dibbs at Forest Hills later (he lost to Manuel Orantes in the round of 16), the tennis world began to wonder if they had a new *wunderkind*, a male Tracy Austin. McEnroe had been ranked 274th, or just better than a public-park player, when he burst on the Queen's tournament. He even had to shoot his way into that one, by winning three qualifying matches.

You need a jeweler's glass to detect the fine points in McEnroe's game. You also need one to find the flaws. "He doesn't over-hit," notes Charlie Pasarell. "Most young players fall into that trap." "He plays the hitter like a good shortstop," says Jack Kramer. "When the ball gets there, he's there."

Young McEnroe has a simpler explanation: "I don't have any weaknesses," he says candidly. Also, thanks to soccer competition in school, he believes he has exceptional stamina.

Still, reaching the semis at Wimbledon before your voice changes can be hazardous to the rest of your career. Tennis is not a game you start out at the top. At 18, you never know how tough any game is. Even girls look simple. So, John's decision to go to Stanford and brave the intercollegiates rather than the pros for the next two years seems well-chosen.

It would be a bit much to expect John McEnroe to win the Southern California Open tennis championship at the L.A. Tennis Club this week. But a young man who has gone from

274th on the computer list of the world's best players to 25th in a little less than a year is going into the history books one way or the other.

For him, 1977 is either going to be, "What was the name of that high school kid who almost won Wimbledon one year, and whatever became of him?" Or "What was that year when John McEnroe almost won his first Wimbledon?"

A REJECTED LANDMARK

MAY 1, 1977

The trouble with Los Angeles is lack of places to go or things to see. It's the only area I know which has to buy an out-of-work ocean liner or a falling down London Bridge as a tourist attraction. Our oranges are imported. Even Hollywood, our only home-grown industry and product, is represented by an edifice called Grauman's *Chinese* (not Hollywood) theater.

Which is why I am constantly surprised that one of our most imposing tourist attractions is not publicized more. I mean, we've had our fill of the Watts Towers, Queen Mary, Disneyland, Pickfair, the Rose Bowl.

Why isn't our most awesome natural wonder in the guide books? Why aren't pictures of it hanging in travel agents' offices? How come nobody sends post-cards back to the relatives posing alongside this Los Angeles phenomenon?

Why isn't Kareem Abdul-Jabbar in the *National Geographic?* Who cares about Sea World, Muscle Beach, Descanso Gardens, the redwoods? Does the Grand Canyon have a sky hook?

Kareem Abdul-Jabbar should be a national monument. The real Civic Center. A law should be passed making it a felony to remove him from the state. He belongs to the ages like Yosemite National Park, as much a part of the lore of the state as Jack London's house or Junipero Serra's missions I mean the Empire State Building, phooey! Glass and brick. Kareem Abdul-Jabbar was put together by the same forces that made Mt. Whitney. Or Farrah Fawcett. Human beings like this come along only once or twice a millenium.

So why aren't people going back to Iowa and popping their suspenders and saying proudly to the in-laws, "Well, the corn is nice, but you should see *our* Kareem Abdul-Jabbar!" Why isn't he one of our proud athletic possessions like Sandy Koufax or

Deacon Jones or Baby Arizmendi or Bob Waterfield or Jigger Statz?

It can't be that he's imported from New York. So were the Dodgers. Not even Balboa was a native. *Everybody* in L.A. is from some place else.

Kareem Abdul-Jabbar is more of a homegrown product than most. He perfected his first low-posts on the campus of UCLA. He's as Californian as the yucca.

He's the best basketball player ever to play the game. And he may be the best athlete ever to play any game. He lives here. He works here. He's happy here.

He's the most visible landmark in the city of the angels. He should be to the city what Babe Ruth was to New York, Vince Lombardi to Green Bay, Mayor Daley to Chicago—or the Eiffel Tower to Paris or Big Ben to London. Our own pyramid.

But people act as if he came to eat Burbank. Crowds part when he walks through. Kids put away their autograph books and stare. Sometimes, it looks as if a western badman has suddenly shown up on Main Street at high noon. Everyone shrinks back. It's almost as if they bang down the shades or hide the women and children.

It's hard to tell why. Kareem Abdul-Jabbar has worked harder to put L.A. on the athletic map than any athlete in its history. You can see him out there night after night exceeding himself, doing everything that can be done by one man to bring a world championship to Los Angeles. With a supporting cast that can best be described as ranging from inadequate to invisible, he blocks shots, grabs rebounds, endures fouls, shoots baskets, makes assists. He is single-handedly taking on the NBA—and beating it. Nothing like it has been seen since Sergeant York.

He shows up for work. Kareem Abdul-Jabbar has never missed a plane, a practice or a tip-off since he came to L.A. He's not "Bad News" Jabbar or "Broadway" Kareem. He never criticizes a teammate, coach, the fans and rarely an official. He has punched out a few oppressors, but only when it was a question of either that or give them your ears. And only on-court. He knows he cannot even do that very much. It scares the customers. If, say, a Cazzie Russell punches somebody, the spectators jump in to help. If Kareem Abdul-Jabbar does, they start nervously for the exits.

Neither is it his size. Wilt Chamberlain was at least as big. But no one in the $13 seats ever thought twice about heaping abuse on big Wilt. A skinny pro golfer once wandered out on the floor threatening to punch him.

Fan abuse is a form of love. It's a sense that the object somehow belongs to you. The chastisement is for his own good, so to speak. Abdul-Jabbar has never heard that song of love wafting from the box seats like Naughty Marietta—"Jabbar, you big donkey, get in the game!"

Kareem recognizes his peculiar relationship with the community and his alienation from it. It is a function of many things, he believes. "First of all, the sports fan is different here. He is not as totally involved as he is in New York. He is able to put sports more in perspective, not take it personally.

"Next, it stems from people not really understanding what I am about as a person. There is misunderstanding. I've never tried to be difficult but people never really know what to expect. They sense a rejection that's not there."

There is a tendency to regard him as a visitor from another planet, almost as if he just stepped from a flying saucer with his space goggles and purple jump suit. Also, "It's harder to meet people here," he says. "Everybody's in his car with the windows rolled up."

He admits his name change frightened some people. "They felt threatened by it," he admits. "They associated it with the Black Muslims." What he actually was, he explains, was a religious convert. People should be no more shaken by it than if he had turned Episcopalian. "Islam is a comparatively new phenomenon in Western culture," he says. His name, by the way, means an unthreatening "Generous Irresistible Servant of God" which is hardly Lon Chaney stuff.

Would it help if he took part in ribbon-cuttings or visited kids in hospitals and promised them 40 points, or if he became the grand marshal in the Rose Parade or a regular on the Johnny Carson show?

Kareem Abdul-Jabbar laughed. "I am always willing to listen to public relations advice. I've never considered myself aloof or in a privileged position in society."

Of course, if he does all those things, wins the championship, cuts ribbons, rides in parades and opens supermarkets, the next thing you know the city of Long Beach will buy him for the harbor, or Disney will make him into a ride. Or they'll make him governor or put him to work doing all the old John Wayne movies.

But no matter what, he'll know he's one of the boys when some baldheaded guy in the box seats balancing a beer leans out some night and bawls. "Call yourself a player, Kareem? You couldn't carry Baylor's sneakers!" Only then will Kareem Abdul-Jabbar know he's not only in L.A. but of it.

THE COWBOY'S LAMENT

NOVEMBER 26, 1977

After 30 years of getting the girl, killing off all the bad guys, and riding off into the sunset singing *That Silver-Haired Daddy of Mine,* Gene Autry, in 1960, founded the then-Los Angeles Angels. And right away, he knew what the rustlers felt like.

The Angels lost more often than the guys in the black hats. They were an Italian movie. Everyone got killed in the end.

Gene was shocked. Every place he looked, there were Indians. Things like this never would have happened in the old days at Monogram and Republic. The wags got busy. Autry's horse in the old days was "Champion," they snickered. If he made a comeback, his horse would be named "Cellar."

The Angels needed a third act. Autry knew what was called for. You call in the cavalry. Only in Autry's case, it was always Custer's.

There's sort of a sporting tradition in Baseball that you build a championship from the ground up. It's kind of like giving the other guy the first draw.

It didn't work for Autry. He kept getting gunned down before he could get his .45 out of its holster. This was an adult Western, not a kiddies' matinee.

So Gene decided to do a little dry-gulching on his own. He began by hiring a manager. This is a dumb thing to do. Baseball is a general manager's medium.

Next, Gene tried players. Gene operated on the theory that what the Angels needed was one good player to put them over the hump. What the Angels needed were nine good players. At least.

In 1971, Gene thought he had finally found his John Wayne. Harry Dalton, an ex-sportswriter from Springfield, Massachusetts, had just led the Baltimore Orioles to four pennants and two World Series in six years, largely because he had acquired a Hall of Fame player (Frank Robinson) for a .500 pitcher (Milt Pappas).

Autry figured the fort was saved. They would cut the league off at the pass. The varmints would swing for their crimes.

But the Angels continued to play it for comedy. Dalton brought in a pitcher who threw no-hitters on his good nights—and walked in the world on his bad.

"Phee-noms" with "can't miss" labels, not only missed, they took called third strikes. Outfielders threw to the wrong base on the infrequent occasions they got to the ball in time to throw anywhere. Jerry Lewis drooled at some of the routines the Angels' infield perfected.

So Autry looked over at George Steinbrenner of the Yankees, who was busy buying an annual pennant on his Diners card, so to speak, and Gene thought, "I can play that game."

Financially, Gene could. The owner of hotels, radio stations, rodeos, and a half-dozen music companies, Autry could have bought the entire American League on the annual proceeds from the royalties of *Rudolph the Red-Nosed Reindeer* alone.

So Gene bought the "on paper" championship of the world. Every available .300 hitter or 20-game pitcher got into him for a bundle. But they kept getting hurt, or fooled—or benched. In other words, they turned into Angels. You had a picture of Autry running out on the field periodically yelling, "Cut! Cut! Now, just a minute, everybody, this is a take! *Be* serious! Somebody put a little makeup on Ryan there. Now, Nolan, we're way over budget. Get this one *in* there!"

The Angels ended up, as usual, surrounded—a remake of *Beau Geste* instead of *Big Sky*. They had arrows sticking out of them all over. Autry began looking at Dalton the way he used to look at the sheriffs who weren't getting the job done. "Marshal, how come you haven't brought in that Billy the Kid yet? Why, women aren't safe in this town!"

The Old Cowboy finally brought in a new man to the territory—Buzzie Bavasi, a man who had built the old Dodgers' dynasty—in other words a man who had cleaned up Dodge City. Tombstone now had two Wyatt Earps.

Dalton got the message and went clear to Milwaukee before he stopped. Buzzie got the star on his chest. The territory was now his, lawlessness and all.

Will this new lawman survive the shootout at O.K. Corral? Or will the Clantons win this one—again? Can the cavalry get there in time? Or will they arrive with back spasms, and pulled hamstrings, and broken hands, and an inability to hit the curve as usual? Will Bavasi run the rustlers out? Will the Cowboy get one more happy ending before he goes to the Big-Bunkhouse-in-the-Sky?

Many years ago—50, in fact—when he was a telegrapher for the railroad in Sapulpa, Oklahoma, Gene Autry was playing his guitar one day when a stranger dropped off a train, patted him on the head, and said, "Keep trying, son." That was Will Rogers and, but for that chance remark, Gene Autry might be now on a Santa Fe pension. But there was another piece of advice that Sitting Bull, the retired Indian chief, used to give everybody in the stageshow *Annie Get Your Gun.* It was the old Indian maxim: "No put money in show business." Old Sitting Bull didn't know Autry. But he sure would have known the Angels.

ALZADO IS RAZOR SHARP

JANUARY 12, 1978

NEW ORLEANS—He looks like something out of the Bible, an Old Testament prophet with fierce, burning eyes, a rabbinical beard, long black locks, a John the Baptist in cleats.

There is a smoldering violence about him. If he came in a box, you'd put him in water before opening. He was a New York street kid, wild, dangerous. Destination: the electric chair. The betting was, if he was playing football by the time he was age 28, it would be for Sing Sing.

He carried a straight razor but not to shave. This was even before he had grown whiskers. On the streets, his nickname was "The Animal," and this was in a jungle full of them.

He was either in a fight or in a cell when the sun went down and, sometimes, when it was up. He threw people out of bars for a living before he was 16. He has knife scars on all his fingers. So do a lot of guys who fought him.

Still, the blood of scholars as well as of mindless violence coursed through Lyle Alzado. Mother was Jewish. Dad, long gone by the time he went to school, was Spanish and Italian, a streetfighter and a brawler of heroic proportions.

One night, when Lyle found himself, as was his custom, in the Nassau County Jail on Long Island, he threw off all his clothes and began to jump up and down naked, screaming through the bars.

An old drunk looked blearily up. "Shut up and sit down, kid. You're just a bum like me. You're going to spend the rest of your life in places like this, just like me."

Lyle Alzado didn't know whether to hit the guy—or kiss him. "The guy did me the biggest favor in the world. Nobody had ever talked to me like that before. I could see it was true."

Alzado put away the razor and opened a book. And began a slow, circuitous route to the 1978 Super Bowl. He took his violence out on the football field instead of the neighborhood and the citizenry.

Lots of people think football is a terrorizing sport. But the first thing Lyle Alzado noticed was that nobody carried knives. Right there, it was civilized to him.

New Mexico State offered a scholarship. When they sent for his record, they only wanted his academic record. Which was bad enough. But his police record was even more hair-raising. They quickly wired him not to bother to come. They had no courses in train robbing.

He hooked on with Kilgore Junior College in Texas briefly, but it was Yankton, South Dakota, College which changed Lyle Alzado from an animal to an artist.

He became perhaps the finest defensive end in football but nobody was noticing because he played in the defensive line of the Denver Broncos and most people didn't think Denver had any defensive line. I mean, you couldn't tell from the scores. To tell the truth, outside of Alzado, they really didn't.

You still wouldn't mistake Lyle Alzado for a guy who reads poems and keeps cats but the chances he will ever spend another night naked in the Nassau County Jail or make the starting lineup at Sing Sing are remote. It's a long way from the mean streets of Manhatten to the center stage of the Superdome and, on Super Sunday, a lot of guys in stir will peer closer at the TV screen and say, "Hey! That looks like the guy who cut me at Rockaway Beach once! See this scar on my nose? He had a straight razor. We used to call him 'The Barber.' But that can't be him. This guy must have long since gone to the chair."

Actually, Lyle Alzado wanted to be a prizefighter. It looked like a pretty easy way to make a buck. I mean, you didn't even have to buy a gun.

Lyle Alzado controls a line of scrimmage the way he used to run the neighborhood, by sheer runaway violence. The man with the face right out of Leviticus is strong enough to lift a freight car and still fast enough to steal fruit from a stand and he couldn't be more effective if he played in a fiery chariot. He weighs several hundred pounds. He plays the game with a archangelic fury that led Tom Landry to complain that the Denver Broncos played as if they had been surrounded with their backs to the sea. His own coach, Red Miller, once explained that he wanted the Broncos to play "like cornered yard dogs." For his part, Alzado plays as if he just heard a cop's whistle and running feet.

Football has its share of stamp collectors, art fanciers, amateur chefs, but Lyle Alzado was a coin collector as a young man—which is to say there wasn't a subway gum machine he could pass up.

If Denver wins Sunday, perhaps the team should consider sending a part-share not only to the clubhouse boy or the team bus driver or equipment man but also to this little old drunk in a drunk tank somewhere on Long Island.

The coach can draw all the X's and O's and pass patterns he wants on the blackboard but without that little old wine-drinker, the Denver Broncos would probably not be in the Super Bowl today. Because, if Lyle Alzado were mugging people in Central Park instead of on the 20-yard line, Sing Sing would have as good a chance to go to the Super Bowl as Denver. Lyle Alzado looked more like a first-round pick of the Mafia than the NFL.

Recently, he invited his mother to see her one and only football game, a head-knocker against the Chicago Bears. Alzado says she was horrified. "I don't know how you can play a game like that, hurting people! It's disgusting!" he says she scolded him.

It's a good thing they didn't sell tickets to what he *used* to do nights. All those times she thought he was at the library. And, when he stayed overnight at "a friend's house," he didn't say the friend was the warden.

FAME BUT NO HALL

JANUARY 20, 1978

As a practicing schizophrenic, the Baseball Hall of Fame makes Jekyll and Hyde look like a model of consistency.

It is divided into two parts. One part is Union League, as stuffy as the Bank of England, as hard to get into as The House of Lords. The other part is as wide open as a frontier dancehall, as easy to get into as the Army, come as you are, and bring your friends with you.

To get into the Baseball Writers' wing of the Hall of Fame, you better be Babe Ruth. Or better. To get in the veterans' wing, all you have to be is a crony. Be able to sing *Mother Machree* over the bar after midnight or be able to tell locker room jokes with the boys at Old-Timers Day.

To give you an idea, the baseball writers voted in one whole player Thursday out of the thousands technically eligible, and the 35 selected by the screening committee. You can bet me the veterans' committee will find a way to put a whole lot of these rejects in the hall anyway. They always have.

I would hate to have to come up before a jury of baseball writers with a noose in the balance. These guys are harder to please than a New York symphony maestro.

Would you believe Joe DiMaggio didn't make the hall the first year of his eligibility? You heard me. Joe DiMaggio. Himself. Lifetime average: .325. Some guys never hit that once. He hit safely in 56 straight games.

First of all, you have to have 75 percent of all ballots cast to get in the writers' hall. You have to have been in baseball for at least 10 championship seasons. You better win 20 games or bat .300—or both—in those seasons to have a chance.

A total of 379 members voted this year. You needed 285 votes to get in (a writer can vote for only 10 of the 35 screened eligibles).

It's a good thing these guys aren't on the gates of heaven. It's all right to be selective, but will someone in the congregation please rise and tell me why Maury Wills only got 115 votes? Will someone please tell why Rabbit Maranville is in the Hall of Fame and Maury Wills isn't?

Maurice Morning Wills not only led the league in base stealing six times, he broke one of the hoariest records in baseball history, Ty Cobb's 1915 record of 96 steals. Maury Wills became the first man ever to steal 100 bases in a season when he broke Cobb's record with 104 in 1962. Maury stole 94 in 1965. He ran the Dodgers into three pennants. He restored a lost art.

Do you realize that the year before Maury Wills came into baseball the total of stolen bases for the American League was 353? The total! The National League total was 368. Only one *club* in baseball stole more than 100 bases. The White Sox stole 104.

When Maury left the game, the leagues were stealing a thousand bases a year. Last year, the American League stole 1,462 bases. And that's the slow league. The National stole 1,555.

I could rest my case. But it should be pointed out, Maury Wills set his records *before* the advent of carpeted ballparks. His records were set mainly on grass and clay surfaces, sometimes heavily watered by the opposition.

The baseball writers are sometimes loathe to reward a guy for a single, incandescent, virtuoso performance over one season. They prefer a guy who keeps doing a predictable thing over and over again. Henry Aaron, who piled up 755 home runs, 30 to 40 at a time over 20 years, will go in the hall by acclamation. Roger Maris, who hit 61 one season, more than anyone ever hit in one season, will never make it.

But, Maury Wills is sixth on the all-time base-stealing list. And he languished *nine* years in the minor leagues before getting his chance. He scored more than 1,000 runs in only a little over 11 full seasons.

He broke a record that had stood for 47 years and, when he stole over 100, he opened the floodgates on a neglected art, like the first 4-minute miler or the first 7-foot high jumper showing the way to a whole generation. He revolutionized the game, electrified audiences, rejuvenated a franchise.

If Maury Wills doesn't belong in the Hall of Fame, Babe Ruth doesn't. He did the same thing Ruth did—change a national pastime, forever. For him to get only 115 votes and finish 11th behind a pack of journeymen players is a joke. The baseball writers would probably pass up Thomas Edison and his discovery of the electric light or the phonograph or moving pictures in favor of some guy who washed the windows in his factory every day for 50 years.

Or, when Alexander Graham Bell invented the telephone, they'd sneer, "Yeah, But I'd like to see him do it again!"

A SALUTE TO GILLIAM

OCTOBER 13, 1978

NEW YORK—I guess my favorite all-time athlete—certainly, ballplayer—was Jim Gilliam.

This is not a post-mortem. I have said it to interviewers, broadcast and print, over the years. I said it while Jim was alive. I lumped him with Ben Hogan. He liked that. He also deserved that.

The reason was simple: I admire most the athletes who didn't wake up one morning with their skill and didn't have to do a damn thing about it to excel. As Jerry Barber, the golfer, said one day to a pupil on the driving range, "Look, Sam Snead rolled out of bed one day with his swing. You and I have to work at it."

Jimmy had to work at it. God didn't give him much of a head start. There were plenty of guys in the neighborhood who could run faster, hit harder, jump higher and dress better. God gave Jim Gilliam qualities that didn't show in a track meet. Patience. Determination. Discipline. Guts. Jim Gilliam was the kind of guy you'd want to get stuck in a submarine with.

Don't misunderstand me. Jim Gilliam wasn't a mediocre ballplayer. He was very, very good. Better than almost every big league infielder in the game in the '30s and early '40s.

But, you see, God not only didn't give Jim Gilliam Honus Wagner's arm, Babe Ruth's swing or Ty Cobb's eye. He didn't even give him the same color skin. Jimmy was bucking into a pat hand right from the start. And he played his cards that way.

The Baltimore Elite (pronounced "Ee-light") Giants were disappointed in him. Not flashy enough. He didn't have any gaudy routines, any hot-dog bat flips or home run struts. Jimmy played it straight. Jimmy wanted to be a ballplayer, not an end man.

They said his arm was too weak for third base. So he shifted to second. They said he was a sucker for a curveball right-handed. So he made himself a switch hitter. They wanted his cap to fly off, his feet to shuffle or his teeth to show. Jimmy told them if they wanted a tap dancer, try Hollywood. As for him, he intended to become a big leaguer.

He became one. One of the best. A joy to watch. As dependable as tomorrow, as quiet as a forest. He outwaited the flashy guys with the buck-and-wing acts and, when they couldn't solve the curveball often enough to go into their act, Jimmy stepped in. The big leagues isn't a floor show and Jimmy was a big leaguer.

He lived in New York but you never found him in any clubs called "Paradise" or "The Kitty Club." That wasn't Jimmy's style. Between games he studied hitting. At the foot of Jackie Robinson.

Much was made of the fact that Jimmy wasn't bitter. Jim Gilliam didn't think he had anything to be bitter about. The Reverend Jesse Jackson hit it right on the nose at the eulogy when he said: "Jim Gilliam gave much to his world but he didn't expect much in return."

A point has been missed about Jim Gilliam, though. A lot of people think he was short-changed in not being named a manager by now. But it didn't bother Jimmy that much. I know. Because he told me. You say, What else would he tell you? But that's not the way it was with Jim Gilliam. He never bothered to lie. About anything. You got nine innings of truth from him, too. And Jim Gilliam was happy in what he did. The old Dodger pitcher, Joe Black, confided ruefully at the funeral about the time he tried to get Jim Gilliam to join him at the Greyhound Bus Company. Recalls Joe: "Jim said to me, 'Joe, you know how far I went in school. No way I could get up in front of all those people and tell them what to do. I'm not qualified.' "

Jim Gilliam was not going to be any man's token. He was going to stay where he was needed—in a baseball uniform. One of Jimmy's favorite sayings was "Never play the other man's game." Jimmy moved within his limitations. He never underestimated anybody. Or overestimated them, for that matter. Jimmy read the pitch.

He took pitches so that Maury Wills could set base-stealing records. Not for Maury, for the Dodgers. He stepped aside as each succeeding "phee-nom" would come along to take his job. One of the first times I ever sat with Jimmy was in a coffee shop back in 1961 as we discussed some now-forgotten young hopeful who was supposed to take over his position. The road to Spokane was clogged with rookies Jimmy sent back to the minors. He never rejoiced in it. He hoped they would come through. They didn't.

He played seven positions on the ballclub and, as Casey Stengel once said, "each one better than the last."

The author, Roger Kahn, a few years ago, wrote a melancholy tome titled *The Boys of Summer*. It was about the 1953 Dodgers, a star-crossed club, the first desegregated team in baseball history, bedevilled by undeserved misfortune. Death and personal tragedy dogged the lives of the individuals—Gil Hodges, Jackie Robinson, Billy Cox, Carl Erskine. Jim Gilliam is the latest. Dead at 49, he makes it seem a ship's company pursued by ill fate.

This is probably the first World Series ever played with a tenth man in one lineup. The Dodgers take the field with a "19" etched in black sewed on their uniform sleeves. It is not a reminder to win. It is a reminder to play well, to play fair and do your best at all times. The number "19" has always stood for that on the Dodgers. The number "19" has stood for a man who was my friend, your friend, baseball's friend, humanity's friend—an American, a major leaguer, a class act all the way.

Two thousand people don't show up at a funeral for a first-base coach. That many don't show up for a league president. But Jim Gilliam was more representative of baseball than any league president. Gilliam was as true baseball as *Take Me out to the Ball Game*. He thought he was lucky to be a Dodger. I thought it was the other way round. And, as he reaches home plate sooner than almost everybody else as usual, I am sure Gil Hodges, Jackie Robinson and the rest of the Boys of Summer will be crowded around there waiting for him with arms outstretched as Junior comes in, standing up as usual.

THE PEOPLE'S CHAMP

NOVEMBER 9, 1978

It was 1935. Bread was a nickel, coffee was, too, and so were hamburgers. Cigarettes were a dime and you could buy a new Ford for $800. Detroit won the baseball championship, Pittsburgh and Fordham played the first of three consecutive scoreless ties, and the only thing we had to fear was fear itself. Shirley Temple was the reigning movie box office star when Will Rogers got killed in a plane crash.

The heavyweight boxing division was a mess. A series of lackluster champions had reduced the title to a series of pillow fights. And that's when Joe Louis came onto the scene.

No one had ever seen a destructive force in the ring like this one. His punches were so fast they were a blur on the fastest Speed Graphic cameras of the day. He fought mostly out of Detroit and Chicago, but word filtered back to New York. A pretty good journeyman fighter named Stanley Poreda had gone out to fight him, and lasted a little over a minute, and, in that time, his manager told the crowd at Stillman's Gym, "My fighter took a count of 39—the ref gave him 20 seconds to get back in the ring, and, when he did, he thought he was catching a bus."

Prior to Joe Louis, black fighters had been principally used to build character or reputations for white ones. They were given fights on the clear understanding they were not meant to win. But to lose. It was either that, or back to the shoeshine stand.

Joe Louis changed all that. Joe was not just another colored fighter. Joe was something for the ages. Joe was to boxing what Barrymore was to acting or Crosby to crooning. He was a national resource.

He had a knack for doing and saying the right things. Every white hope he ever knocked kicking, he described afterward as "another lucky night." When someone suggested World War II wasn't his people's war, Joe rebutted, "There's a lot of things wrong with this country—but nothing Hitler can fix." He never did a malicious thing in his life. Nine out of nine pugs were scared to death of him in the ring, but every panhandler on Broadway knew he was a pushover for a hard-luck story. Joe went through life leaking money. Every two-handicapper in the country tried to get on his dance card on a golf course. It was like finding money. Jim Braddock, who had been on relief when he won the heavyweight championship, cut 10 percent of Joe Louis' purses for 10 years.

Ticket sellers, ushers, program printers, hot-dog vendors, cab drivers, headwaiters, hustlers—you name it—all benefited from the Joe Louis years at the top. All, that is, except Joe. Joe wound up owing the government more than Germany. Joe got into such a hole that every time he made a nickel, he wound up owing six cents.

It was a well-played olio. Black fighters throughout history had ended up holding a sack with a hole in it. Sam Langford, one of the best, wound up blind and broke in a flophouse in New York, bumming quarters for coffee. Jack Johnson starred in a flea circus. And Joe Louis took to wrestling. It was like watching Abraham Lincoln bus dishes.

Capitalism is heartless. Joe Louis' education had stopped in the sixth grade. In fact, it had started in the sixth grade. The shack in Alabama he attended before the family moved to Detroit was a school in name only. In Detroit, they told Joe he'd better learn to work with his hands. He did.

Joe Louis earned $4,675,795.40 in the ring. He made probably another $4 million out of it. He raised $103,246.94 for Army and Navy relief during the war.

Somehow, he wound up owing the government all of it—even more.

Las Vegas is not exactly America's idea of Heartline, U.S.A. It's not supposed to be where folks are folks, where the heart is, where your happiness lies right under your eyes, and where seldom is heard a discouraging word. Vegas is not for tap-outs. It's not meant to have a heart, but a slot machine, and an either pay-or-play philosophy. Well, would you like to see Joe Louis selling pencils in the lobby of the Garden? Like to see the Brown Bomber taking care of somebody else's golf shoes?

Neither would Vegas. And that's why, when a newspaper

campaign to raise Joe Louis' back taxes came up with the magnificent sum of $4,000 some years ago, Vegas took up the slack. Vegas took care of Joe Louis while the rest of us looked busy. And tonight, at Caesars Palace, they are staging another A Night With The Champ fund-raiser for Joe. Everyone from Muhammad Ali to Frank Sinatra, Dean Martin, Howard Cosell, both Reggies, Smith and Jackson, Jim Rice to Alice Cooper will be there. But the biggest sports hero of them all will be the one in the wheelchair. He did more for more people than all the others put together.

TROUBLE
HITS TAPE

MARCH 16, 1979

Nobody—with or without a football—ever ran faster than Bob Hayes. The only thing in the world that could ever keep up with him was trouble. Trouble runs an 8.6 100.

It beat him again the other day in Dallas. Hayes hit a broken tape for, like, the second time in his life.

The first time I saw Bob Hayes was in the Olympic Village in Tokyo in 1964. Now, American sprinters, on the eve of Olympic heats and finals, can be pretty uptight human beings. Even their eyeballs are clenched.

You would have thought Bob Hayes was going to the beach. He had his shades on and a tape deck blasting Cannonball Adderley, and he was as cheerful as a kid going fishing.

The U.S. had a disaster in the sprints at the Olympics four years before when Ray Norton finished last in the 100 and 200 and dropped the baton in the relay.

Was Hayes, therefore, worried? Hayes flashed a smile. "I'll run a 10.1 100 if I have to, don't worry," he said cheerfully.

He ran a 10-flat 100 meters. The runner-up was several yards behind. I remember sitting behind Jesse Owens at the time and Jesse was bug-eyed. "That's the first time anyone won this race by daylight since I did it in 1936!" he exclaimed.

Hayes not only didn't drop the baton in the relay, he made up more ground than a cheetah after a square meal. The U.S. was a beaten fifth when Hayes took command, and he ran an 8.6 anchor on four clocks.

Hayes traveled faster than bad news. He had more moves than Little Egypt. He was one of the few Olympic stars who didn't have to move only in a straight line.

So, when the Dallas Cowboys drafted him, all they wondered about was whether he might have "bad hands." In pro football, this is the euphemism for a dozen other more serious maladies.

Your sainted grandmother can hold on to a football. It's not "bad hands," it's bad eyes, or bad nerves, or bad teeth, or bad vibes that makes you drop a football. Mostly, it's not bad hands at all, it's good hearing. You hear Jack Tatum coming. It's fear that makes you drop passes, not fingers.

Hayes didn't have that trouble. His trouble was not his hands, it was his feet. They outran the football.

Still, Bob Hayes drew more coverage that the White House.

But, even a random search of Dallas Cowboy statistics turns up some boggling records. Hayes in a Buffalo Bills game, two receptions for 91 yards; Hayes against the Patriots, three for 83; Hayes against the Rams, one for 51; Hayes against the Giants, four for 154, Hayes in the Super Bowl, two for 23, and Hayes against Houston, four for 246 yards and a Cowboy record.

Once, before fame, and, presumably, misfortune came his way, Bob Hayes found something he couldn't outrun—a warrant. He was in the company of a fellow undergraduate at Florida A&M one night in 1961 when the fellow turned to a life of crime. That is to say, he pulled a water pistol on another undergraduate and pulled off an 11-cent armed robbery—a nickel, a penny, and a package of chewing gum. A police car pulled around the corner just as this big heist was in progress. The Brink's robbery, they blew, but this one they were right on top of.

Bob Hayes took off. The police fired, but Bob won this one by daylight, too. But, the next day, he was arrested. The football coach, Jake Gaither, got him off.

The story would have died on a police blotter. Bob Hayes, a sophomore running back from a segregated college leaving the scene of the crime, was not news. But an Olympic gold medalist coming home four years later, was. They dusted off the story when Bob came back with his gold medal and put it on page one, along with the hijackings, influence-peddling, break-ins, and Mafia hits, and the other great crimes of the decade.

The governor of Florida pardoned Hayes then, I guess for keeping company with a man carrying a concealed water pistol. But Bob needs the governor's pardon even more today. He pleaded guilty to three charges of delivering cocaine and something called methaqualone before a district court in Dallas the other day.

It's a pity that the one time Bob Hayes should have used his great speed—to set a world record getting away from a pusher—he slowed down. In Texas, he could get life. If he's got the habit they say, he's already signed up for that. Still, the thought of an Olympic gold medalist and Super Bowl superstar behind bars is a sad commentary on our times. And the thought of the world's fastest human in a cell barely wider than the margin he won the Olympics by is too terrible to contemplate. That was one baton Bob Hayes should have dropped.

LIEUTENANT FAIR-AND-SQUARE

AUGUST 14, 1979

When Roger Staubach was named the Most Valuable Player in a Super Bowl a couple of years ago, and the sponsoring *Sport* magazine offered him a snazzy souped-up sports roadster that looked like a traveling bomb, just perfect for picking up chorus girls and speeding tickets, racing at Watkins Glen, or arriving in style at the disco, Roger frowned and asked if he could have a station wagon instead.

The sports world cracked up. If Roger Staubach won two weeks at St. Tropez and the French Riviera, they said, he would ask if he could swap it for two days in Cleveland. Staubach would rather win a cow than a yacht. He was a guy who, when he saw his first *Playboy* centerfold, didn't know what it was. He saw a pornographic movie and thought it needed subtitles; he didn't understand anything they were talking about. Roger Staubach was as square as a piece of fudge. He made Pat Boone look kinky.

They couldn't understand why, as a star high school quarterback, he didn't pick Alabama, Nebraska, Penn State or SMU like any other self-respecting all-stater. Why he chose instead the U.S. Naval Academy. They figured he had been bitten by too many screenings of *Navy Blue and Gold*, that he thought Frank Merriwell was a real person, or maybe, among his other drawbacks, he was patriotic.

The pros regard Navy as just another Ivy League school with delusions of grandeur. No one from the Naval Academy had ever really made the NFL, and, when Staubach won the Heisman Trophy as a junior, they were convinced he was not going to spoil that record. Heisman Trophy winners are notorious busts in the NFL.

When Staubach graduated from the Academy and insisted on serving his four-year hitch, the pros just figured he preferred seasickness to scrimmages. The Cowboys had drafted him in the 10th round, which is a little like sending somebody an anonymous letter, and when Staubach spurned the pros' offers of aid in getting him out of his Navy commitment, like offering to find him a girl for a mock marriage, the pros just considered him as lost at sea.

Staubach spent four years in Vietnam while the Cowboys got good at losing to Green Bay and the Cleveland Browns. When he showed up at training camp to remind them he was their draftee, the pros tried to be polite. "Look, sailor, why don't you just re-up and see if you can make the Quantico Marines? You have about as much chance of making admiral as you do the Dallas Cowboys." They wondered how a guy could come walking off a destroyer and into the Dallas backfield. How could you spend four years mapping the Gulf of Tonkin and understand a Green Bay defense?

But it wasn't only the Heisman Trophy, the four years at an ammo dump or on a gunboat in the Mekong that seemed to make Staubach unfit for the role. That was an era when quarterbacks were nicknamed "Broadway" or "Dandy" or "Whisky." It was an era when quarterbacks were supposed to buy drinks for their offensive line, get dates for their wide receivers, and pick up the tabs for the hotel parties. Roger Staubach could hardly do this. He was at early Mass at the time.

Besides, Tom Landry's offense was so complicated, only persons who also understood Einstein's theory could master it. It was popularly supposed it would take your average wizard seven years to fully understand it. And Staubach had already lost four.

The Navy had lost a promising officer, and the Cowboys had gained a placekick-holder, was the consensus. The Cowboys of the day were portrayed in almost every football novel that came out of Texas—and there were a raft of them at the time—as more of a traveling stag movie than a team, an orgiastic, ribald set of young men. They were popularly believed to be the prototypes of the cast in such works as *Semi-Tough*, *North Dallas 40* and *The Hundred-Yard War*. It was incongruous because the team's coach was a man who had no more vices that a vicar, in fact, had the morals of a minister, the dignity of a deacon, and the lifestyle of a lay leader in the church.

No one knows if Tom Landry liked Roger Staubach for his morals or his arm. But not much was wrong with either. The week before he reported Don Meredith had announced his retirement, the club had traded away Jerry Rhome, and all Staubach had to contend with was Craig Morton.

Staubach found the Cowboys' backfield as easy to make as Navy's. He found coach Landry's calculus no more complicated than the Naval Academy's midterms, as soon, that is, as you figured out the cosines of the angles, and, pretty soon, he was leading the Dallas Cowboys to their first Super Bowl win ever, in fact, their first big-game win ever.

It was a plot Burt L. Standish couldn't improve upon. Merriwell routed the bullies. The U.S. Navy was arriving in the nick of time. It was, wave the good ol' red, white, and blue all over again. Hit up *Anchors Aweigh* and cut to shots of the Pacific Fleet slicing its way through the Sea of Japan. Hit the statue of Tecumseh with a penny.

Eleven years ago Staubach was just another returning Vietnam vet looking for a job. Today he's the premier quarterback in the NFL. To be sure, the Dallas Cowboys have lost two Super Bowls under his direction—by a total of eight points. They have also won two—by a total of 38 points.

Staubach would now be starting his 15th year as an NFL quarterback had he not done his duty for God and country. He has not changed appreciably, save for the slightly longer haircut, from the ramrod-straight young officer who showed up at the Cowboys' Thousand Oaks camp 11 years ago. He still looks like a Navy recruitment poster. And he still leans more to the station wagon than the roadster with the belt on the hood and the room positively for only two people. Nor does he feel uncomfortable on the team which has inspired more *roman à clef* novels than any other in pro football history.

"Either I don't get invited to those parties, or they are simply figments of the authors' imagination," Staubach said the other day.

Lieutenant Staubach's victory is one of the Navy's proudest. Asked the other day if he didn't regret not resorting to subterfuge to get out of his Navy commitment, Staubach shook his head. "If I had ducked my responsibilities then, I would have spent the rest of my life ducking responsibilities," he explained.

I ask you, could Admiral Farragut have said it better? Commodore Perry? Instead of checking USC for quarterbacks, perhaps the NFL scouts should be checking the S.S. Antietam. They sure should be on the lookout for a guy who shows up at training camp in a station wagon.

A COLLEGE
GRADUATE

OCTOBER 25, 1979

Bud Wilkinson doesn't look like your basic native American football coach. No broken nose. No limp when the weather turns bad. No shrieking tantrums from the top of the practice-field football tower. He doesn't look as if he'd ever punch a kid in the helmet, jerk on his facemask or teach him to use an arm cast to break teeth.

He looks rather the way, well, the way you might expect a U.S. senator to look. He looks like he ought to be in the White House. Which is interesting, because he ran for the U.S. Senate. He got beat. And he was in the White House. In the Nixon White House, but Bud Wilkinson was not in the dirty tricks department. And his appeal transcended party lines. In 1961, John F. Kennedy appointed him national director of the President's Council on Physical Fitness. And President Lyndon Johnson reappointed him.

So, when he left college football in 1963, most people figured Bud Wilkinson was taking dead aim on the Executive Mansion on Pennsylvania Avenue. People kept telling him when he was football coach at the University of Oklahoma that he was bigger than the governor of the state. And, when the voters rejected him for the Senate in 1964, no one was sure whether it was because they didn't want him as senator or because they wanted him back as coach.

With his silver hair, twinkling blue eyes and rugged, dimpled profile, Wilkinson would seem to make the Perfect Candidate. Hollywood would cast him as a frontier marshal, as a destroyer captain in wartime, as a Marine lieutenant, bomber pilot or cavalry officer.

But in 1978 Bud Wilkinson proved he would rather be

191

wrong than be president. After a 15-year hiatus, he went back into football coaching. With the St. Louis Cardinals, no less, who are not to be confused with the great aggregations of NFL history.

His friends couldn't have been more shocked if he had run off with a French floozie or joined the circus. Football, they said, had passed Bud Wilkinson by. They said you might as well make Walter Camp coach of the Cardinals. Football had become an esoteric mumbo jumbo in the intervening years, the arts and mysteries of which would surely elude Bud, who had spent the intervening years in board rooms, not locker rooms. Bud, they warned darkly, would not have Oklahoma State to beat, but the Dallas Cowboys. And the Cardinals! Bud was going up to do battle with jets in old moth-eaten Sopwith Camel.

But it still looked like blocking and tackling out there to Wilkinson. It still looked like a game being played by kids who had to be motivated. So far as he could see the last telling invention in the game still was the forward pass, and that was at least 70 years old. When the Cardinals started out losing eight games in a row, the smart money figured this was just another college football coach trying to do it with pep rallies and bonfires and band music.

It is part of the mystique of pro football that no college coach can succeed at this level of competition. And yet, every great pro coach, with one exception, came up from the colleges. The great Vince Lombardi came to the pros off the coaching staff of West Point. Paul Brown, his nearest rival, came up out of Ohio State. Earle (Greasy) Neale one of the greatest innovators of the modern game, came, of all places, out of Yale!

Nor was Wilkinson any ordinary college coach. His records put him in the lodge with Rockne, Pop Warner, Amos Alonzo Stagg or Bear Bryant. His Oklahoma record from 1947 to 1963: 145 victories, 29 defeats and 4 ties. His teams had four undefeated seasons, won 13 consecutive conference titles, three national championships, two Sugar Bowls and four Orange Bowls. They once had a 47-game winning streak, the longest in college history.

Still, when Wilkinson's first pro team was 0–8, he appeared like a guy sailing out to meet ironclad battleships in a three-masted schooner. A guy with a lance going after a machine-gun nest.

Then, Bud Wilkinson's Cardinals won six of their last eight, duplicating what the Super Bowl-bound Dallas Cowboys were doing, and the game was impressed. Suddenly, there was a bull market in college coaches again in the NFL.

1979 was supposed to be like the good old days at Norman, with parades down the main stem in open convertibles with people throwing confetti and streamers and shouting "We're No. 1!" It was to be more like a stumble down a dark but familiar alley. In the opening game, the Cardinals played the Cowboys to a virtual standstill only to see a field goal attempt hit the crossbar and fall between the uprights for a one-point Dallas victory. The Cardinals lost to the Pittsburgh Steelers by only three points. Philadelphia beat them by four points.

The Cardinals are 2–6, instead of 5–3. But Bud Wilkinson's stock in trade is optimism. Positiveness. The man who once won 47 games in a row in college sees no reason why he can't win 14 in the pros. "This is no mysterious contest," he allowed as he stood in a locker room after a recent defeat, as composed as though he had just won the Orange Bowl. "Everybody's playing two wide receivers, a tight end, two running backs and a quarterback. Defensively, you've either got a 4–1 front basically or a 3–2 front because everybody's got two outside linebackers, two cornerbacks, and a weak and strong side safety."

What then was the basic difference in college and pro coaching? "Numbers," said Wilkinson. "In college you have 90 to 100 players on the practice field, let's say you have 90. Forty-four are going to play and 46 are going to help get ready to play. In this league your best offensive team runs the scout plays for the defense. So you're on the practice field longer than you wish you were, trying to get the number of repetitions you will need to excel. The time factor and the body weight of the players and just plain weariness takes its toll."

Can coach Wilkinson become the scourge of the pros he once was in the Big 8? A man who can run for the U.S. Senate in cleats with a whistle around his neck and as a Republican in Oklahoma is not easily discouraged. Or turned away by odds. At 62, one may not only not have enough time on the practice field, but not enough time on the calendar.

In the view of those who have watched over the years or played for him, the only thing that could keep Bud Wilkinson from going to at least one more bowl, would be a Republican landslide. And that looks like a much longer shot than the Cardinals.

A TOUGH LITTLE LADY

JANUARY 5, 1980

When you think of a fight promoter you think of this Damon Runyon character who talks out of the side of his mouth through an unlit cigar, sleeps with his shoes on, eats with his hat on.

He talks grandly of his "property," but chances are he's wearing it. He lives in a room with a bath down the hall, offices out of his pocket, his English would have to improve to be described as "broken," and, on a crowded day, his room looks like a parole office.

His friends are camera-shy, and the only pictures of them in existence have numbers across the front. He refers to the fighter as "I," as in "The night I stopped Mauriello in three," and he regularly takes the Fifth when commissions get nosy.

He hardly ever wears lipstick, nail polish or high heels. And he doesn't get his hair done because he ain't got any, and the only jewelry he wears is a hot watch.

Prior to Aileen Eaton, this was the profile of a fight promoter. She was the first one in history to make fights wearing a Dior suit, bracelets and Chanel. It was a great part for Roz Russell.

When Aileen Eaton was growing up in British Columbia, her mother thought she was going to turn out like every other girl on the block. She gave her piano lessons, put ribbons in her hair, bought her dancing pumps and shopped around for finishing schools. She thought she might have another Isadora Duncan on her hands, not a Tex Rickard. Fighting was something you did on barges till the cops raided. Pugilism was for piers, not parasols.

All went well until Aileen went to work in Los Angeles as private secretary for Frank A. Garbutt, president of the Los Angeles Athletic Club which owned the Olympic Auditorium, which staged weekly prizefights, often at great cost to management. Garbutt loved fights, but not at a weekly tab of $2,000. He dispatched his secretary to see why the house always lost this wheel.

Aileen didn't know much about boxing but she knew a lot about money. Also she knew double-entry bookkeeping when she saw it. Aileen fell in love with boxing. It appealed to her high instinct for combat and for its high potential for making money off people less bright and energetic than she—which included most of the civilized world.

She married Alvah (Cal) Eaton, who was a boxing-commission inspector at the time, which meant his job was to go down to the locker rooms before the fight and make sure there wasn't any gin in the water bottles or horseshoes in the gloves. Aileen installed her husband as promoter, but among those not fooled was the matchmaker, Babe McCoy. "I don't work with dames," he growled. Told she came with the lease, he relented. "But the first time she cries, I go!" McCoy was still waiting till the day he died. And after, for that matter.

Aileen didn't exactly put curtains on the windows or ruffles on the ring ropes, and the piano and tap-dancing lessons were largely lost, but she ruled the game with a well-manicured fist for three decades in her own town and beyond. Red-haired, blue-eyed, pound for pound she was as tough as any welterweight who ever came down the aisle. She was as hard to handle inside as any infighter who ever fought a semi-main at St. Nick's. The Mafia didn't scare her. She told Blinky Palermo once he'd seen too many Edward G. Robinson movies.

Competitors arose and she fought them inside and hard, but always through the commissioner's office, not with goons or gangsters. And she paid off in the light. She dealt sharp, but she took her losses like Nick the Greek and never paid off in markers or at 10 cents on the dollar.

In an industry whose crest should be a field of double-crosses rampant on a shield of blackmail, where, it is said, even an archbishop could come out with dirty skirts, Aileen managed to come out as clean as a soap commercial. Not innocent—clean. Fritzie Zivic, maybe, but Gentleman Jim Corbett when it came to the payoff.

She once refused to do business with mobster Mickey Cohen. And Mickey protested, "But 96 percent of my business is legitimate!" And Aileen told him 96 percent of Jack the Ripper's dates were platonic, and only 1 percent of the Russians were Communists.

A week ago, Aileen Eaton, up to her earrings in the promotion of the bantamweight championship fight between titleholder Lupe Pintor of Mexico and challenger "Superfly" Sandoval of Pomona, which takes place at the Olympic Saturday, checked into the UCLA Medical Center to find out why she got tired playing just seven hours of gin rummy at a time.

"I don't even enjoy fighting with managers," she complained, adding that she even skipped the blackjack tables in Vegas when she was there as part-promoter of the Wilfredo Benitez–Sugar Ray Leonard fight.

When Aileen Eaton got bored haggling over percentages, the medics knew it was serious. They slapped her in an oxygen tent and undertook seven-hour quadruple-bypass heart surgery.

It's one of those operations where they saw your chest in half, and put veins from your calves around your aorta, and, since Aileen will be 71 years of age next Tuesday, the staff at the Olympic thought they would not hear the red telephone ring for a month.

The operation was Tuesday. The phone was ringing in the Olympic Thursday. The call was from intensive care. The caller was still listed in "serious" condition. Aileen sure was.

"Listen! Are all the tearsheets out? Why don't we get more publicity in the papers? We got two champions and an unbeaten fighter on the card! Count the advance and call me back in an hour. And whatever you do, don't give the fighters an advance!"

Aileen wasn't even taking a count. Louis and Dempsey may be the greatest heavyweight champions who ever lived, but the greatest promoter may be a good, game welter out of Vancouver who keeps getting up.

FIRST
TEST-TUBE
LINEBACKER

JANUARY 17, 1980

NEWPORT BEACH—The first time you see Jack Lambert, you're tempted to ask what he did with the fangs. Is that really tomato juice he's drinking or something he bit out of the neck of Earl Campbell? Was his coffin comfortable last night and what time does he turn into a wolf? The pro from Pittsburgh, Transylvania. If hair starts growing out of his face, get a mirror. Or get out.

All middle linebackers are a little crazy, but Jack Lambert is the Dracula of the lot. Bela Lugosi gets the part. Karloff in cleats. Lambert didn't come out of a college; he escaped from the laboratory.

He is carrying a glass of red juice in one hand and a glass of amber fluid in the other. Ginger ale. It's sovereign for the "touch of the flu" he is feeling this morning. The kind you get sitting too close to a bar rag.

He is wearing a hat emblemed "Pittsburgh Police." "Did you get that before or after you were booked?" someone wants to know. Lambert doesn't even smile. "I do a lot of pistol shooting down at the police station and I have some very good friends on the force," he explains evenly.

Lambert is the NFL's resident Jack the Ripper. A girl in a London fog had a better chance with the original than a guy carrying a football has with the Pittsburgh counterpart in the neutral zone. Four years ago, on national TV, in front of 80 million people, the viewers saw an enraged Jack Lambert pick up a Dallas safety man, Cliff Harris, hold him aloft, then send him crashing to earth like a guy throwing mail off a train. And Cliff Harris didn't even have the football.

198

A referee instantly shouted, "You're out!" and football was almost treated to its first Super Bowl starter being thrown out of a game for roughness. The official later changed his mind. Some say because he looked over and Cliff Harris was still alive. That's one way you know Lambert didn't really mean it.

Jack Lambert plays football the way Attila the Hun sacked villages. When he's in there, the middle of the line looks like a shark frenzy. A man with a football drives him into the kind of towering rage most people reserve for wife stealers or kidnappers. The resultant reaction looks like a reformer busting up a saloon, or a cop jumping through a skylight into a crap game.

Jack Lambert is a man with a deep sense of what is right—and a 15-yard gain isn't. He's outraged when anyone trespasses on his property, whether it's a bar stool or the 50-yard line. He should wear "Violators Will Be Prosecuted" instead of No. 58 on his Pittsburgh Steelers uniform. And teams would do well to hang a "Do Not Disturb" sign on Lambert's sphere. Even if it's a bar stool, except that the last time Lambert attempted a zone defense there, he wound up with four stitches. Some NFL teams have been attempting to find the perpetrator ever since. Not to punish him, to sign him.

"Middle linebackers," the late Curly Lambeau used to say, "are people who start out in life tying tin cans to dogs' tails. They develop a fondness for train wrecks, and they can be spotted in the crowd because they're the ones smiling when everyone else is crying. Their idea of a good time is a mass funeral."

Other coaches think you can detect a middle linebacker at birth. Other babies put bowls of porridge on their own heads. A middle linebacker puts it on yours.

Middle linebackers have to have very bad tempers. They have to be easily offended and have little patience with intruders. They play the game in a cold rage. Their area of influence is not as clearly defined as other players', and they regard a successful enemy play anywhere on the field as a personal affront.

Lambert flung Harris to the ground simply because his own placekicker had missed a field goal, and somebody had to be punished. They are football's avengers.

Dick Butkus was a middle linebacker, for instance. So was Ray Nitschke. So, no doubt, was Genghis Khan. To play the position you have to have all the compassion of a Chinese war lord or a Mafia hit man. You play the game at a low smolder. You scowl a lot, and growl even more. It's suicidal. Other guys have "assignments." Your assignment is the ball. A middle linebacker swoops like a hawk over a chicken. And he takes no prisoners.

Which is why you're surprised when you meet Lambert. In thongs and jeans, he looks rather like that disc jockey on TV's *WKRP*. Harmless. Dissolute, even. He's tall (6'10") but not big (212). He has long blond locks, talks in a soft baritone whisper. (He leads the Super Bowl interviews in "Whadeesays?") That stuff in the glass is indeed tomato juice, not somebody's Type O. He looks for all the world like an undergraduate at Kent State (which he was) and not the center of a defense so formidable that running on it is considered in the NFL as hazardous as swimming a piranha river in South America.

It's no accident Pittsburgh started winning its Super Bowls when Lambert joined the defense as a rookie in 1974. "Before him, the Pittsburgh line was tough. With him, it also became crazy," a rival coach explains. "The junkyard dog began to froth at the mouth, too."

At game time, Lambert is like Lon Chaney when the moon comes out. It's as if the nice man next door, who always comes home with the briefcase and a lollipop, suddenly began getting down on all fours and barking.

Lambert accepts the image. If it makes a running back get up on his tippy toes when he crosses Jack's no man's land, this Ripper approves. And he admits it takes him hours after a game before he can come down and trust himself in polite company, where you can get 1 to 10 for doing what he does to Roger Staubach. Besides, he is emotionally spent. "It takes me an hour just to get my shoes off."

Lambert made 116 tough tackles this year. And resented every one he didn't make. He was in on 46 others. His fingerprints were on the necks of hundreds of other ball carriers. He intercepted six passes, giving him half as many receptions as his tight end.

By his own admission, Lambert has proposed to "227 girls." They all said no, he sighs. "I'm no day at the beach," he protests, "but I'm not that bad looking."

It is possible they don't believe he is Jack Lambert. It is the notion here that the real Jack the Ripper spent his whole life in pubs bragging he was Jack the Ripper. And everyone said, "Sure, sure, Jackie. Drink up."

And maybe someday Pittsburgh's Ripper may try to tell a bartender he is Jack Lambert and the barkeep will say, "Sure, sure. Listen, mister, the real Jack Lambert was between 7 and 9 feet tall and he had these funny eyes and furry ears and white fangs, and he used to hang Earl Campbell by his heels while he felt around for the ball. You don't look to me like you could hang a mirror, so give it a rest, will you?"

MAKING OF A MAN

FEBRUARY 24, 1980

"Tom appeared on the sidewalk with a bucket of whitewash and a longhandled brush. He surveyed the fence and all the gladness left him and a deep melancholy settled on his spirit. Life to him seemed hollow and existence but a burden. Work consisted of what a body is obliged to do. Play is what a body is not obliged to do."
—The Adventures of Tom Sawyer

"I'm in the gunsights now. It's not a game, it's a responsibility. It means no more breakfasts alone. It means ringing phones and you're a louse if you have to say 'No.'"
—The Adventures of Tom Watson

Fortunately for Mark Twain, Tom Sawyer is always going to be 15 years old and whitewashing that fence. Huck Finn is always going to be barefoot and fishing.

Imagine what a sad sight it would be to see Tom Sawyer working in a bank, wearing a tie and carrying a briefcase. Like to think of Huckleberry Finn in an office with shoes on?

Their fellow Missourian was not so lucky. Ten years ago, when young Tom Watson came on the golf tour with his freckled face and shock of red hair, he looked like something that stepped right out of the imagination of Samuel Clemens. Or, arrived by raft with a runaway slave. You kept looking around for Becky Thatcher. He looked as if he had just landed a string of catfish. If he had a wood in his hands it should have a string and a hook on it. You looked at him and you could hear the steamboat whistles.

Alas, he is now no longer young Tom Watson, he's Thomas Watson, Esquire. He's not a country kid from the banks of the Mississippi, he's a corporation, earnings last year $462,636 from the golf division alone, probably double that from all sources.

He's the most improbable-looking captain of industry you'll ever see. He looks like he's playing hooky. Not too long ago, if you saw him on the street you would have bought him a balloon and told him not to cry, that you'd find his folks for him.

The Watsons go back as far in Missouri lore as Twain or the James boys. Horse traders, likely, maybe river men, they were a fearless lot. Great grandfather Isaac Newton Watson broke up the Prendergast machine in Kansas City in the '30s when that was about as easy—or as advisable—as breaking up a Mafia picnic.

"I. N.," as he preferred to be called, put FBI men on his payroll (at $50 a week) and brought so many truckloads of affidavits and depositions to court that old Tom Prendergast himself went to jail. If you think that wasn't brave, you don't know Kansas City. While the rest of law enforcement concentrated on Bonnie & Clyde, I. N. went after the real public enemies.

That's probably why Tom Watson never saw anything to be particularly afraid of in a 10-foot putt or a 3-wood over water. When you come from a long line of people who have to be careful starting their cars or standing in a lighted window at night, what's a double bogey?

Competitors say the thing which distinguishes a Watson round of golf is his inability to sulk over a bad shot, a bad hole or a bad round. He plays an attacking game and, like a fighter who comes on, he expects to take some punishment. I don't know whether you know it or not but golfers, as a class, tend to what an old Missouri mule-skinner might call crybabying. They'll blame the grass, the gallery, the weather, the curvature of the earth, even sun spots for a shanked shot, a missed putt.

It's a good thing Tom Watson didn't let erratic golf send him sobbing into the clubhouse, otherwise he'd be in a rubber room somewhere today. Tom threw away tournaments like a bank embezzler race-track bets when he first came on the tour. He would play three rounds and 13 holes of impeccable golf—and then would start hitting the ball sideways. The joke was, Tom Watson had two lumps in the throat—one put there by Adam and the other by the last three holes. He went into the last round of the 1974 U.S. Open at Winged Foot leading by one stroke. He came out of it trailing by five. He shot a 69 on Saturday and a 79 on Sunday. People thought the experience might scar him forever. He won his first tournament two weeks later.

Tom Watson has won 14 tournaments in the last three years while earning almost as much as the chairman of the board of General Motors. Old I. N. Watson would probably want to prosecute him for taking money without working for it, except that putting for a living is harder on you than robbing a bank for one.

So, Tom Watson went from the pro-from-the-fishing-hole to the next Jack Nicklaus, from Mark Twain to marked man. He's not just a freckled face in the crowd anymore. With two British Opens, a Masters and playoffs in the PGA and the Masters, among his 14 tournament wins in three years, Watson is going to find out what it is to carry golf. If Watson shows up, it's a championship. If he doesn't it's just a tournament. If Touring Pro 18 doesn't show up, the sponsor shrugs. If Tom Watson doesn't show up, he sues.

Life in the gunsight doesn't seem to bother Tom Watson, who is second in the Glen Campbell L.A. Open after three rounds, any more than a triple bogey. Even if it means eating out of a bag or taking the phone off the hook. "Anyway," he says, "I'm really a ham at heart. And, all things considered, it beats the alternative, which was 'What did you say that Watson's first name was again?' "

THE ONE
AND ONLY

MARCH 13, 1980

PALM DESERT—The man on the first tee looked suspiciously like the winningest football coach of all time (short of the late Amos Alonzo Stagg). If you saw him in a houndstooth hat and the all-purpose slump of a guy who had to play Tennessee and LSU on alternate weekends, being escorted off the field by two Alabama state cops in Smokey the Bear hats, you'd swear it was Paul (Bear) Bryant, the legend, himself.

The voice, when he spoke, was an indistinct rumble like the sound of a distant avalanche, or a thunderstorm 10 miles away. The blue eyes squinted as if they were trying to see who missed the block down in one corner of the game films. The pants were characteristically baggy.

The man has been a refugee from a steam iron for 40 years. The swing was that of a man who has other things on his mind. If he were on a tower in Tuscaloosa, drawling down, "Callahan, you went after that man like you were going to ask him to dance," you'd swear this was the one and only Bear Bryant of Alabama.

Then he hit a golf ball into the water, and, when he didn't walk over the top of it to play the shot, you knew you had an impostor on your hands.

The real Bear Bryant, as they will tell you down in Mobile, wouldn't need a boat to go to Cuba. He could have saved the Titanic. Not only that, he can beat Auburn.

The man playing golf in the National Football Hall of Fame tournament at Monterey Country Club here would be the first to tell you he's not that Bear Bryant, that the resemblance is not even close.

The real Bear Bryant has won close to 300 football games. Nobody else but Pop Warner and Stagg—not Rockne, Howard

Jones, Woody Hayes, Walter Camp, or Tom Landry—has come close.

This Bear Bryant won but one game. "I ain't won but one," he admits. "My team won the rest in spite of me."

The one game he won, the historic game, will hardly go in the Hall of Fame. It was scarcely a strategic masterpiece. It was 38–0 over Auburn. The week before Bryant had frittered away the Georgia Tech game, by his own admission, breaking his team's 27-game winning streak by ordering the ball to go to the wrong back in a two-point conversion.

He had a quarterback at the time who was hardly known for his running. Therefore no one was expecting it. It was before quarterback Namath would become "Broadway Joe," and Coach Bryant ordered the team to muscle up for the fullback to carry it.

"I told the team afterward I blew it. If I gave the ball to Namath, no one was expecting it, he could have walked in." Which was a good thing, because that's all Joe could do even if his pants were on fire.

Bear Bryant won the Auburn game because he recanted on this confession. A study of the film showed it was not a coach's error. It was the offensive line's. "Nobody blocked," Bryant told the team on the eve of the Auburn game. "I didn't blow that game, you did." Mortified, the team chased Auburn clear to Biloxi the next day.

Bryant takes the position that Alabama, year in and year out, must be the best team in the country because it overcomes his mistakes. "Most coaches study the films when they lose. I study them when we win. To see if I can figure out what I did right."

One of the things he does right is not overmatch himself. Bryant got his nickname rassling a bear in a carnival once and the wags say Bear has been careful ever since whom he puts on his schedule.

Bear Bryant is at great pains to portray himself as a country bumpkin, anyway, a barefoot boy from Moro Bottom, Arkansas. He shambles through life like a grizzly through a berry patch. He talks like a man under 12 feet of water, but he's like a guy who is always turning up four aces—and apologizing because there aren't five. "I don't suppose these are any good," he'll sigh.

The pose conceals a high intellect. As John McKay, a rival

coach, once said, "When you scrape away all the hayseed, you find you're looking at the royal flush underneath. You can beat the Bear once, but never the same way twice."

Lots of college football coaches think they can go on to become a U.S. senator or chairman of the board. Bryant never wanted to be anything but the winner of the Orange Bowl. He even turned down the Miami Dolphins. "I bet they're glad," he says in a characteristic putdown of Bear Bryant.

This man that walks like a bear is as academically pure as a Latin prof. A sportswriter succinctly summed it up once: "Bear annually gets 40 of the best players in the Southeast and Pennsylvania without ever getting caught at it."

Bear himself says, "The only transcript problem Alabama ever had was me. They had to put me in a Tuscaloosa high school to make up algebra and Spanish. The Fordyce (Arkansas) Redbugs' lineup didn't have too many guys who could conjugate Spanish verbs or find the unknown in X equals Y."

Bryant's dream for college football is not a playoff system, it's televised intersectional spring practice games. "Everybody needs money now with inflation. We lost money, for instance, taking the team and the band to the Sugar Bowl." The beauty of his plan, Bear thinks, is that it will not only make money, it will help spring practices.

Bryant explains his scheduling teams like Wichita State as just common compassion for his athletes. "After all, they ain't gettin' much help from me," he explains.

Of his 50 years in football, Bear, 66, frowns. "I ain't never had much fun," he says. "I ain't never been two inches away from a football. Here guys go fishing on the day of the game, hunting, golfing, and all I want to do is be alone, studying how not to lose."

Bear would like to win one more game before he dies to make it an even two for a career. He would also like to coach his 300th team victory and break Stagg's record. "If somebody's got to do it, I'd just as soon that somebody be me. After all, I ain't never done nothin' else."

PERFECT TIMING

MAY 2, 1980

You'd recognize him immediately if he had a ray gun in his hand. Or if he'd just crash-landed a spaceship on the evil planet, Argon, ruled by the wicked queen, Arbadella, and her army of blobs.

He looks out of place in this century. You're half expected to say, "Haven't I met you in the future someplace before?"

Is it a bird, a plane, a man? No, it's Super Buster—Clarence Lynden Crabbe, the first, the only, the original Flash Gordon, Buck Rogers, King of the Jungle, the granddaddy of the star wars, the original Trekie, the king of the Saturday afternoon serials, the envoy from Fantasy Island, visitor from outer space, America's time warp.

You say the name "Buster Crabbe" and you immediately think of Tarzan yells, eight men swimming through a sea of crocodiles with chimps on their shoulders, or you think of long lines at the Saturday matinee in the days when popcorn was a nickel and candy was a penny, and you had to see how the 25th-century man got out of the disintegrator tunnel run by the dia-bol-ical master of the purple people, Dr. Death.

Buster Crabbe belongs to the lore of America, the age when heroes were possible, the bad guys always lost and moon landing were comic book stuff.

But Buster Crabbe the legend came within 1/100th of a second of, if not obscurity, the next best thing to it, a lawyer for a sugar combine.

Part Hawaiian, part fish, and all athlete, Crabbe was a law student at USC in 1932 when the Olympic Games came along. Had there been a boycott then, he would have spent his life litigating torts for pineapple growers. As it was, he had been spending his mornings sorting out stock in a men's downtown clothing store, and his afternoons pulling school kids out of riptides at Santa Monica beach when he was catapulted into fame as the only American man to win a swimming gold medal in the 1932 Olympic Games, breaking the Japanese monopoly of the Coliseum pool that summer.

Crabbe had competed in the '28 Olympics, winning a bronze medal in the 1,500-meter freestyle at Amsterdam. Between Amsterdam and Los Angeles, he broke 16 American and world records, won 35 national championships and broke all the records set by Johnny Weissmuller over 200 meters. He broke Weissmuller's half-mile record by 12 seconds.

Hollywood came running. The "Clarence" was changed to "Larry" and as Larry (Buster) Crabbe, he became a marquee draw in loin cloth and space boots all over the world. He was the undisputed king of the science-fiction serial.

"Hollywood found out that, by spreading a space-fantasy feature into 13 chapters, you could fill the theater 13 times while a feature-length film filled it only once," Buster explains.

Crabbe escaped from more exploding planets, brought law and order to more galaxies and strangled more lions than anyone in Gower Gulch in those years. His roles ranged from one million B.C. to 2500 A.D., and he never knew whether he was going to be wearing a leopard skin or a space helmet, carrying a club or a rocket, dodging a shower of arrows or a shower of meteorites.

"I thought when those fellows landed on the moon they put Flash Gordon and Buck Rogers out of business but, if anything, they revived them." Buster toiled long before the days of residuals, but his career continued apace on TV in New York, via a health club, the manufacture of swimming pools and in lectures at colleges.

Now 72, and only a pound or two over his weight when he was swinging through sound stages on vines, Buster is touring the country campaigning for his *Buster Crabbe's Arthritis Exercise Book*. Not because he has the disease but because so many of his friends do.

He notes that Hepburn, Cagney, Betty Ford, Rock Hudson and Henry Fonda suffer from arthritis, along with 360 million other people. Crabbe has written with Dr. Raphael Cilento a (Simon and Schuster) book on exercises and a lifestyle to relieve arthritic pain without medication.

Crabbe's success story points up again the ripple effect an

Olympic boycott can have on those whose lives are swallowed up in it. Out of the Olympic pools and the skating rinks of the past to make show-business millions came Sonja Henie, Eleanor Holm, Weissmuller, Crabbe, Herman Brix (the decathlete who became Tarzan as "Bruce Bennett"), Carol Heiss and Peggy Fleming.

The gold you take out of an Olympics cannot always be hung on a ribbon. One-100th of a second in an Olympic pool can mean more than eight years in a law school classroom or library.

WORLD CLASS LEPRECHAUN

MAY 8, 1980

Whenever you meet Eamonn Coghlan, your first temptation is to ask him how are things in Gloccamorra, and to wonder if he came by rainbow.

There is no need to ask, did your mother come from Ireland? Aye, you can see, and his mother's mother's mother—and so on, all the way back to Brian Boru. The eyes are as blue as the waters off Donegal, and when he talks you can hear the ripple of the trout stream, all right, and when he runs, he's the original barefoot gossoon from the turf fire in the cabin.

Ireland is a poor country, and there's not much to cheer about in its benighted provinces these days, but Eamonn Coghlan is the nearest thing to an all-Ireland hero since Danny Boy. From the Liffey to the Bogside, O'Connell Street to Drumlin Jail, he's done more for Ireland than Gladstone and Home Rule. As the man in the pub on Galway Bay puts it, "If he was any more popular, they'd have to hang 'im!"

Running has always been a national sport in Ireland, where the natives got plenty of practice leaving the scenes of exploding troop trains, or house-to-house searches by the dreaded "Black and Tans" of English constabulary. But the country was not electrified by the sport till 1956 with the winning of the gold medal in the Olympics by Ron Delany, a native of the Auld Sod, who beat the mighty John Landy, the New Zealander Murray Halberg and, saints be praised! the representative of Perfidious Albion itself, master Brian Hewson.

But Delany had caught the country by surprise. He had earlier emigrated Ireland—not in the coffin ships as in the Great Famine, but in a great winged aeroplane—to learn the tricks of international running at Villanova University in the USA.

Eamonn Coghlan is a runner who came into Irish consciousness much more gradually. He followed much the same route as Delany but, by the time the Montreal Olympics rolled around in 1976, he was as popular a topic of Irish conversation in the late-night pubs as The Trouble in Ulster itself. Eamonn Coghlan had twice won the American NCAA mile championships by that year and had stepped off a near-record 3:53.3.

When the Africans shunned the Olympics at Montreal, Ireland got the shamrocks out and, when Eamonn won both his mile heats breezing, they made ready to break out the good stuff along the Shannon. Alas! The hope of Ireland tied up in the last 300 meters, even losing a bronze medal in the closing strides to a German, Paul-Heinz Wellman, whom he had safely beaten in the heats. Coghlan had not faced the ultimate gold medal winner, John Walker, in the heats, but he had beaten the second-place finisher Ivo Van Damme, of Belgium, and it was popularly thought on the eve of the final that Walker had burned himself out in his blistering 3:36 heat.

When Eamonn lost, Ireland was philosophical. "He may not have won," a policeman in Dublin told his father. "But, by Jove, for four minutes he united all of Ireland!"

"That in itself is a record," a bystander observed.

Eamonn himself was less consolable. "You know," he told a friend, "fourth place is the absolute worst place to finish in an Olympics. Far better to be last."

He then had a choice: to take to Irish dreaming of what might have been, adopt a stream of Celtic fatalism, and to brood on a fate that let him finish three-tenths of a second off a gold medal—or to get back on a track and see if he could whittle those three-tenths down in four years. He could go back to social running with the Dunsmore Harriers—or he could come to America and challenge the world again.

Years of running on Villanova's outdoor board track had made Eamonn the undisputed bull of the woods, master of the indoor track, or, as track writers had it, Chairman of the Boards. He put up the world indoor record at 3:52:4, prompting an Irish journalist to remark, "If the Olympics were moved indoors, we could have another gold medal at last."

For Eamonn, the Olympics just may have been moved to the moon. On the surface, he would seem to be the safest of the world-class runners in the boycott controversy. The head of the International Olympic Committee, Lord Killanin, is an Irishman, nee William Morris. "That cuts no ice with the Irish," notes Eamonn sadly.

With Wellman out of the running, John Walker plagued with calf injuries, Ivo Van Damme tragically killed in a traffic accident and Africa's Filbert Bayi toying with the notion of running the 5,000 meters, and the rest of the top 1,500-meter contenders either boycotting or about to boycott, Eamonn wouldn't even need the boards to win at Moscow. "But," he gloomily admits, "the Irish government is applying pressure on the Irish Olympic Committee." The chances of Ireland being united for four minutes again this summer appear dimming.

This Sunday, at the UCLA-Pepsi Invitational track meet at Drake Stadium on the Westwood campus, Eamonn will don the green and gold of Ireland once again and meet up with four other forlorn athletes for whom Moscow is as long gone a dream as Camelot. Steve Scott, who chased Britain's Sebastian Coe to his world record 3:49 mile at Oslo, running 3:51.2 himself, Craig Masback, who was third to Scott and Coe in 3:52.1, Don Paige, the NCAA mile champion, and Steve Lacy, who ran a 3:54.7 indoors, will run in a great what-might-have-been race. If Eamonn wins, then doesn't go to the Olympics, it may turn out to be worse than finishing fourth. And there'll be no loud singing in the public houses along the Liffey this summer and the banshees will be heard as usual in that troubled land.

THE ONE THAT COUNTS

NOVEMBER 18, 1980

Everybody wants to be something, whether it's president of the United States or lead tenor at the Met. Some people want to be first-string quarterback, or a heavyweight contender.

Me. I always wanted to be barred from a casino.

I could just see myself, patch over one eye, red-lined black silk cape, white tie, a man of mystery, aloof, contemptuous. The Man who Broke the Bank at Monte Carlo. A guy who could do anything with a pack of cards, a pair of dice, a wheel. A tango dancer, the scourge of the croupiers, a man with numbered accounts in Swiss banks, the most-feared player on three continents. Every police force in the world has my picture, from Interpol to the French Surete. The greatest backgammon player who ever lived. A master at baccarat.

Well, I met the man who is living out my fantasy the other day. Half Japanese, half Austrian, Ken Uston cannot call for cards in any blackjack game in the world unless he wears a false beard or poses as a cowboy from Texas. Actually, he's from New York by way of San Francisco, and he learned odds at, of all places, Harvard and Yale.

You're supposed to learn Chaucer at those institutions, not when to say "Hit me." I mean, Nick the Greek never made Skull and Bones, but Ken Uston learned the laws of probability of blackjack at Harvard Business School while his classmates were wasting their time on the Dow Jones.

He went to work on the Pacific Stock Exchange after graduating but, one time, a bunch of computer analysts enlisted him in a scheme to break the blackjack dealers of Vegas. They didn't exactly do it, but Uston suddenly found he could make a month's salary on a turn of a card and he put away his pin-striped suit and subscription to *The Wall Street Journal* forever.

Now, in the rest of life, a "counter" can be something you sell pie a la mode or unlisted securities over. In a casino, it's a dirty name. A counter is a guy who keeps track of all the cards played out of the shoe at the blackjack table. When he bets, he knows what cards are likely to come up. He knows when to stand and when to take a hit. He's pretty sure what the dealer has. He destroys the house edge.

You don't beat the house going one-on-one. You have to go into a zone. You put together a "team." Not to cheat, mind you, just to count the cards.

Ideally, a team should be made up of guys who look like morticians on a holiday. But, Nevada has ways of spotting counters even if they look out of place without a coffin between them. Ken Uston began to get barred from casinos from one end of the Vegas Strip to the other.

In Reno, they did even worse than that. A casino goon broke his cheekbone and almost put his eye out one night. Uston was posing as a big loser from Texas at the time, but the pit bosses got suspicious when he began doubling-down on sure winners. He is, of course, suing.

He's also suing a casino in Atlantic City which barred him and his teammates after a $145,000 score. He also got knocked down by a passing car in the snow there, but it may have been an accident.

Casinos do not like the image of being open only to losers. But neither do they want to go broke. But, now, comes forward a Vegas operator named Herb Pastor, owner of the Treasury Hotel and Casino there, who has actually invited Uston to teach his patrons how to beat the house at blackjack. It's part of the old Western policy of making the roughest, toughest guy in town the marshal. I mean, give Wyatt Earp the tin star, and you clean up Dodge City in a hurry.

Will Ken Uston become Establishment? And teach his pupils how to lose? Ken Uston shakes his head emphatically. "A math teacher who teaches his classes two and two make five isn't going to be a math teacher very long," he argues.

Besides, counting cards is not illegal. Neither is recruiting a squad to count cards, although it's interesting that Uston's own rules for his teams provide that team members periodically take a lie detector test. To be sure they're trying for the home team, as they say around the racetrack.

It's hard for anyone who never even got a cherry on a slot

machine to drum up any sympathy for the casinos. Personally, I would rather Vegas ban losers, not winners. I would really rather they barred me. And not because I want to be a big glamorous mysterious international Raffles. Just because I can use the money elsewhere.

ANOTHER ROCKY STORY

DECEMBER 4, 1980

The first time I saw Rocky Bleier, 11 years ago in a hotel in Los Angeles, he didn't look much like a pro prospect. They had just brought him back from Vietnam, where they had carried him down a hill in a rubber bag with his right foot blown up, the one he used to cut on when he played in the backfield for Notre Dame.

When he began to talk about going back into pro football, I thought he must still be delirious. I turned to our companion, Joe deFranco, with my eyebrows raised, he put a finger to his lips as though we were in the presence of a guy who thought he was Napoleon.

Rocky was as emaciated as a Cypriot placekicker. He walked with a limp. He had about as much chance to play running back for the Pittsburgh Steelers as a guy who had a platform on roller skates for legs and sold pencils.

You see, Rocky had not exactly been Red Grange before that Vietnamese hand grenade shattered his foot. True, he had been elected captain at Notre Dame, but on the second ballot. George Gipp, he was not. There was no part for Ronald Reagan in Rocky Bleier's life.

Rocky rattled on that afternoon about his future in the pro ranks and, afterward, I wrote a Pollyanna-ish piece, upbeat, optimistic, hopeful. I don't want to say I didn't believe a word of it—I don't write anything I don't believe a word of—but I made it clear the opinions expressed were not necessarily those of the writer but merely those of Robert Patrick Bleier, and any resemblance to real people or events was purely coincidental. Not real, but imagined.

Well, there was a helluva part for Ronald Reagan, after all. And for Robert Urich, who'll play it when it's aired on ABC this

Sunday. It's the heart-warming story of the poor little crippled kid who made it all the way to the Super Bowl—four times.

Even at this late date, I find it difficult to believe Rocky made it from that rice paddy in Que San to the Super Bowl. He had no more business being in a backfield with Franco Harris than Don Knotts, but he lifted weights, ran sprints, worked out and ignored the skepticism of the world till he became a vital part of the best backfield in all of football.

He needed the encouragement of an owner, Art Rooney, skillfully played in the movie by Art Carney, an encouragement that drew resentment at first from other members of the Pittsburgh Steelers. There is a scene in the film where a burly lineman bitterly reproaches management for keeping the "cripple" in the lineup at the expense of younger, faster, but, ultimately, less dogged, determined players. "You think if this team wasn't owned by a Catholic and Rocky didn't play for Notre Dame, he would be around here?" he asks a quarterback belligerently in the film.

But Art Rooney didn't keep Rocky Bleier around because he was a Notre Dame man. He kept him around because he was a wounded serviceman. It's a better reason than most.

Incredibly, Rocky Bleier became, not the team charity, but the team star. For one thing, he was fearless. A guy who finds out that 4'9" Asians with hand grenades are more than a match for 11 Mean Joe Greenes is not apt to flinch at a block or drop a pass because he hears the footsteps of an unarmed man.

The measure of a great ball carrier is a 1,000-yard season. And Rocky put one up in 1976. He caught passes for 294 more that year. He is the fourth leading rusher in all Pittsburgh Steelers history. There isn't an orthopedic surgeon in the M.A.S.H. unit that brought him out who would believe it. He is the only guy in the history of the franchise whose speed in the 40 increased as he got older—from 5 flat down to 4.6.

Four Super Bowls are vindication enough, but loyalty paid off for Art Rooney. It usually does. Rocky Bleier was not about to let a Viet Cong patrol or an NFL secondary knock him out of football.

The Channel 7 flick, which has a love interest besides boy meets football, is derived from Rocky's book *Fighting Back*. I have a copy of that 1975 book in my library. The flyleaf is inscribed to me with the following words: "Jim, You started it six years ago with your fine article—I will always be indebted, thanks for everything, Rocky Bleier."

I'm embarrassed, Rocky. Like everyone else, I thought your career ended in that poncho liner they used to haul you down Million Dollar Hill. I thought the casualty list of the original 32 who went on the rescue mission August 20, 1969, included 9 dead, 2 missing in action, 21 seriously wounded and 1 career. I never thought you'd get to be the first Notre Dame man since Gipp to have a movie made of his life. But I didn't make you look good. And neither did Art Rooney. You made *us* look good. You made America look good.

MASTER OF THE CITY GAME

FEBRUARY 15, 1981

You look at No. 33 of the Boston Celtics and you think you've got the picture. Big white kid. All that goldilocks blond hair and a scraggly moustache. Skin so fair you could almost see through it. The big honest blue eyes of the rube at a shell game. He looks as if he's standing in a load of corn shucks.

OK. He's a rebounder, right? Comes in the game to get you a few boards while The Big Guy takes five to rest up. He sucks up a few fouls for you and knocks a few people around, not because he's mean, because he's clumsy.

He tries, oh, Lord, how he tries! But the Lord didn't give him much to work with. He'd need a run to jump over an egg, if you know what I mean. Comes in there late in the game when it's already out of hand one way or the other. A mop-up pitcher.

You look down the roster. Just as you guessed. He's from French Lick, Indiana. Went to Indiana State. Cow college. Moo U.

You don't get basketball players out of French Lick, Indiana. You get them off the playgrounds. The projects. The sidewalks of New York. Or the sidewalks of Chicago. Or North Carolina. Marquette. UCLA. You get apple pickers out of French Lick, Indiana. You find it on the map under "G—4." Go to Young's Creek and turn right.

What do the Celtics want with this kid, anyway? Somebody will sell him the Brooklyn Bridge. The Celtics want magicians like Bob Cousy. Cool cats like Sam Jones. The glowering Tom Heinsohn. Street-smart immortals like Bill Russell. Hondo Havlicek. Not some guy shooting baskets in the sycamores.

OK, he's too white, too slow, too dumb and too untested. Is this what put all those championship flags up in the rafters of

Boston Garden? Red Auerbach would faint. Or would he? Isn't he the one who signed this guy? Why isn't he getting Darrell Griffith or Joe Barry Carroll or somebody whose nickname is "The Glide" or "Dr. Dunkenstein" or "The Truck" or "Magic," for crying out loud?

Celtics fans want to know. Does this guy come with a load of pumpkins? What do we need him for? We already got a piano mover.

Well, that was the shower of skepticism under which Larry Bird came into the National Basketball Association a year ago, walking out of the tall corn, getting lost in the Callahan Tunnel. He had played his collegiate basketball at Indiana State University, which is not to be confused with UCLA, or even DePaul.

He had enrolled briefly at Indiana but quit there because he had never seen so many people in one place before ("Thirty-three thousand is not my idea of a school, it's a country.") and not, as some said, because he got his first look at the fast break as practiced by a Bobby Knight-coached team, and thought he might get run over.

The word was out—if you took Larry Bird, you got him, cornsilk and all. He was Down Home, moonlight on the Wabash, and he said "We wuz" and "You wuz" or "Me and my father, we . . . " American gothic. All he needed was the pitchfork.

But, when you put a basketball in his hands, this guy turned into the slickest article who ever sold a watch to a tourist or cut a deck on a boat. The kids under the street lights in Harlem had nothing on him. He wasn't flashy. He wasn't "Dr. J." Or "Magic." He was just there. Wherever the ball was. He wasn't fast. But, when you got the ball, they have to wait for you anyway, don't they?

A lot of people were upset when he was chosen Rookie of the Year over Magic Johnson—but not anybody who had seen him play a lot. And, in Boston, that came to around 14,490 a night, a Celtics record.

The Celtics had won only 29 games and lost 51 the year before the hick from French Lick got there. They won 61 and lost 21 with him on the boards. This year they're 46–14.

The other night, the Boston Celtics came into L.A. to play the world champion Lakers. The Forum was packed to the roof.There is no team the Laker fans would rather beat than the lordly Celtics. About half those pennants hanging from the Boston Garden roof were put there at the expense of the Lakers.

No player from the glory years of the Celtics ever put on a better exhibition against the world championship club than Larry Bird—not Cousy, Russell, Heinsohn, K. C. or Sam Jones, Ramsey, Sharman, Havlicek or Cowens. "Birdie", as the Celtics call him, even stole the ball from the imposing Kareem Abdul-Jabbar. And scored it each time.

He threw in 36 points, 8 field goals in a row, some from $2^1/_2$ point range, and he pulled down 21 rebounds. He had six assists. His outlet passes whistled to receivers like Jim Plunkett's. He beat the Lakers the way Cousy used to. The way Russell used to. The way the Celtics used to.

In the locker room later, he surveyed the crowd of interviewers brandishing microphones, notebooks and tape recorders as if they were all two-shot fouls. "Can I please just get dressed first?" he pleaded politely.

The press watched while he pulled on a pair of work pants, a lumber shirt and jogging shoes. "It looks like he's going out to put the hay in," whispered a print journalist. Around him, the street boys were putting on their spangled night costumes that they most prefer. Jewelry flashed in the lights. Bird didn't even have a wristwatch. In French Lick, they tell time by the cows.

The questions had their usual low in-depth quotient. Was this his best game ever? Well, he didn't like to compare. Did he especially like to beat the Lakers because of comparisons between him and Magic Johnson? No, he wanted to beat the Lakers because the Celtics had lost their last four games on the road, and they didn't want it to become a trend.

Did he feel the specialness of the Celtics tradition and want to carry it on? Well, he had never been a Celtics fan, particularly back home in Indiana, but, when he got to Boston and saw those pennants and numbers hanging from the ceiling, and heard the fans, he had come to appreciate the pride of being a Celtic. He was proud to be part of it, to be carrying it on.

The problem now for all the wiseguys of the NBA is going to be, how you gonna keep 'em down on the farm after they've seen L. B.? Do the scouts now have to fly into Terre Haute and rent a dog? Are there more basketball players under the harvest moon than there ever were under the neon? Or is the Bird in the hand just a needle in the haystack?

Either way, it's for sure his jersey will one day hang from the Boston Garden rafters, too. You'll have no trouble recognizing it—it'll be the one with hay on it.

AN AMERICAN
LEGEND

MARCH 15, 1981

"Legend—That which is characterized as something wonderful that occurred in the past, a series of remarkable events occurring to an individual or group believed to have historical basis in fact."
—Webster's New 20th Century Dictionary

INDIAN WELLS—Ever regret you didn't see DiMaggio hit? Gehrig homer? Hubbell pitch?

Feel cheated you never got to see Dempsey punch, Grange run, Jesse Owens jump, Nagurski block? Like to have seen Jones putt, Luisetti shoot, Sande ride or Seabiscuit race? Maybe you wish you could have seen Nijinsky dance, Barrymore act, Tilden volley?

All those are yesterday's roses. Faded dance cards in the attic. The memories of old men nodding in the sun over cobwebbed chess pieces. Heirlooms of the mind.

The old-timers watch the moderns, shrug, shake their heads and say, "Yeah, but you should have seen Cobb." Or Pie Traynor.

Sam Snead belongs to that past. Sam Snead came up when DiMaggio did. Gehrig and Ruth were still around. So were Jones, Sande, Hubbell, Grange and Owens. None of them was a bigger legend than Snead.

No one ever swung at a golf ball with the purity, the poetry Sam Snead did. Snead on a tee was a thrilling thing to watch.

It was pure Americana. The barefoot boy with the trap lines and the fishing pole with a cork on the line came walking out of the Blue Ridge Mountains of Virginia, the trail of the lonesome pine, to shock the sports world. He came from a long line of people who slept with their hats on and their rifles by the bed. His first golf club was a swamp maple limb with a knot in the

224

end and the bark left on for a grip. He didn't have boxes of new Titleists to hit—he had round rocks.

Sam could have been anything—soda jerk, farmer, prize-fighter. Or moonshiner. The sky was the limit down there in that army of North Virginia country where, Sam says, the hollows were so narrow "the dogs had to wag their tails up and down."

No one ever taught him how to hit a golf ball. He was double-jointed, rhythmical, had wrists like wagon tongues and could coil like a spring. No one had ever hit the ball as straight as Samuel Jackson Snead. He drove into the president of the Chesapeake & Ohio Railroad on a green one day and the man was apoplectic.

"Son, don't you know better than to hit a fairway shot into an occupied green?" he shrieked. "Mr. Bradley, that wasn't no fairway shot, that was my tee shot," Snead said. Since Alva Bradley had never seen a 345-yard tee shot, he made him do it again. Snead did.

What is so remarkable about Samuel Jackson Snead is, he's not in a wax museum someplace with his porkpie hat and Popeye arms. He's on a golf course, where he's been for over 50 years. He's 68 years old, and he shot a 69 in the opening round of the Vintage Invitational here the other day in a field that should be a patsy for Samuel Jackson—everyone in it is over 50. Sam is more used to shooting 69s in fields that include people 48 years younger.

Sam won the L.A. Open in 1945—and finished second in the same tournament on the same course in 1974. He won the Greensboro Open for the first time in 1938—and for the 12th and last in 1965. At age 52 years 10 months, he was the oldest ever to win a tournament.

They never got Sam out of the hills—or the hills out of Sam. He'd still rather hunt squirrels than tour Europe. He came to Hollywood periodically but it didn't take. Sam made the film, and then went home to soak his feet, and then back to Virginia to shoot ducks. His pleasures are biblical and simple. Once, when he went to a nightclub, he ordered soft drinks all night— then took the bottles home in his pocket to claim the deposit.

He played in a hat to cover his bald head and, today, only about 11 people in the world know he is bald. He won't wear a wig, just a hat. His humor runs heavily to barnyard, but his vocabulary has the "oot" and "aboot" of the Old Dominion. His handwriting, in Elizabethan script, would gladden the heart of the oldest schoolmarm in the land. But, otherwise, not the social graces for Sam Snead.

You might think you would find this legend of golf in fading old movie clips, or on the yellowed pages of a scrapbook. After all, he did win his first tournament the year DiMaggio broke in with the Yankees. But Snead, through the miracle of his own remarkable genes, is present, in person and intact in a palmetto hat and a 1-iron at the Vintage golf course this weekend.

He won 84 PGA tournaments, 22 more than anyone else, and 135 tournaments worldwide. He shot a 66 when he was 67 and a 68 when he was 69. It was figured out that, had he been able to shoot 69 in the last day, he would have won six U.S. Opens and tied four more. He never won any. But that was Snead.

No one was more exciting to watch on the golf course, with the possible exception of Arnold Palmer. No one had the trouble shots Snead had. Once, playing the Masters, on the third hole, a well-wisher, Freddy Corcoran, his manager, wondered where he was.

"He's over in the trees in the middle of all the squirrels and pine cones and needles and rocks," someone advised. "Good," nodded Corcoran, "he knows how to play that shot. I was afraid he was in the middle of the fairway."

He's an athletic marvel you might want to see before one of you dies. He's not gonna drive the ball into railroad barons 345 yards away anymore, but the singing swing is still there. He can still kick a doorsill 7½ feet up, he still crabs about photographers clicking on his backswing, he hasn't mellowed and he still won't give you strokes. "Every time a guy tells me he's 'between a 12 and a 14 handicap,' I say 'Oh-oh, here I go again.'"

If you missed DiMaggio and Hubbell and Gehrig and Owens and Grange and Barrymore and Garbo and Tilden, catch Snead. And stand when he enters the room. He's a genuine, dyed-in-the-wool-hat American legend, Dan'l Boone with a 1-iron, Huck Finn in a hat. Mark Twain would have loved him. Sam Snead, coonskin golfer. We shall not see his like again. A legend past his time.

TRACK AND FIELD'S HOTTEST DOUBLE FEATURE

JULY 31, 1981

The last time the world had anybody who could run faster and jump farther than anyone else on earth at the same time, Hitler was ruling Germany, Roosevelt was running for a second term, and the King of England was giving up his throne for love.

That's how hard it is to do.

The running is a joyous thing. You fall out of bed with the ability to do that. God is your partner. The jumping, you are bucking the theories of a bunch of German doctors in white smocks and wire glasses, running around with micrometers and test tubes and blood-pressure machines. They want to make a jump as refined and complex an operation as a Mars shot. They believe in their experiments in Europe. Anything that occurs in nature can be duplicated in the laboratory, they think. Just bring them the athlete and a slide rule and these Dr. Frankensteins will produce a world and Olympic record. If you look closely, maybe you can see the sparks coming out of the record setter.

Americans don't agree. "Do you teach a gazelle to jump?" they challenge. They have seen too many youngsters come wandering over to the long jump from the sprint paths, drop a handkerchief out at the world-record mark, and reach it with no more form than a guy leaving a raided crap game. In 1968, in Mexico City, a long jumper who had to be ranked no better than 10th in the field on form, rocketed so far through the air he almost overjumped the pit.

Bob Beamon, who never took off on the same foot twice, who had never bested 27'4" before, broke the world record by almost two feet and the Olympic record by almost three. His style had all the technique of a guy falling out of an airplane, but his 29'2½" was so astronomical it may not be broken in this century, and it was 12 years before anyone even jumped *twenty-eight* feet.

Still, when Carl Lewis, of the New Jersey Lewises, came along in the Year of our Lord 1980, proposing to run faster and jump farther than anyone else in the world, the wise men with the stop watches shook their heads. Not since Jesse Owens in Berlin in 1936 had anyone brought off this package. And Jesse himself thought it was a bad idea. "You're too small to jump, kid," he told Carl Lewis when Lewis was a schoolboy and still growing. "Stick to the ground."

The scam was, the jump had become too scientific, it was an engineer's proposition, not an athlete's.

Carl Lewis didn't believe it. The son of a father who sprinted and long-jumped and a mother who hurdled at Tuskegee Institute, he grew to be bigger—and faster—than Jesse Owens, and longer off the tee than any jumper in the world. The jumper from Germany, Lutz Dombrowski, probably a product of the test tubes, finally broke the 28-foot barrier in the Moscow Olympics last summer. (Dombrowski wanted to be a soccer player but the state had other ideas.)

Only 19, Carl Lewis became the first athlete since Jesse Owens to win the NCAA long jump and the 100-meter sprint this year. He set the world sea-level long-jump record of 28'-3½" in The Athletics Congress meet in Sacramento, where he also jumped 28'7¾" before a slight aiding wind. Carl also holds the sea-level 100-meter record of 10 flat. Jimmie Hines set the world mark of 9.95 in the same rarefied air of Mexico City that Bob Beamon sailed through.

But Carl Lewis does not think he can chicken-scratch or frog-leap his way to a world record or a gold medal the way earlier sprinter-jumpers in this century may have. In his own way, his assault on the world mark is as carefully orchestrated as the invasion of the low countries.

"I take a longer run, 147 feet 6 inches, than almost any other world-class jumper," he explains. Velocity is important to his jump, because altitude is not, he says. "I take exactly 21 steps and step number one is important as step 21. You have to lift off vertically, but I try to keep running through the air. I take two full turns with my legs, because the thing is not to lean your body foreward. That moves your legs backward and shortens your jump."

Lewis' key to jumping is not to soar too high. He's rather like a low iron punched under the wind to a holding green.

"He wins because he breaks the world 40-yard record going down the runway," insists a British coach. "Even if you put a drag chute on him, he'd go 28 feet with that speed."

When Carl Lewis wins a sprint, he can say "Thanks, pop," or "Thanks mom and pop." When he wins a jump, he can thank Thomas Edison. That is because he has seen so many reruns of Bob Beamon's Mexico City jump movie, he can recite it the way a *Star Trek* groupie can recite the plot of any episode. The walls of his room at the University of Houston are festooned with charts of Beamon's jump, with arrows indicating the air-drag. He knows what foot Beamon took off on, what he did while aloft, and how and on what foot he came down.

He is going to run in a special "World Record 100 Attempt" Saturday at the Arco Jesse Owens Games at UCLA. These games are a national competition put on by the oil company for youngsters age 10–15 and, as a boy, Carl Lewis participated in four of them. It was here that the late Jesse Owens advised him to forget jumping.

In a way, though, Carl Lewis is lucky. He has applied scientific techniques to his jumping and will continue to do so. Owens and Beamon relied more or less on what they were born with. If they knew what they were doing, Carl might be looking at 33 feet to break today.

YOU'D NEVER THINK SHE IS ONE OF THEM

DECEMBER 27, 1981

You can tell right away that Mary Decker Tabb isn't a world-class runner. A world-class chorus girl, perhaps. World-class model, maybe. Brooke Shields in cleats.

Mary is 23 years old now, but if you saw her in Disneyland looking lost you would probably buy her a lollipop and prop her up on the sergeant's desk and take her picture with a police cap on and page her mother.

If you don't think this is unusual, you haven't been to any international women's track meets lately. To give you an idea, Mary went into the women's locker room in Hungary last year and rushed right out, blushing. "I thought I told you I wanted the *women's* dressing room!" she wailed to officials. "That is the women's dressing room," she was told. Mary recalls she was flabbergasted. From the muscular builds she had seen from the rear, she had thought she wandered into a touring troup of the Green Bay Packers by mistake.

Women's international track and field stars are beginning to look like someone you might call "Bubba." At a time when 90 percent of the adult female world wants to look like Bo Derek, they're working more towards looking like Bo Schembechler. In a world of perfect "10s," they're "minus 3s."

The kind they're turning out in Eastern Europe, America's girl athletes are not even sure they're human, let alone female. They're about as human as a tractor, they believe. They're not born, they're assembled. If you listen closely, they believe, you can hear the hum. If they cough, a printout may emerge. Or so their American counterparts believe.

The world record holder in the 1,500 meters is Russia's Tatyana Kazankina. When Mary Decker Tabb ran her American record 1,500 of 3:59.4 in Zurich, Tatyana beat her by a full seven seconds. "When I first ran against her as a young girl in Moscow years ago, I used to beat her in the 800. The girl I ran against now looks like her brother," Mary says.

A lot of people thought Mary Decker had retired. That's because she was one of the most precocious athletes in American history. At age of 14, running in teeth braces, she was beating the world's best in the half-mile and, in fact, set the American half-mile record. She ran the mile in 4:37, the half in 2:02.4. She set the indoor half-mile record and she did this as an "Amazon" of 89 pounds and 4 feet 11 inches tall. "Wait'll she grows up!" said the track-and-field world.

When she grew up—she gained 25 pounds and seven inches by her 17th birthday—Mary Decker could hardly walk, let alone run. She was the youngest person in the history of Orange County to need a cane. When she tried to run, it felt as if her shins had caught fire.

What had happened was that the muscle sheath surrounding her shin bones had lost its elasticity and couldn't expand. One filled with blood which created such pressure it was like having gout along the entire leg. Mary could not only tell when it was going to rain, she could tell when it was going to be high tide.

A New Zealand Olympian, Dick Quax, persuaded Mary to have an operation that had proved successful with him. It was an operation on the sheath, or fascia, which had so alleviated his suffering that he won a silver medal in Montreal and broke the world record in the 5,000 in Europe later.

It worked for Mary, too. She returned to the track and became the first woman to break two minutes for the half-mile, and to break the world record, indoors, for the 1,000-yard race.

Mary won the 1,500 at the Olympic trials in 1980 and would have been our best bet at the middle distance in Moscow if President Carter didn't decide to get the Russians out of Afghanistan by placing an embargo on foot racers, which proved to be like telling a naughty kid he couldn't have his spinach if he didn't shape up.

Mary would not have beaten the Soviet wonder runner Tatyana Kazankina (who Mary calls "Ted," for what she feels are obvious reasons) at Moscow, but she might certainly have won a medal. She will set out on her campaign for the 1984 Olympics next month at the 23rd annual Sunkist Invitational track meet at the Sports Arena. She married marathoner Rob Tabb last September, the legs are fine—in fact she looks more like a ballerina than a miler—and if anyone wanders into her dressing room by mistake, he will be quite sure it is not the Green Bay Packers.

COACH OF THE LIVING DEAD

DECEMBER 5, 1982

It starts like a horror movie. The man comes into focus wearing a look of horrified resignation. It is the face of a man who knows there is no longer any use in screaming.

There are 60,000 people going crazy around him, but he crouches there on the sidelines, hands on knees. He appears to be staring under the wheels of a train at some unspeakable horror. His mouth is turned down, his nose is wrinkled in disgust and disdain and his eyes register sheer terror. His is the face of a man tied to a plank with a buzz saw slicing its way toward his torso. His eyes are slightly bugged, as though a tombstone just talked to him. His face is haunted. God knows what evil terrors lurk in his mind. He is a man looking at his own corpse. Dr. Jekyll looking at Mr. Hyde. A great part for Lon Chaney.

He is Don Coryell and your heart goes out to him. This is a man who has been hanging on a cross or a tree or the highest yardarm in the British Navy too long. The flesh is loose, the pallor evident. The look is a cross between that of a man who just had his pants stolen or who just ate a plate of cold cucumbers with spoiled sour cream. Or both. I have seen guys look happier throwing up.

And what is Coryell staring at? His own coffin? A skeleton? A squad of police come to take him kicking and screaming to the funny farm?

No. Coach Coryell is staring at nothing worse than the San Diego Chargers. They are a high-spirited bunch of young men as carefree as puppies in a meadow. They do not look like a menace to society. Most of them just look like the boy next door, not choir-boy murderers.

Coryell is not fooled. His face shows it. He knows this is a football team that has its back to the wall if it is leading 24−0. He knows that they are reckless squanderers of points, that they throw leads around like sailors throw money.

You see, Coryell painstakingly draws these complicated formulas on blackboards for his players, all these foolproof get-rich-quick plays. He's like a father who sends his kid off into the world with 50 grand and, in a week, is getting a wire from a Baltimore flophouse asking for money. These guys are the prodigal sons of football.

No wonder Coryell has the look of a guy who has just been asked by the detectives, "All right, coach, after you killed the mother, what did you do with the baby?" Coryell starts to hang his head *during* the game. If his team is ahead only 14−0 at the end of the first quarter, he wants to concede. He is like a politician who knows he needs to pile up big pluralities in the big cities before the upstate vote moves in, or the master chess player who can see he is going to be mated even when he appears well ahead.

The Chargers have more good players than anybody who played this game since the 1940 Chicago Bears. How many franchises could lose John Jefferson and Fred Dean and not even notice they're missing?

But they are the playboys of the Western world. They can't stand prosperity. Easy come, easy go. You all saw what happened last Saturday. They had a 24−0 lead by the first commercial break. By the half, or shortly thereafter, they needed a comeback to get back in the game with the Dolphins. That's the Chargers for you. Five times this year San Diego scored 40 or more points a game, once more than 50. But three times they allowed 40 or more points, and three other times they allowed 30 or more points. They haven't shut anybody out in years.

So you can see Coryell knows what he's looking at. He notices the blue lips and the pointed teeth of the guy who opens the castle door. He knows enough to look under the bed and deadbolt the door and not go down in the cellar. You'd look like Don, too, if you worked all your life to build up a fortune in points for these profligates and then watch them throw them off balconies to the rabble. How'd you like to go into every hand knowing you needed four aces or better to break even?

PATCHING
AN IMAGE

DECEMBER 16, 1977

In 1968, when he announced he was going to jump the Grand Canyon, Evel Knievel was the toast of America. The greatest authentic Western hero since General Custer. Wyatt Earp on a motorcycle. George Hamilton made a movie on his life. Crowds followed him. State fairs competed for his services. So did The Tonight Show. The Today Show. The White House. They brought out a line of Evel Knievel toys. And they outsold Mickey Mouse's.

In 1974, when he finally jumped a canyon—sort of—he became the second-most identifiable American of his day. He bought airplanes by the squadron, cars by the fleet. He had more boats than the Chilean navy. He jumped his motorcycle over sharks, snakes, trucks. He dressed himself in gold and diamonds. He marched to a different drummer than the rest of the world. He was America's Accident. He had to be put back together again more often than a museum dinosaur. He had more broken bones than a slaughterhouse. He was either in a spotlight or in traction. He had more press agents than MGM in its heyday. He was copy.

Then, on September 21, 1977, this multimillionaire folk hero bought a $2 baseball bat at Sears Roebuck and broke the arm of a relatively puny, 140-pound, cheerful little press agent named Shelly Saltman in a methodical, seemingly senseless, one-sided beating in the parking lot of 20th Century Fox's commissary— and the music promptly stopped.

The royalties on the toys fell to the vanishing point. Nobody wanted a doll that went around beating up people.

The guy on the phone wasn't the President, it was the district attorney. The offers dried up. Evel had missed this jump, all right. This was not a part for George Hamilton. This was a part for Conrad Veidt—a guy in jackboots and a monocle.

Suddenly, Uncle Sam was at the door with a bill for $1.5 million in back taxes. Bankruptcy loomed. The $10,000-a-month payroll was in jeopardy. So were the $20,000-a-month payments. The diamond-headed cane went into mothballs.

Nobody wanted the image of a red, white and blue hero beating up a little publicist with a ball bat. Evel had really broken his back this time. He wouldn't clear these sharks.

What had happened? Well, Shelly Saltman had written a seemingly harmless little diary-type book on his adventures as Evel's press agent on the Snake River Canyon jump. It was hardly *Roots* or *Gone With The Wind*. Bob Kirsch didn't review it. Neither did *Time*. Nor the *New Yorker*. It never even came out in hard cover.

Among the people who didn't read it was the guy it was about. Evel Knievel says he didn't even know it was published till one day he went to a news stand in Hollywood to buy a book on Elvis Presley. Right next to that, he saw a book about a person he knew better. *Evel Knievel On Tour*, it was titled. "The Inside Stuff On The High-Living Daredevil Hero No PG-Rated Movie Could Ever Show!"

The man who had tried to jump the Snake River in a wingtip fuel cannister, who had orbited sharks in a sputtering Yamaha, who proposed to jump 40,000 feet into a haystack without a chute, was driven into a rage by a paperback. Once again, he hit the wrong lever. He did the one thing you shouldn't do with a damaging book: put it on page one.

I got a call from Evel the other day. Once again, he is trying to put the bones back together, to reconstruct the image. Once again, Evel Knievel has scattered pieces of himself all over the parking lot. His image is at ground zero.

"First of all, I will respect what you write," he began. "I hope so," I told him. "Next," he said, "what would you do if someone said you didn't like your mother, were a booze hound, anti-Semitic, a womanizer and a drug addict?" (For the record, the Saltman book accuses Knievel of no more serious drug addiction than putting aspirin in a bourbon and water, or an occasional Librium under the tongue in periods of stress.)

"Well," I said, "after I stopped laughing, I would probably sue."

"I sued Dell Publishing for $200 million!" roared Knievel. "Meanwhile, my wife, my mother, and my kids have to read that about me!" Then he mellowed. "Listen!" he said. "Nobody ever accused me of being sane. Nobody ever accused me of going along with society."

There are those who would say society is going along with him. Under a unique "work furlough" system worked out by his attorney, Paul Caruso, and Judge Edward Rafeedie, Knievel is merely an overnight guest of the county of Los Angeles. He reports to jail in a chauffeur-driven Stutz, submits each night to a strip and change into prison nightgown, and is behind bars only from 9:30 p.m. to 6:30 a.m. His days he spends at the Sheraton Universal Hotel like any other movie-struck tourist.

But Knievel says he is using his days at the office to plot a 40,000-foot free fall from the bomb bay of an airplane into a pile of haystacks. Some believe there is a large needle in this haystack from the favoritism shown this prisoner in jail. Others however feel the judge has precedent in the Bible: "Sufficient unto the day is the Evel thereof."

HE NEEDN'T TAKE NUMBER; IT'S HIS

JUNE 12, 1981

When the historians of the future get together to decide which athletic numbers to retire in that great clubhouse in the sky, they're going to have a great deal of trouble assigning No. 32.

Whom does it belong to? Jim Brown? Sandy Koufax? O. J. Simpson? Magic Johnson?

No. 44 belongs to Henry Aaron, right? Well, what about Jerry West? Reggie Jackson?

No. 3 was Babe Ruth, of course. But wasn't it also Bronko Nagurski?

Is No. 6 irrevocably Bill Russell? Or is it Stan Musial?

But, No. 43 is, was, and always will be, the Right Honourable Richard Lee Petty, the chairman of the board of auto racing. Richard is not, like, the Babe Ruth of auto racing. He's more like the Joe DiMaggio. He does what he does effortlessly, gracefully, without undue flash, with such a quiet perfection it's almost as if he's making a mockery of his game. A "look, ma, no hands!" approach.

Twenty-four years of the most hairy wheel-to-wheel racing and he doesn't have a mark on him. He has all his teeth, marbles, limbs, walks without a limp, can eat steak and corn, doesn't need glasses and his thick, black hair doesn't look as if it was ever set afire.

You'd probably never guess Richard Petty's profession if you didn't read the papers. He doesn't look like a guy you'd ever call Fireball or Shorty or Smokey or Speedy or Junior. He looks like a guy you'd call Clarence or Richard.

The squire of Randleman, N.C., would be right at home

catching the 4:02 to Westport with *The Wall Street Journal* under his arm. Race drivers all come from Carolina, but not very far. They wear wool hats, carry wrenches in their pockets, keep a sharp eye on the rear-view mirror for revenue agents and have a dog. So does Richard, but Richard Petty's been known even to wear a tie. And, no one ever called him "Dick."

The Pettys have been in racing so many generations now it's a surprise they don't come with clutches for feet. Richard Petty has climbed in more car windows in his time then 50 auto thieves.

This Sunday, he'll climb into the family sedan, a red and blue Buick with the familiar 43 on it, and take out after victory No. 193 in race No. 852. The only guy who's made more money out of a stock car than Richard Petty is Henry Ford. Richard Petty has won $4,210,000 and he habitually picks up more money in a car in a month then Bonnie and Clyde's getaway driver. It is a career he took over from daddy and is being taken over by his son, Kyle, giving rise in the mountains of Carolina to the saying, "If its got wheels, get a Petty."

Like his car, Richard is 43. But since his only dissipation is big, fat cigars, he isn't looking to park old No. 43 in the near future. "Retire at 44? Heck, I won't even be slowing down!" he scoffs. He points out that Bobby Unser won Indy this year at age 47. So far as Richard Petty is concerned, Unser *did* win.

"In stock car racing, if you commit a violation, they let you know right away," he says. "They black-flag you off the track on the next lap and tell you to get back in position or get disqualified. Unser would have lost his eight car lengths under NASCAR, but not the race."

In view of his success in cars with roofs on them, people often wonder why Richard Petty didn't get bored with the tamer closed-chassis racing and try the open-cockpit running at Indy.

"Because," says Richard sunnily, "racing is like any other sport. You have to make up your mind what you're good at and stick to it. You can't be good at baseball and football, too. You can't be a good tackle and a good fullback. Guys who try both are either good in one, adequate in the other—or adequate in both. I plan never to be 'adequate.'"

No. 43 takes dead aim on No. 193 this Sunday in the Warner Hodgdon 400 Race at Riverside, with $180,460 at stake. If Petty doesn't get win 193, maybe he'll be in the top five for the

506th time or in the top 10 for the 602nd time. No one has ever dominated his sport more than Old No. 43 has, not Babe Ruth, Jim Brown, Knute Rockne, Joe Louis or even Bjorn Borg.

Ruth once hit 20% of all the home runs hit in his league. Richard Petty has won 27% of all the races in his career.

Around the garages in Dixie, they say Richard wasn't really born, he was assembled and modified. When he won the Firecracker 400 once, the presenter tried to praise him for his "great heart." A rival driver, Marvin Panch, shook his head. "Richard doesn't have a heart," he explained. "It's a fuel pump."

AN ACTOR ON CANVAS

DECEMBER 15, 1977

Lots of people think that Alex Karras, the left tackle turned thespian, learned to act when he came to Hollywood to make George Plimpton's *Paper Lion*. He didn't. Alex Karras learned to act in the center ring at the old Olympia Arena in Detroit, and in a traveling roadshow that played the bright lights of Iowa, Indiana, Illinois and Wisconsin.

It wasn't the Old Vic, and they didn't learn method acting. But it was a tough school. It wasn't the old Orpheum circuit. It was the wrestling circuit.

Anyone who doesn't think pro wrestlers are consummate actors doesn't know wrestling. To be sure, every performance is bravura. You don't play to the critic from *The Times*. You play, as Alex Karras says, "to the guy in the 75-cent seat."

You have to be able to do *Camille, King Lear* or even *Carmen*. The gestures are operatic, but you have to have some Hamlet in you. You have to be an acrobat. You have to learn how to fake a punch, pretend to be hurt, writhe in simulated agony—in short, a stunt man.

The guys in the white hats always win, but the black hats make all the money. The Lon Chaney parts are in demand. A wrestling match is part morality play and part Disney nature study, and it is beamed to the same audience. It is an acted-out comic book. It's also kind of true to life. The good guys never lose in the end. But the bad guys get all the money.

Alex was right at home in this milieu. He started as a "baby face," the wrestlers' own term for the good guy. "I started out wrestling to supplement the terrible income I got from football," he explains. "I was making $17,500 from the Lions and Merlin Olsen was making $68,500 from the Rams." Alex dropped the good-guy pose in the ring as soon as he saw where the money was. "I went from 'Cuddles' Karras to 'Killer' Karras in one night."

Wrestling wasn't quite as strictly rehearsed as, say, the Metropolitan Opera. The characters had a certain amount of leeway. "They (the promoters) would say to us 'OK, tonight, you win, and you lose. You guys figure it out between you.'"

It didn't always work. One night, Killer Karras and his partner in crime, "Crippler" Konovski, also a defensive lineman in the real world, climbed in the ring against a couple of baby faces, twins by birth, and All-American boy types by features. "They looked like two John Davidsons with all those dimples and hair spray, and Crippler Konovski, he went, like, ape. He didn't have too far to go. Anyway he went over and he was shaking his finger at these two and he was screaming 'When you come out you come out for freakin' real!' And they like to have jumped into each other's arms, they were so scared. Well, there was a real riot that night. There was a whole bunch of sailors and farm workers and somebody ripped Konovski's leg open with a knife, and the cops came, and this rookie cop (Karras hated rookie anything) came in, and he was shaking and I said 'Your gun! Pull your gun!' And he pulled his gun and I lifted him up, and pointed him at the crowd."

The wrestling troupe, snarling and bullying in the ring, actually traveled around as sedately as nuns on a picnic. "They would read a lot between shows and call up their brokers and all," Karras says. "We had this one guy, Gypsy Joe, who used to buy up land wherever he went. At the end of his career, he owned, like three states, and you had to be careful. If you said the scenery looked nice, he'd go out and buy it. He ended up with more land than the Interior Department. Sometimes he'd forget what state it was in."

The audience, Karras says, was "hard-core illiterate—which is a step up from football crowds." He adds: "It's a wonderful form of entertainment. It's been around for 400 years, and you can still go in for a dollar-fifty and work all your aggressions out. You don't have to plunk down $12 as you do to watch football, which is so boring now. I never go to football games, but I go down to wrestling and watch the crowd."

Karras will be wrestling for pay as usual and to a script as usual again Wednesday on CBS. As usual, he won't be playing a baby face. Iago Karkus, the character he plays, will come easy to him. But, then, most do. Karras was as born to act as Alfred Lunt. It's not your basic night-before-Christmas show, but is the story of the eccentric world of pro wrestling called *Mad Bull*. They could have written a part in it for Crippler Konovski but, if the leading man turned out to look anything like a quarterback from Princeton, he would have spoiled the ending.

THE ETERNAL COWBOY

JULY 13, 1981

You'd know him if he were on TV in a cowboy hat lipping snuff. If you were a rodeo buff, you'd know him if he was flopping under the horns of a 700-pound running steer and dragging him to the ground or roping and tying a bawling calf. If you are a Green Bay Packer, you'd know him if Dallas had the ball on the four-yard line because he'd be the one with the ball.

He looks like 190 pounds of trouble just sitting there. He's coiled. You'd imagine the members of the Dalton Gang looked like this. He looks as if he might have a price on his head somewhere west of the Brazos. Wyatt Earp would get nervous if he rode into town.

He was the genuine spurs-on-the-boots, chaps-on-the-Levis, hammered-copper-on-the-belt-buckle article, the only cowboy on the Dallas Cowboys.

He wasn't fast, he wasn't big. He was just dangerous. He hit with the outraged fury of a surprised mountain lion.

The Cowboys were "America's Team," and Walt Garrison was as American as a coyote's howl. The team had Calvin Hill, Duane Thomas, Robert Newhouse, Bob Hayes, Golden Richards and Don Perkins in his years, but Walt Garrison was the guy they gave the ball to when the play had to work or the game was lost.

He was raised deep in the heart of Texas, but he had to go to school in Oklahoma, at State, because he was considered too slow for offense and too small for defense in the Lone Star State. The Cowboys waited clear till the fifth round to draft him because he ran the 40 in only 4.75. And, in Dallas, defensive tackles ran faster than that. Even when he slowed to 5.2 in the 40 he was still the Cowboys' bread-and-butter player. Garrison, like Billy the Kid, was quick on the draw. He shot you first. You had to reach quick or you were dead.

Don Meredith, his quarterback, put it in perspective with his tongue in cheek: "If you needed four yards, you'd give the ball to Walt Garrison, and he'd get you four yards. If you needed 20 yards, you'd give the ball to Walt Garrison—and he'd get you four yards."

The unusual part was, Walt Garrison didn't want to be a football player. He wanted to ride bulls, not buses. When some of the guys sign with the Cowboys, they want the team to buy them tax-free bonds or oilfields. Garrison wanted a horse trailer. When the team publicist reached him in a phone booth one time and told him he had a number for him to call, he asked "Do you have a pencil?" "No," Garrison said, "but I have a pen knife."

When he first played for the Cowboys, the club would have a team meeting the night before a game. Garrison would attend. Then he would get in his pickup truck and ride to a nearby town where they had a rodeo. He would bulldog dagger-horn steers on the evening before he would wrestle the Los Angeles Rams the next day. Anything without horns held no terror for Walt, and Merlin Olsen only had his painted on.

Still, Garrison was not your basic *Sports Illustrated*-cover, inspire-a-novel pro football star. The Cowboys made him get off horseback—and bulls' horns—during the season. But during the off-season, Walt got out his snuff box and lasso and went chasing steers and calves again. He starred in a film showing unusual off-season occupations of football players and, in the course of the filming, the narrator became fascinated with his snuff-dipping. The announcer had never seen anyone do it, outside of costume movies by guys wearing wigs or dancing the minuet.

Garrison extolled the virtues of smokeless tobacco and the U.S. Tobacco Company saw the footage and signed "that Cowboy" to a contract on the spot. Garrison was able to quit pro football on the spot.

He was able to quit everything when he married the daughter (Pam) of one of Texas' richest men, B. F. Phillips. Walt is in Los Angeles this week for the running of the Skoal Dash For Cash Futurity at Los Alamitos Saturday night.

So Walt Garrison's life is no *Cowboy's Lament.* He got the hat, the horse, the girl, the gold watch and everything. Also, the *Home on the Range.* Nor was it *The Kid's Last Ride* for the last Cowboy to play for the Cowboys. He still goes out lassoing dogies on the college circuit and is a certified card-carrying Cowboy, No. 32, in the Rodeo Cowboys Association. Only now, he doesn't have to get Tom Landry's permission. He also gets to spread the joys of smokeless pipe tobacco. "Jist a pinch between your gum 'n cheek . . . "

Fond
Farewells

LIFE FINALLY CAUGHT MARCIANO WITH A SUCKER PUNCH

SEPTEMBER 2, 1969

When news of the death by shooting of Stanley Ketchel reached Wilson Mizner in 1910, his response was swift. "Start the count, he'll get up," he said.

A lot of us today are wishing there were an honest referee in a cornfield in Iowa. We'd never seen Rocco Francis Marchegiano go to more than one knee before. The count never reached three. To get to 10 over The Rock, you'd have to multiply.

Alas! Rocky Marciano, of all people, got a short count from life. The count has reached 11. The Rock has lost his first fight.

"He could fight an airplane," they used to say of Rocky in the better New England gyms. Ironic. It was the one thing he couldn't fight.

Rocky lived life lately as if it were the 15th round and he was behind on points. Every time I saw him of late, he was on the dead run. Rocky chased a buck the way he chased Ezzard Charles. It finally caught him with a sucker punch. It must have been a tremendous punch.

You could throw a loaded safe at Rocky in his prime and not make him stop coming in. He was as unstoppable as a flood. The night he fought Ezzard Charles, his nose was so split in two, and spurting, he didn't need a doctor, he needed a plumber. Sixty seconds later, Charles was crumpled on the floor like a mop with a broken handle.

Rocky didn't take people out with one punch. That was the trouble. He didn't induce nice clean unconsciousness the way Joe Louis did. Rocky put people in a wheelchair. He paralyzed one poor fellow who tried to mix with him. It is melancholy to consider also that Ezzard Charles, who fought 23 savage rounds with Rocky, is walking around today with the aid of an orthopedic cage.

It was not that Rocky meant to cripple people. He just meant to win the fight. He couldn't do it with a dazzling left hook. He didn't have one. He had a club for a left and an ax for a right. He sawed people in half.

I always thought, if you could cut Rock's hand off at the wrist and weigh it, it would weigh twice as much as the ordinary fist. His nickname was part description. His fists were like boulders swung on strings. Velocity punchers, like Joe Louis and Sugar Ray, knocked you out for the same reason a car going 70 mph will kill you while one going 2 mph might not even knock you down. When Rocky's fists hit you, the speed didn't matter. It was like cracking nuts with a anvil.

Outside the ring, he was the gentlest athlete I have ever known. There is a new breed of snarling winners today, but Rocky was apologetic. Who can ever forget the concern and kindness with which he bent over to pick up the helpless Archie Moore in 1955? The compassion was genuine. Even though a minute before Rocky was a dervish of furious onslaught. His boxing style was crude. His lifestyle was championship all the way.

I have caught up with Rocky many times over the years. But the definitive recollection I have of him is the first time. It was at Grossinger's in New York State in 1953 when he was training to turn Roland LaStarza into six feet of lumps.

It was Rocky's day off from sparring and he was sitting shirtless on the porch reading *A House Is Not a Home*. I was playing catch with Dr. Iannone, a Brockton pal of Rock's.

We saw a black Mercury with Pennsylvania license plates

drive up outside the hanger which served as a gym. I chased an errant toss from the doctor, and I heard four Negroes laughing softly as they came back to the Mercury from the gym with the sign "Sorry, No Sparring Today" on it. "Drive all the way up from Philly to read a sign," one of them sighed as they stepped in the car prepared for the 250-mile trip home.

I ran to Rocky. "Those guys drove all the way up from Philly," I told him. Rocky was immediately concerned. He put the book down, hurried over to them.

It was an odd little scene. I remember the fellas all took their hats off to shake hands with the champ as I introduced them. Rocky chatted with them for a half-hour. *They* broke it off.

It was near enough to fight time so that Rocky should have been on edge. He should have snarled, "Don't you know it's my day off?" or "Can't you see I'm reading?"

Rocky retired undefeated. He died the same way. "Champ" will never have quite the same meaning for me.

LAST OF THE VICTORIANS

SEPTEMBER 19, 1970

Someone once said of the late Perry T. Jones that he was a "combination of Marie Antoinette and Stanley Ketchel."

He was the last of the Victorians. He came from a prosaic-enough background. He was never what you might call rich, but whenever you were around him you could almost hear the sterling silver tea service rattling.

Perry drank out of china cups, and he had the exaggerated respect for "manners" one finds in the over-privileged. He was bridge-party American. Pasadena Gothic. But, inside, he was like a fighter who never stops moving in. He had some of the instincts of a guy who hops freights.

It took awhile to know Perry—like, a decade if he liked you, a quarter of a century if he could tolerate you, and never if he considered you common.

He had standards but they were not rigid. Hardly anyone ever called him "Perry." He met with kings and prime ministers, movie czars and real czars, dukes and earls. He knew every dowager on Orange Grove Avenue as well as Doheny Drive. But his world was bounded on the south by Clinton Avenue, on the north by Hollywood—and on the east by Wimbledon and the west, Australia. The Los Angeles Tennis Club was his castle, but all tennis was his domain.

He could never play the game very well. He couldn't teach it at all. He just loved it—the way a widowed mother loves her only child. He never had time for anything else once he found tennis—neither a wife nor a fortune. Not politics, diplomacy, government or philosophy. His idea of a foreign policy was "Win Wimbledon!"

He could look out his office window any afternoon and see the crowned heads of tennis. It must have made him feel like Talleyrand—because he crowned them.

He made Southern California the tennis incubator of the world—by providing the best competition, facilities, cooperation and instruction. A tennis player might grow up in Cincinnati or Montebello; Richmond, Virginia, or Arequipa, Peru; or the Philadelphia Main Line. He was nothing till he had tested and honed his game against the California superstars who came out of Perry Jones' assembly line. Everywhere he looked on his desk was an autographed picture of tennis greats of the half-century who owed this man a great deal. The Davis Cup itself was on it for awhile.

Fussy, arbitrary, demanding, he wore bow ties and tinted glasses and no day was too hot for him to appear with his collar unbuttoned or sleeves rolled up. He could spot a tennis player 20 blocks away—but he was not like some mentors who didn't care if their proteges pulled wings off birds or dealt blackjack in the dorm as long as they could score an ace or bring the Davis Cup back to America. Perry once barred Pancho Gonzalez because he was a school drop-out, an antic which almost got him picketed and prosecuted. But Perry stood his ground and held his serve and, years later, someone asked Pancho if he forgave him and Pancho growled "For what? For making me go back to school?"

I thought Perry was the most exasperating old man I ever met for the first 10 years of our acquaintanceship. The last 10, I always looked forward to our meetings. He never gave up trying to reform me. I found his devotion to a game that America seems to have passed by, at first, quaint, and then, admirable. In a world of reeds, he was a tree. He didn't run his empire by poll. He took a sampling of one man—a Mr. Jones.

They jimmied up the game in recent years. They tried to get it on the Eye and over by midnight. It must have been traumatic for Perry but he would have put in points-after-touchdown to advance tennis. "Some people think the game is shot through with gold," he once told me. "But I can tell you, since 1923, tennis has been a struggle. We have never made as much as $10,000 from our (Pacific Southwest) tournament. I would have to beg, borrow, and, if not steal, at least juggle to keep the other 70 tournaments going and send our great players to Wimbledon and Forest Hills."

Perry Jones was tennis' door-to-door salesman. It was not a job he liked, but it was for a game he loved.

There was an empty chair at the recent Pacific Southwest tournament and no answer on a phone which would always be busy this time of year. Perry Jones had carried the match with Death to deuce as long as he could. I hope tennis survives him. And, though I loathe the stuff, I hope, too, that the "tea committee" survives. I'd even serve on it for Perry's sake.

HE NEVER GREW UP

JULY 19, 1974

Well, we're all 10 years older today. Dizzy Dean is dead. And 1934 is gone forever. Another part of our youth fled. You look in the mirror and the small boy no longer smiles back. Just that sad old man. The Gashouse Gang is now a duet.

Dizzy died the other day at the age of 11 or 12. The little boy in all of us died with him.

Dizzy was not your manufactured American eccentric. He was the real article. He came out of a time and a place, the *Grapes-of-Wrath* America, that today's two-cars-in-the-garage, television-aerial America cannot even conceive.

The part of the country that spawned Dizzy Dean also gave delivery to Bonnie and Clyde, Baby Face Nelson, the Joads, Jukes, Huey Longs, the share-cropping '20s, Dust Bowl '30s, Brother can you spare a dime, Eddie Cantor on Sunday night, Father Coughlin, NRA, breadline America.

I once had an editor who insisted Dizzy Dean was the invention of a St. Louis newspaperman named J. Roy Stockton, but not even Ring Lardner could dream up a Dizzy Dean. He had a third-grade education, in his own language, and, fortunately for all of us, he never grew up. I don't think anyone ever saw him scowl. I'm positive he died laughing. Or eating. Or both.

He got in the Hall of Fame because he was Dizzy Dean. He only won 150 games. But he won them in a little over five years. The only right-handed pitcher I have ever seen who was any better was Satchel Paige. It tells you a lot about Dizzy when you know he was one of the few, if not only, white pitchers who cheerfully went on barnstorming tours with Satch.

Dizzy never knew for sure what his right name was or where or when he was born. He chopped cotton, ate sowbelly and went barefoot till he was old enough to join the Army. Someone gave him a baseball and it was like giving Caesar a sword or Napoleon a cannon.

He was as vain as a movie star, as amiable as a dolphin. He pitched for $3,000 a year in that Depression time and won 20 games. He used to laugh at the hitters. "Son," he once asked a hitter he'd struck out all day, "what kind of a pitch would you like to miss?"

In the World Series of 1934, when Hank Greenberg, one of the feared sluggers of the American League, came to bat, 0 for 4 against Dizzy in the final game, Dizzy went to the manager, Frankie Frisch. "What kind of a pitch did you say he likes to hit?" "High, inside fastball. Don't throw him none," said Frisch.

Dizzy threw him a high, inside fastball. Greenberg singled to center. Frisch screamed, "What'd you do that for?" "I was beginning to think he couldn't hit nothin'," said Diz serenely.

The late Detroit columnist, Doc Greene, tells of the time Dizzy reported that the people who scouted him thought he was left-handed. "That was because they seen me killing squirrels with stones th'owing left-handed. If I'd of th'owed right-handed, I would have squashed them."

Dizzy let death dig in on him, something no other batter could do. His life, like his career, was too short. He was still a 60-year-old barefoot boy when he died.

But, for one brief shining afternoon in 1934, he brought a joy to that dreary time when most we needed it.

Dizzy Dean. It's impossible to say without a smile. But, then, who wants to try? If I know Diz, he'll be calling God "podner" someplace today. I hope there's a golf course or a card game or a slugger who's a sucker for a low outside fastball for old Diz. He just might have been what baseball's all about.

DEATH OF AN HEIRLOOM

OCTOBER 1, 1975

Well, God is getting an earful today. I hope He understands the infield-fly rule, the hit and run, how to pitch to Hornsby with men on, when to platoon, when it would do you some good to bunt, and what really happened in the 1913 World Series. He will get an illustrated lecture on the hook slide, the best place to play Babe Ruth, when to order the infield in, and how to steal on left-handers.

At the end of this, the narrator will doff his cap and a sparrow will fly out.

They finally slipped a called third strike past Casey Stengel. He can't argue the call. The game is over. Dusk is settling on the bleachers, the lights are turned on in the press box where "my writers" are putting "30" to the final bits of Stengelese they will ever type, and, if you look in the gloom, you can probably see the ghosts of John McGraw, Uncle Wilbert Robinson, Cobb, Ruth, Gehrig, and Frisch, and Ring Lardner and Damon Runyon. Someplace, it's 1912 again, and there isn't a lawyer, agent, ad executive or TV camera in sight.

I hope they've got a team that needs platooning, a pitching staff that bears watching in the late innings, a pugnacious umpire or two. I hope the sun is out, the grass is cut, and they have somebody who can make the double play. Above all, I hope they have a sportswriter or two to translate. Casey takes his language with him.

A lot of people are going to be surprised that Casey died. Because they didn't think he was born. Casey just came walking out of the pages of *Grimm's Fairy Tales* years ago. He escaped the wicked old witch's oven, or jumped the club on Snow White. Disney invented him. Part moose, part mouse, sometimes he was all seven of the dwarfs. His rubbery face, his rumbling voice that sounded like a distant artillery barrage, those gnarled old legs so full of lumps from balls bouncing off them looked like two socksful of plums.

Casey had a terrible hang-up. He thought baseball should be fun. World Series or spring exhibition game, either one. He used to infuriate the types that thought baseball was a solemn High Mass. Casey treated the high priests of the game with the disrespect they deserve, whether they were 50-homers-a-year hitters, or chewing gum magnates.

There was a lot of little boy in Casey, the eternal kid-at-a-circus. He was the world's oldest nine-year-old. He was always leading a parade. He was a genuine American heirloom, like a railroad watch. What Fernandel was to the eternal Frenchman, Cantinflas to the poor put-upon Mexican, Chaplin to tramps, Stengel was to Americana.

Watching this rumpled Rumpelstiltskin waddle bowleggedly to the mound and lift a pitcher with the elaborate courtesy and manners of a maid being presented at court was as much fun as a carful of clowns.

They said he was a bad manager because he never won till he got to the Yankees, but I always liked the answer Doc Green gave to some humorless types who were complaining about Stengel's inability to manage one night. "I can't," commented Doc, "imagine anything more beside the point."

A lot of laughter goes out of baseball with Casey. I know the upcoming World Series is going to have a big hole in it. One of the delights of the Series buffet and hospitality room was always old Case holding court in a corner in a monologue which the hearer couldn't tell to the nearest decade which World Series he was talking about. There's going to be one corner of this Series with a deafening silence to it.

I hope they don't cut the whisky where Casey's going because Casey liked a glass with his maunderings. I don't expect the keeper of the gate up there will come out too well in the translation. If I know Case, and I do, he'll come out as "Peterson." Casey dropped proper names about the time baseball put numbers on players' backs, and even 10-year veterans came out as "my switch-hitter" or "the big fella hisself."

Heaven won't need much for old Case. A lineup he can juggle, an ill-fitting uniform, a dependable relief pitcher and a hotel bar that stays open after night games.

The scouting report on his entrance to that big-clubhouse-in-the-sky must be eye-opening. "There's an applicant out here of indeterminate national origin, speaking a language we do not know, non-stop, wearing a wrinkled uniform with the logos of 10 teams on it, bright blue eyes which he winks incessantly, cereal bowl haircut, and a straw suitcase, carrying a bottle and bat and says he knows Heinie Groh personally and has a lineup card in his hand."

And over the intercom will come the voice of The Owner himself. "Why, that must be Casey Stengel! Tell him to come right in. Mr. Hornsby and Mr. Ruth and the 1923 Giants and the 1912 Dodgers are all waiting. Tell him to come in and make himself right at home, platoon Ruth and Hornsby, and lift Mathewson for a pinch hitter in the eighth inning, and after the game, I'll send over my writers, Matthew, Mark, Luke and John so he can tell them how he won the 1953 World Series by holding Robinson on."

A PORTRAIT IN COURAGE

DECEMBER 15, 1976

Well, I see where Danny Thompson has played out his option in baseball, too. But Danny's option wasn't to become a millionaire or a New York Yankee. Danny's option was to live. To stay on the team. Danny didn't make it.

Leukemia is hard to knock out of the box. It has a winning streak unsurpassed in the annals of disease. For years, it toyed with Danny. Fed him an assortment of slow curves, changeups, junk pitches he thought he could hit. Finally, it busted that third strike in there. Knowing Danny, I don't think it was called. He was battling all the way.

I have heard the word "courageous" loosely used in sports to describe a guy who plays with a limp or pitches with a sore finger, who fights to stay in the game by sitting in the whirlpool bath or under a heating pad till just before the game starts.

But a whirlpool bath does nothing for chronic granulocytic leukemia. Danny had more than a limp. Danny was dying.

Danny thought he could make it. He thought he had "the best kind of leukemia to have if you have to have leukemia." Danny thought the leukemia was slow acting. It was merely patient.

Danny didn't want to talk about it. If there's anything a ballplayer hates, it's to be thought sickly. It's all right to have he-man things like sprained ankles or bad backs. But a white blood cell disease is something little kids have and ballplayers go to cheer them up. Danny had two pennant races going— one in the American League and one in the Mayo Clinic.

Danny thought he could carry leukemia into extra innings. But he was up against the 1927 Yankees of diseases. Still, as far

259

as Danny's contribution to leukemia research was concerned, he was the real MVP of the league.

Danny was a pioneer in new research on the way to fight the disease. Basically, the treatment was based on the theory that Danny's defense mechanism against the leucocytic migration of the disease had gone to sleep on him, or into appeasement. It didn't seem to get the message it was under attack. The docs decided to inject further leukemia cells into the system to wake it up, to alert it to the Fifth Column, to get it to fight back.

I went down to see Danny in the dugout at Anaheim Stadium last May to see how the battle was going. None of us suspected what a late inning it was. Danny showed me the hideous craters in his arms—they looked like moon photos—where the medics had made the injections he needed whenever his white blood cell count soared up into the 200,000s.

I whistled. "What do they do it with—a broadsword?" I wondered. Danny ruefully confirmed that the treatment was a nightmarish experience. Some of the scars, the size of 50-cent pieces, he said, remained unhealed for months. "I don't have an unstained T-shirt," he admitted.

Danny's system also was flushed out with other powerful, apocalyptic drugs. His body was a battlefield. In this state, Danny was asked to hit 100 mph fastballs from Nolan Ryan, or to stop 125 mph ground balls, and turn them into double plays. A lot of fine red-blooded guys around the league couldn't do it. But Danny did.

I remember I had to wait outside the clubhouse while Danny conducted the prayer service for the Christian group on the club. Danny knew that leukemia kept loading up the bases on him for four years, but it hadn't scored, and he was sure prayer had a lot to do with that.

I remember writing that major league baseball only had a dim view of Danny's desperate fight, that it regarded leukemia as something that happened to "little boys who had to have Christmas early because they wouldn't be around for the real one."

Well, now, Danny won't be around for the real one either. In the best traditions of Babe Ruth and baseball, Danny was visited by a slugger in his illness. Only teammate Harmon Kille-brew didn't leave an autographed baseball. He left an autographed check for $6,000. You can, too. Make it out to the University of Minnesota Leukemia Research Foundation.

I remember the last thing Danny Thompson said to me, "I'm really lucky, you know. How many guys get to be big leaguers?" Not many. As big league as Danny Thompson anyway.

THE CALL OF A SIREN

NOVEMBER 25, 1980

In 1972, I wrote the following:

"One of the saddest things in life is to see a human in the grip of unrequited passion. Frequently, it's an inhuman bondage.

"In the movie version of the Somerset Maugham book, it was Leslie Howard and Bette Davis in the star roles. In real life, it's Lee Taylor and a jet boat.

"You will remember that in the original *Of Human Bondage,* the young medical student kept giving his affection—and time and money—to a sluttish waitress who was scornful of his attempts to embrace her and kept kicking him around till he was broke, beaten and battered. Well, in this scenario, the Philip Carey character, that's Lee Taylor. Mildred, the waitress, that's the water speed record.

"Anyone else would call the cops on her, but Lee keeps showing up with his black eye and a bouquet of flowers which she promptly throws in his face and yells at him and kicks his hat out the door and him after it."

Well, they fished Lee Taylor, what was left of him, out of 200 feet of water in Lake Tahoe last week. He died as he had lived, chasing that awful harlot, Fame, to the last. He never could see that, if you scraped off all that paint and powder and lipstick, she was an awful old bawd, destructive, extravagant, not worth throwing your life away over. But Lee Taylor thought she was a "10." She wasn't. The "1" doesn't belong there. She was a zero.

When I met Lee Taylor 16 years ago he was almost the handsomest specimen I had ever seen. He had been a football player, 6'2", 200 pounds. A walking collar ad. Robert Redford in a jet boat. He was in the grip of his obsession, mad about the girl.

The next time I saw him he looked as if he had aged 20 years, overnight. One of his eyes stared off at right angles to the other, the hair had receded where the skull had been fractured, one of his legs was shorter than the other, and 18 days in a coma had impaired his speech function and God knows what others. Mildred had thrown him out a window again. He had tried to set a water speed record at Lake Havasu and had gone aground. And the helicopter that picked him up crashed, cracking his skull, his legs and parts of his jaw.

As soon as he got out of the hospital, 6½ months later, he went limping up the stairs to Mildred's apartment. This time, he got her briefly in his arms. He did set the world speed record at Guntersville, Alabama, 282.2 mph.

But it wasn't long before she was two-timing him again. An Australian, Ken Warby, set a new record, 317.6 mph.

It would have seemed like a good time to tear up Mildred's phone number and change the locks on his doors and put a notice in the paper that she had left your bed and board, you were no longer responsible for any debts or actions taken by your ex-beloved, but Lee called me down to his lab one day, all excited over a mock-up of a boat he thought would ultimately break the sound barrier and recapture the speed record.

Lee died where he always knew he would, in the rusting cockpit of a rocket boat on the floor of a mountain lake. It took them a week to get his body. But that's nothing. In January, 1976, Sir Donald Campbell crashed in the waters of Lake Coniston, England, and they haven't found him yet.

Lee was 46. Twenty years with the wrong woman may seem like a lot to the rest of the world, but Lee—and Donald Campbell and John Cobb—must have seen something in her that the rest of us can't. She must have looked to them like the most desirable, beguiling creature on land or sea, a siren on the rocks.

If Lee had survived the crash, I have no doubt he'd be back under her balcony again with a rose in his teeth. As I wrote so long ago, "I get a picture of Philip Carey (read Lee Taylor) limping up the staircase with his club foot and glowing hopes, a corsage under one arm, a box of candy under the other, and the lovelight in his eyes. I just hope she doesn't throw a drink at him." But she did.

HE MADE
A NAME OF
RED SMITH

JULY 16, 1982

His name was Walter Wellesley Smith, and if my name were Walter Wellesley Smith you can bet I would use every syllable of it. Except, I might be W. Wellesley Smith, even though a sage once remarked that you never trust a man who parts his name in the middle.

Know what the real Walter Wellesley Smith preferred to be known as? Red. He had a moniker right out of the pages of Ivanhoe and he preferred a name that sounded as if he had just climbed down from a truck.

You don't have to be all that good if your name is Westbrook Pegler. Or Grantland Rice. Who the hell is ever going to forget that? But, if your name is Smith, and all you have to go with it is Red (or Jack), you better be good.

Red Smith was good. People knew the name. And what it stood for. Uncompromising integrity. A surgical deftness with words that made some of us wonder if Red wrote with rubber gloves.

To give you an idea what a class act Red Smith was, there was another Red Smith and he was a baseball wheeler-dealer in the '40s. One night in 1948, the real Red Smith was awakened from a sound sleep by the real Leo Durocher. I mean, the voice was unmistakable. It was either Leo Durocher or a bullfrog. He wanted to discuss a baseball deal. It would have been a real scoop for Walter (Red) Smith, but he realized Leo the Loud wanted Richard P. (Red) Smith, then a scout for the Chicago Cubs. Leo was with the Giants, and a three-way deal was in the works. "You've got the wrong Red Smith, Leo," Walter Smith told Durocher, "but don't worry, only next time check the room number. I don't want to wind up with one of your pitchers to feed." And he hung up and went back to sleep. Red didn't pick up stories by eavesdropping. You got one call to your lawyer with him.

I bring this up both because Red has a book out posthumously (he died last January) and because I have a somewhat more personal interest. I was honored immeasurably by my craft by being presented with the Red Smith Award by the Associated Press Sports Editors last month. And when I tell you the only other winner of that award to date is Red Smith, you know how proud I am.

But I come not to self-praise. I come to tell you what kind of a craftsman Red Smith was, the standards he set and why they named an award after him. (Actually, I warned the APSE that Red should have been consulted. Red considered that anything that came out of California should be divided by 11. He might have thought that they had got a short horse again if he knew about me.)

Red's book is called *To Absent Friends* (Atheneum), and it's vintage Smith.

Red was the master of the pithy quote. For instance, the bookmaker who booked himself on an ocean cruise in quarters so palatial that a rich passenger—Red thinks it may have been an Astor or a Rockefeller—asked the bookie how he could afford to go so first-class. "Odds-on favorites," the bookie told him laconically.

Red could pick the quote that was an oration. Like the time the great Yankee slugger, Tommy Henrich, was told by Manager Joe McCarthy to lay off a certain pitch. Henrich couldn't. Several misses later, Marse Joe told him, "Henrich, either lay off that pitch, or you'll learn to hit it in Newark."

Another time, the Newark farm team of the Yankees was so good, it won its pennant by 27½ games, and when Henrich went up to the Yankees somebody wondered why, and Joe Gordon, Newark's second baseman at the time, cracked "because he couldn't make the team here."

Red explains his own career choice—"I went on newspapers because I disliked lifting things." Everyone's sure glad of that.

He told of the time his great good friend, Granny Rice, was telling a young reporter that his favorite race track was not lordly Belmont, regal Santa Anita or storied Hollywood Park, but Sunshine Park in Tampa, Florida, which Red described as "a sort of slum-clearance project in a rattlesnake colony." The young reporter couldn't understand Granny's affection for it. "Well, then, what's your favorite city?" he asked. "Quebec, " answered Granny. "You go there for snow, you'd get it."

Red tells of the time Heartley (Hunk) Anderson was warming up the interior linemen for practice on the Notre Dame field as assistant to Knute Rockne and Rockne finally hollered over, "All right, Heartley, will you be good enough to bring those behemoths over here?" And Hunk answered, "Hell, Rock, they ain't even bleeding yet!"

Red remembers the time a colleague, Tom Meany, described the fabled Rudy York as "part Indian, part first baseman." And Red remembers the time Rudy was pulling away from an inside pitch when a sudden blackout hit the Polo Grounds in wartime, and he fell away and hit the ball into the right-field seats. "The scorer ruled it self-defense," Red wrote.

He remembers Pegler in his non-political phase as almost as savage as when he was chastising the Roosevelt White House. Pegler once wrote that a horse owner's silks should be "a dirty shirt with a louse in it."

Red could puncture pomposity with the most invisible and painless of needles. Of Avery Brundage, he said: "Avery Brundage stood as a monument to Avery Brundage's concept of sport. It did not trouble him that what he stood for existed mainly in his own mind." Avery, he said, had "an integrity equalled only by his insensitivity."

Red could keep an eye on his own craft too. Of Jimmy Cannon, he wrote, "At his best, he could make any writer wonder what was the use?"

So could Red. He wrote that another writer said of Cannon: "Jimmy, you remind me of a young left-handed pitcher with all the stuff in the world and no control."

Red had control. He was like the grizzled old Grover Alexander, who could keep the batters (read readers) off balance on sheer artistry. With Red, if you were guessing curve, you got fastball. I got his award. But I never got his touch.

Index

A

Aaron, Henry, 11, 54, 68, 130, 133, 157, 176, 238
Abdul-Jabbar, Kareem, 144, 146, 156, 165–168, 222
Adams, Don, 109
Adams, John Quincy, 94
Adderley, Cannonball, 184
Ade, George, 149
Alexander, Charles, 113
Alexander, Grover Cleveland, 68, 101, 266
Alger, Horatio, 141
Ali, Muhammad, 24, 25, 27, 38, 55, 63, 183
Allen, George, 44
Allen, Richie, 133
Alou, Matty, 130
Alston, Walt, 38, 101
Alzado, Lyle "the Animal", 111, 172–174
Anderson, Heartley "Hunk", 266
Andretti, Mario, 27, 28
Angell, Roger, 96
Arizmendi, Baby, 166
Astaire, Fred, 129, 130
Astor, Lady, 92, 94
Attila the Hun, 199
Auerbach, Arnold "Red", 126–128, 221
Austin, Tracy, 163
Autry, Gene, 169–171
Avery, Scott, 6

B

Babilonia, Tai, 81
Barber, Jerry, 178
Barber, Red, 39
Barnum, P.T., 148, 149, 157
Barrow, Clyde, 62, 203, 239, 254
Barrymore, John, 181, 224, 226
Baugh, Sammy, 10, 144
Bavasi, Buzzie, 170, 171
Bayi, Filbert, 213
Baylor, Elgin, 144, 168
Bealey, John, 36
Beamon, Bob, 158, 161, 228, 229
Beatty, Clyde, 26
Beethoven, 40
Bell, Alexander Graham, 177
Bench, Johnny, 96, 112, 154
Benitez, Wilfredo, 197
Benjamin, Guy, 113
Bennett, Bruce, 210
Bernhardt, Sarah, 113
Berra, Yogi, 41
Billy the Kid, 62, 170, 245
Bird, Larry, 220–223

Black, Joe, 179
Blankers-Koen, Fanny, 158, 161
Bleier, Rocky, 217–219
Bloch, Arthur, 40, 42
Bodie, "Ping", 68
Boe, Ray, 145
Bolt, Tommy, 157
Boone, Daniel, 226
Boone, Judy, 106
Boone, Pat, 187
Booth, John Wilkes, 2, 8
Borg, Bjorn, 240
Boros, Julius, 111
Boudreau, Lou, 104
Braddock, Jim, 182
Bradley, Alva, 225
Brando, Marlon, 138
Brewer, Gay, 21
Brezhnev, Leonid, 79, 121
Brix, Herman, 210
Brodie, Steve, 62
Brooks, Mel, 151
Brown, Jerry, 40
Brown, Jim, 37, 109, 238, 240
Brown, Larry, 10
Brown, Mordecai, 84
Brown, Paul, 192
Browne, Mary K., 136
Brudzinski, Bob, 99
Brundage, Avery, 266
Bryant, David, 78
Bryant, Paul "Bear", 192, 205–207
Buchwald, Art, 62
Budge, Donald, 135, 162
Bundy, Dorothy, 135
Bundy, May Sutton, 135–137
Bundy, Tom, 136, 137
Burroughs, Edgar Rice, 25
Butkus, Dick, 199
Button, Dick, 81
Byron, Lord, 141

C

Caesar, 94, 255
Cagney, Jimmy, 69, 138, 144, 209
Calamity Jane, 62
Caldwell, Bruce, 69
Camp, Walter, 192, 206
Campanella, Roy, 101
Campbell, Clarence, 81
Campbell, Earl, 41, 198, 201
Campbell, Sir Donald, 263
Cannon, Jimmy, 266
Cantinflas, 257
Cantor, Eddie, 254
Capra, Frank, 139
Caray, Harry, 96
Carew, Rod, 50, 54, 101, 133

Carney, Art, 218
Carroll, Joe Barry, 221
Carroll, Lewis, 31
Carson, Johnny, 62, 133, 167
Carter, Jimmy, 120, 231
Carter, John, 39
Caruso, Enrico, 63, 144
Caruso, Paul, 237
Cashman, Terry, 102
Castro, Fidel, 108
Cey, Ron, 86
Chamberlain, Wilt, 108, 144, 157, 167
Chambers, Dorothy Douglass, 136
Chaney, Lon, 150, 167, 200, 233, 241
Chaplin, Charlie, 129, 136, 144, 257
Charlemagne, 32
Charles, Ezzard, 248–249
Chaucer, 214
Chavez, Cesar, 60
Chiaravalle, Antonio, 106
Chopin, 145
Churchill, Winston, 112, 144
Cilento, Dr. Raphael, 209
Clark, Jimmy, 9
Clarke, Bobby, 80
Clay, Cassius. See Ali, Muhammad.
Clemente, Roberto, 54, 100, 130, 133
Cobb, John, 263
Cobb, Ty, 37, 75, 83, 96, 101, 176, 178, 224, 256
Cochet, Henri, 162
Coe, Sebastian, 213
Coghlan, Eamonn, 211–213
Cohen, Mickey, 196
Collins, Floyd, 49
Comaneci, Nadia, 158–161
Connolly, Little Mo, 135
Connors, Jimmy, 163
Coolidge, Calvin, 51
Cooper, Alice, 183
Corbett, Gentleman Jim, 196
Corcoran, Freddy, 226
Cord, Chris, 66, 67
Cord, E.L., 66, 67
Corrigan, Wrong Way, 62
Coryell, Don, 233–234
Cosby, Bill, 39, 109
Cosell, Howard, 48, 183
Coughlin, Father, 254
Cousy, Bob, 144, 220, 222
Cowens, Dave, 222
Cox, Billy, 180
Crabbe, Buster, 208–210
Crenshaw, Ben, 153–155
Crosby, Bing, 181
Csonka, Larry, 27, 153
Cunningham, Bill, 127
Curie, Marie, 25
Custer, Gen. George Armstrong, 169, 235

D

Daley, Mayor Richard, 166
Dalton, Harry, 169, 170
Davidson, John, 242
Davis, Al, 118–119
Davis, Bette, 20, 262
Davis, Jefferson, 2
de Portago, Marquis, 9
Dean, Dizzy, 39, 69, 70, 96, 101, 254–255

Dean, Fred, 234
DeFranco, Joe, 217
Delany, Ron, 211, 212
DeMille, Cecil B., 136
Dempsey, Jack, 24, 25, 69, 81, 86, 103, 144, 153, 154, 197, 224
Dent, Bucky, 104
Dent, Phil, 163
Derek, Bo, 75, 230
Dibbs, Eddie, 163
Dickens, Charles, 95
Didrikson, Babe, 158
Dillinger, 129, 130
DiMaggio, Joe, 39, 50, 68, 83, 85, 86, 100, 175, 224, 226, 238
Disney, Walt, 149, 159, 168, 241, 256
Disraeli, 48
Doby, Larry, 148
Dombrowski, Lutz, 228
Dorsett, Tony, 87
Dowdeswell, Colin, 163
Dryer, Fred, 99
Drysdale, Don, 54, 101
Duncan, Isadora, 195
Durocher, Leo, xvi, 96, 129, 264

E

Earp, Wyatt, 144, 170, 215, 235, 244
Eaton, Aileen, 195–197
Eaton, Alvah "Cal", 196
Eddy, Nelson, 77
Edes, Gordon, 81
Edison, Thomas, 58, 177, 229
Einstein, Albert, 33, 38, 188
El Shafei, Ismail, 163
Elder, Lee, 11, 138–140
Erskine, Carl, 180
Erving, Julius "Dr. J", 144–146, 221
Esposito, Phil, 34

F

Farragut, Admiral, 190
Fawcett, Farrah, 165
Feller, Bob, 51, 70, 100, 137
Ferragamo, Vince, 99
Fields, W.C., 157
Finley, Charlie, 84
Fisk, Carlton, 104
Fleming, Peggy, 81, 210
Florence, Mal, 114
Floyd, Raymond, 112
Flynn, Errol, 48
Fonda, Henry, 209
Ford, Betty, 209
Ford, Doug, 21
Ford, Henry, 239
Ford, Tennessee Ernie, 39
Ford, Whitey, 101
Foreman, George, 10, 24
Foxx, Jimmie, 69
Foyt, A.J., 27, 28
Frazee, Harry, 104
Freud, Sigmund, 12, 50
Frisch, Frankie, 255, 256

G

Gable, Clark, 69
Gaither, Jake, 185
Garagiola, Joe, 96
Garbo, Greta, 144, 226
Garbutt, Frank A., 195–196

Gardner, Ava, 24
Gardner, Randy, 81
Gareau, Jacqueline, 62, 64
Garner, Jim, 27
Garrison, Pam Phillips, 245
Garrison, Walt, 244–246
Gehrig, Lou, 101, 224, 226, 256
George V, King, 136
Gibson, Billy, 117
Gibson, Bob, 55, 108, 133
Gibson, John, 133
Gielgud, John, 113
Gilliam, Jim, 96, 178–180
Gipp, George, 217, 219
Gleason, Jackie, 111
Gomez, Lefty, 70
Gompers, Samuel, 60, 61
Gonzales, Pancho, 135, 252
Gordon, Joe, 265
Goring, Butch, 36
Graham, Lou, 162
Graham, Otto, 10
Grange, Red, 37, 87, 137, 217, 224, 226
Green, Doc, 255, 257
Green, Hubert, 112
Greenberg, Hank, 255
Greene, Mean Joe, 17, 110, 111, 218
Griffith, Andy, 39
Griffith, Darrell, 221
Grimm, Charlie, 147
Groh, Heinie, 258
Grove, Lefty, 70
Guest, Edgar A., 141

H

Haden, Pat, 111
Halas, George, 117
Halberg, Murray, 211
Hale, Dr. Creighton, 12–14
Hale, Nathan, 8
Hall, John, 38
Hamill, Dorothy, 106
Hamilton, George, 235
Hammerskjold, Dag, 25
Harris, Cliff, 198–199
Harris, Franco, 218
Harum, David, 106
Hattie, Hilo, 39
Havlicek, Hondo, 220, 222
Hawkins, Jim, 133
Hayes, Bob, 184–186, 244
Hayes, Woody, 40, 44, 206
Hearst, William Randolph, 93
Heinsohn, Tom, 220, 222
Heiss, Carol, 210
Hemingway, Ernest, 25, 144
Henderson, Hollywood, 48
Henie, Sonja, 80, 210
Henrich, Tommy, 265
Hepburn, Katherine, 209
Herman, Billy, 69, 70
Hewson, Brian, 211
Hill, Calvin, 244
Hines, Jimmie, 228
Hirsch, Elroy, 55
Hitler, Adolf, 12, 63, 72, 73, 159, 182,
    227
Hoad, Lew, 162
Hobson, Butch, 104
Hodgdon, Warner, 239
Hodges, Gil, 180

Hogan, Ben, 23, 37, 151, 153, 178
Holm, Eleanor, 210
Holmes, Larry, 63, 86
Holmes, Oliver Wendell, 102, 118, 119
Hope, Bob, 79
Hornsby, Rogers, 256, 258
Horowitz, 145
Howard, Leslie, 19, 20, 262
Hoy, "Dummy", 68
Hubbell, Carl, 70, 224, 226
Huber, Bill, 87
Huber, Katie, 87
Hudson, Rock, 209
Husing, Ted, 39
Hutson, Don, 144

I

Iannone, Dr., 249
Irving, Clifford, xvi

J

Jack the Ripper, 197, 198, 200, 201
Jackson, Jesse, 179
Jackson, Reggie, 50, 51, 54, 133, 183,
    238
Jackson, "Shoeless" Joe, 84, 101
Jacobs, Mike, 24
James, Jesse, 117, 139
Jefferson, John, 234
Johnson, Byron Bancroft, 116, 117
Johnson, Jack, 24, 182
Johnson, Lyndon, 127, 191
Johnson, Magic, 221, 222, 238
Johnson, Martin, 26
Johnson, Osa, 26
Johnson, Walter, 132, 134
Johnston, Little Bill, 135
Jones, Bobby, 3, 23, 89, 90, 224
Jones, Deacon, 166
Jones, Ed "Too Tall", 111
Jones, Howard, 143, 205–206
Jones, James Earl, 151
Jones, K.C., 222
Jones, Parnelli, 28, 29
Jones, Perry, 251–253
Jones, Sam, 220, 222

K

Kahn, Roger, 180
Karloff, Boris, 198
Karras, Alex, 241–243
Kasavubu, 25
Kazankina, Tatyana, 231, 232
Kelly, Grace, 24
Kennedy, John F., 191
Ketchel, Stanley, 248, 251
Khan, Genghis, 199
Kieran, John, 39
Killanin, Lord (William Morris),
    212–213
Killebrew, Harmon, 260
King, Billie Jean, 135
Kirsch, Bob, 236
Knievel, Evel, 235–237
Knight, Bobby, 221
Knotts, Don, 218
Konovski, Crippler, 242, 243
Korbut, Olga, 158, 159–160, 161
Kosygin, 121
Koufax, Sandy, 27, 54, 68, 100, 144,
    165, 238

Kramer, Jack, 135, 162, 163
Kuhn, Bowie, 83

L

Lacy, Steve, 213
Lajoie, Napoleon, 68
Lambeau, Curly, 199
Lambert, Jack, 111, 198–201
Landers, Ann, 87
Landry, Tom, 173, 188, 189, 206, 246
Landy, John, 211
Langford, Sam, 182
Lanier, Bob, 156–157
Lardner, Ring, 38–39, 254, 256
Larned, Bill, 136, 137
LaStarza, Roland, 249
Lautrec, Toulouse, 144
Laver, Rod, 162
Lazzeri, Tony, 101
Lemmon, Jack, 109
Lemon, Meadowlark, 109
Lenin, 60, 72
Leonard, Sugar Ray, 197
Lewis, Carl, 228–229
Lewis, Jerry, 170
Lincoln, Abraham, 39, 94, 109, 140,
    157, 182
Liston, Sonny, 24
Little, Floyd, 10
Lizana, Anita, 135
Loes, Billy, 101
Lombardi, Vince, 143, 166, 192
London, Jack, 165
Long, Huey, 254
Louis, Joe, 38, 69, 139, 181–183, 197,
    240, 249
Louis XIV, 112
Luckman, Sid, 10
Lugosi, Bela, 198
Luisetti, Hank, 224
Lumumba, 25
Lunt, Alfred, 243
Lupescu, Magda, 160
Luzinski, Greg, 83
Lynn, Freddie, 103, 104

M

Mahaffey, John 111
Mallory, Molla Bjurstedt, 136, 137
Malone, Pat, 147
Mangrum, Lloyd, 139
Mantle, Mickey, 100, 102, 154
Mara, Tim, 117
Maranville, Rabbit, 37, 147, 176
Marble, Alice, 135
Marciano, Rocky, 53, 54, 248–250
Marie Antoinette, 251
Marin, John, 21, 22, 23
Maris, Roger, 62, 176
Marshall, George Preston, 118
Marshall, Mike, 133, 134
Martin, Dean, 183
Martin, Harvey, 111
Martin, Pepper, 162
Marx, Karl, 71
Masback, Craig, 213
Mathewson, Christy, 258
Maugham, Somerset, 262
Mayer, Sandy, 163
Mays, Willie, 53, 54, 68, 83, 96, 100,
    102, 129–131, 133

McCarthy, Joe, 265
McCoy, Babe, 196
McDonald, Jeannette, 77
McEnroe, John, 162–164
McGraw, John, 98, 117, 256
McKay, John, 206–207
McKenzie, Dr. Ed, 39
McLoughlin, Maurice, 135
McNamee, Graham, 39
Meany, Tom, 266
Meiler, Karl, 163
Melville, Herman, 16
Meredith, Don, 188, 189, 245
Miller, Johnny, 153
Miller, Marvin, 60–61
Miller, Red, 173
Mizner, Wilson, 248
Mobutu, 25
Monroe, Marilyn, 157
Moody, Orville J., 162
Moore, Archie, 249
Morgan, Bob, 150–152
Morgan, J.P., 60
Morgan, Joe, 96
Morris, Mercury, 10
Morris, William, 212–213
Morton, Craig, 189
Mungo, Van Lingle, 68–70
Murphy, Bob, 4, 111
Murray, Geraldine, 29
Musial, Stan, 54, 96, 100, 238
Mussolini, 73

N

Nader, Ralph, 11, 50
Nagurski, Bronko, 224, 238
Namath, Joe, 19, 74, 188, 206
Napoleon, 94, 217, 255
Nave, Doyle, 43, 162
Neale, Earle "Greasy", 192
Nelson, Baby Face, 254
Newhouse, Robert, 244
Newman, Paul, 27
Nick the Greek, 196, 214
Nicklaus, Jack, 11, 23, 41, 111, 112,
    140, 154, 204
Nijinsky, 224
Nitschke, Ray, 199
Nixon, Richard, 41, 191
Norton, Ray, 184

O

O'Connor, Pat, 28
O'Malley, Peter, 96
O'Malley, Walter, 96, 119
Oakley, Annie, 62
Oldfield, Barney, 27
Olivier, Laurence, 145
Olsen, Merlin, 241, 245
Orantes, Manuel, 163
Ott, Mel, 69
Owens, Jesse, 158, 161, 184, 224, 226,
    228, 229

P

Page, Dynamite, 90
Paige, Don, 213
Paige, Satchel, 109, 132–134, 148, 254
Palermo, Blinky, 196
Palmer, Arnold, 3, 11, 23, 112, 153,
    154, 159, 226

Panch, Marvin, 240
Pappas, Milt, 170
Parker, Bonnie, 62, 203, 239, 254
Parker, Dan, 39
Parker, Dave, 50
Pasarell, Charlie, 163
Pasteur, Louis, 58
Pastor, Herb, 215
Patton, General George, 138
Pegler, Westbrook, 264, 266
Penna, Toney, 20
Perini, Lou, 148
Perkins, Don, 244
Perry, Commodore, 190
Perry, Dr. John, 47
Petty, Kyle, 239
Petty, Richard, 238–240
Philip, Prince, 109
Phillips, B.F., 245
Pickford, Mary, 136
Pico, Governor (California), 135
Pintor, Lupe, 197
Plimpton, George, 241
Plunkett, Jim, 222
Poffenberger, Cletus Elwood, 68
Poreda, Stanley, 181
Prendergast, Tom, 203
Presley, Elvis, 236
Pretty Boy Floyd, 62
Price, Jack, 93

Q

Quax, Dick, 231

R

Rafeedie, Judge Edward, 237
Ramsey, Jack, 222
Reagan, Nancy, 79
Reagan, Ronald, 217
Redford, Robert, 262
Rembrandt, 51
Revere, Paul, 62, 104
Reynolds, Jack, 99
Reynolds, Leo, 80, 81
Rhodes, Cecil, 26
Rhome, Jerry, 189
Rice, Grantland, 38, 264, 265
Rice, Jim, 50, 104, 183
Richards, Golden, 244
Rickard, Tex, 24, 195
Riegels, Roy, 43, 44
Riggs, Bobby, 137
Riley, James Whitcomb, 143
Rindt, Jochen, 9
Ritz Bros., 151
Roberts, Cliff, 90
Robertson, Oscar, 137, 157
Robinson, Edward G., 196
Robinson, Frank, 170
Robinson, Jackie, 96, 179, 180, 258
Robinson, Sugar Ray, 38, 55, 249
Robinson, Uncle Wilbert, 256
Rockne, Knute, 143, 192, 205, 240, 266
Rockwell, Norman, 95
Roebuck, Eddie, 130
Rogers, Will, 171, 181
Rooney, Art, 218, 219
Roosevelt, Eleanor, 39
Roosevelt, Franklin, 60, 144, 227, 266
Roosevelt, Teddy, 136, 144
Rose, Pete, 50, 54, 61, 96, 100

Rousseau, Jean-Jacques, 61
Rozelle, Pete, 43–45
Ruiz, Rosie, 62–64
Runyon, Damon, 195, 256
Rupp, Adolph, 143
Rusk, Dean, 127
Russell, Bill, 109, 126, 128, 138, 220, 222, 238
Russell, Cazzie, 166
Russell, Rosalind, 195
Ruth, Babe, 11, 34, 37, 50, 53, 84, 87, 96, 101, 137, 144, 157, 159, 166, 175, 176, 178, 224, 238, 240, 256, 258, 260
Rutherford, Johnny, 27
Ryan, Nolan, 170, 260

S

Saltman, Shelly, 235, 236
Sandoval, "Superfly", 197
Saperstein, Abe, 108–109
Sayers, Gale, 137
Schaefer, "Germany", 68
Schembechler, Bo, 230
Schroeder, Ted, 135
Schumacher, Hal, 70
Schweitzer, Albert, 11
Scott, George C., 138
Scott, Steve, 213
Scully, Vin, 96
Serra, Junipero, 165
Shakespeare, William, 145
Sharman, Bill, 222
Shaw, George Bernard, 92, 94
Shaw, Robert, 151
Shero, Fred, 80
Shields, Brooke, 230
Shoemaker, Bill, 75, 157
Shore, Eddie, 80
Sifford, Charlie, 2–4
Sime, Dr. David, 47
Simmons, Gary, 35
Simmons, Pat, 19
Simpson, O.J., 10, 154, 238
Sinatra, Frank, 183
Sisti, Sibby, 68
Sitting Bull, 171
Skeoch, Danica Erin, 75
Slaughter, Enos, 37, 96
Smith, Reggie, 183
Smith, Richard "Red", 264
Smith, Walter "Red", 39, 264–266
Snead, Sam, 19, 21, 22, 23, 111, 178, 224–226
Snider, Duke, 68, 102
Snyder, Jimmy the Greek, 47
Souchak, Mike, 21
Spitz, Mark, 136, 158, 161
Stagg, Amos Alonzo, 143, 192, 205, 207
Stallworth, Dave, 145
Standish, Burt L., 189
Statz, Jigger, 166
Staubach, Roger, 47, 112, 187–190, 200
Steinbrenner, George, 96, 170
Stengel, Casey, 55, 96, 101, 130, 180, 256–258
Stevenson, Robert Louis, 16
Stewart, Jackie, 8
Stockton, J. Roy, 254
Stradivarius, 20
Stravinsky, 144

Sutton, Capt. Adolphus, 136
Swann, Lynn, 75, 112

T

Tabb, Mary Decker, 230–232
Tabb, Rob, 232
Tatum, Jack, 185
Taylor, Elizabeth, 19
Taylor, Lee, 262–263
Tchaikovsky, 81
Temple, Shirley, 159, 181
Terry, Bill, 70
Terry, Ralph, 130
Thomas, Duane, xvi, 244
Thompson, Danny, 259–261
Thompson, Titanic, 139
Thorpe, Jim, 137, 158, 161
Thurmond, Nate, 156
Tiegs, Cheryl, 78
Tilden, Bill, 137, 162, 224, 226
Toscanini, 129, 130
Tracy, Spencer, 113, 129, 130, 144
Traynor, Pie, 86, 224
Treacy, John, 72
Trotsky, Leon, 73
Tshombe, 25
Tunney, Gene, 81
Twain, Mark, 202, 204, 226

U

Unitas, Johnny, 55
Unser, Bobby, 239
Urich, Robert, 217
Uston, Ken, 214–216

V

Vachon, Roger, 35
Valentino, Rudolph, 86, 144
Van Alen, Jimmy, 32
Van Buren, Abigail, 87
Van Damme, Ivo, 212, 213
Vander Meer, Johnny, 70
Veeck, Bill, 96, 109, 147–149
Veidt, Conrad, 235
Victoria, Queen, 136
Viren, Lasse, 72
von Trips, Count Wolfgang, 9

W

Wagner, Honus, 178
Walker, John, 212, 213
Wall, Art, Jr., 4
Walton, Bill, 146
Wambsganss, William Adolph, 68
Warby, Ken, 263
Warneke, Lon, 70
Warner, Pop, 192, 205
Washington, George, 94, 141
Waterfield, Bob, 10, 55, 166
Watson, Isaac Newton, 203, 204
Watson, Tom, 202–204
Wayne, John, 39, 48, 168, 169
Weiskopf, Tom, 91
Weissmuller, Johnny, 209, 210
Welk, Lawrence, 87
Wellman, Paul-Heinz, 212, 213
Wertz, Vic, 100
West, Jerry, 238
Westmore, Pere, 150
White, Randy, 111
Wightman, Hazel Hotchkiss, 136
Wilder, Billy, 139
Wilhelm, Hoyt, 132, 134
Wilkinson, Bud, 191–194
Willard, Jess, 24
Williams, Lee, 156
Williams, Ted, 96, 103, 134
Williamson, Roger, 8
Wills, Helen, 135
Wills, Maury, 37, 53, 54, 96, 176, 179
Wilson, Hack, 147
Wind, Herbert Warren, 89
Wooden, John, 141–143
Wright, Beals, 137
Wright, Harry, 116, 119
Wright, Wilbur and Orville, 58

Y

Yastrzemski, Carl, 103, 104
York, Rudy, 266
York, Sgt. Alvin, 166

Z

Zivic, Fritzie, 196